MEDICINAL AND NUTRITIONAL VALUES OF PLANTS

ENV BOOKS SERIES

MEDICINAL AND NUTRITIONAL VALUES OF PLANTS

Editors

Dr. Alka Chauhan

Society for Environment, Health, Awareness of Nutrition & Toxicology (SEHAT)
1775, Sohan Ganj, Near Clock Tower
Delhi - 110 007 (India)

&

Dr. Pawan Kumar 'Bharti'

Society for Environment, Health, Awareness of Nutrition & Toxicology (SEHAT)
1775, Sohan Ganj, Near Clock Tower
Delhi - 110 007 (India)
E-mail: gurupawanbharti@rediffmail.com

DPH

DISCOVERY PUBLISHING HOUSE PVT. LTD.
INDIA

Published by:
Namit Wasan
DISCOVERY PUBLISHING HOUSE PVT. LTD.
4383/4B, Ansari Road, Darya Ganj
New Delhi-110 002 (India)
Phone : +91-11-23279245, 43596064-65
Fax : +91-11-23253475
E-mail : discoverypublishinghouse@gmail.com
namitwasan9@gmail.com
sales@discoverypublishinggroup.com
web : www.discoverypublishinggroup.com

***First Edition:* 2017**

ISBN: 978-93-5056-883-5

Medicinal and Nutritional Values of Plants

Printed at:
Infinity Imaging Systems
Delhi

ENV Books Series, India

Calls descriptive and error free chapters for upcoming volumes of books on various environmental issues. Send your manuscripts to envbooks@gmail.com

Founding Editor **(*Editor-in-Chief*)**

Dr. Pawan Kumar 'Bharti'

Society for Environment, Health, Awareness of Nutrition & Toxicology (SEHAT-India)
1775, Sohanganj, Near Clock Tower, Delhi-7, (India)
E-mail:*gurupawanbharti@rediffmail.com*

Other Important Titles by Editor-in-Chief:

1. **Advances in Biotechnology and Ecological Sciences**
   Bharti, P.K., Chauhan, A. and Ray, J. (eds.)
   (ISBN: 978-93-5056-358-8).
2. **Advances in Agriculture and Ecology**
   Bharti, P.K.; Chauhan, A. and Ezeaku Peter Ikemefuna (eds.)
   (ISBN: 978-93-5056-362-5).
3. **Agriculture and Environmental Biotechnology**
   Bharti, P.K. and Chauhan, A. (eds.)
   (ISBN: 978-93-5056-479-0).
4. **Agriculture Crops and Food Security**
   Bharti, P.K. and Chauhan, Alka (eds.)
   (ISBN: 978-93-5056-881-1).
5. **Agriculture Development and Sustainable Environment**
   Ray, J. and Bharti, P.K. (eds.)
   (ISBN: 978-93-5056-759-3).
6. **Agriculture Ecology and Environment**
   Bharti, P.K. and Olubukola O. Babalola (eds.)
   (ISBN: 978-93-5056-480-6).
7. **Agriculture Ecology, Sustainable Development and Agribusiness Management**
   Mehta Piyush; Sharma Pankaj; and 'Bharti' P.K. (eds.)
   (ISBN: 978-93-5056-851-4).
8. **Agriculture, Environment and Nano-science**
   Bharti, Pawan K. (ed.)
   (ISBN: 978-93-5056-760-5).

9. **Agricultural Practices and Crop Disease Control**
Chauhan Alka and Sharma Anubhuti (eds.)
(ISBN: 978-93-5056-859-0).

10. **Agro-biodiversity: *Conservation and Sustainable Development***
Sharma, Pankaj; Singh, Narayan; and Bharti, P.K. (eds.)
(ISBN: 978-93-505-782-1).

11. **Agro-forestry and Climate Change**
Bharti, Pawan K. and Singh, Narayan (eds.)
(ISBN: 978-93-5056-514-8).

12. **Agro-forestry and Sustainable Agriculture**
Sharma, Pankaj; Bharti, P.K. (eds.)
(ISBN: 978-93-5056-786-9).

13. **Air Pollution and Ecosystem Health**
Swami Abhishek and Bharti, P.K. (eds.)
(ISBN: 978-93-5056-877-4).

14. **Aquaculture and Fisheries Environment**
Gupta, S.K. and Pawan K. Bharti (eds.)
(ISBN: 978-93-5056-408-0).

15. **Aquatic Biodiversity and Pollution**
Bharti, P.K.; Chauhan, A. and Kaoud, H.A.H. (eds.)
(ISBN: 978-93-5056-359-5).

16. **Aquatic Ecology and Biotechnology**
Bharti, P.K. and Zaki, M.S.A. (eds.)
(ISBN: 978-93-5056-451-6).

17. **Aquatic Environment and Toxicology**
Bharti, Pawan K. (ed.)
(ISBN: 978-93-5056-236-9).

18. **Biodiversity, Biotechnology and Environmental Conservation**
Bharti, P.K. and Bhandari, G. (eds.)
(ISBN: 978-93-5056-750-0).

19. **Biodiversity, Biotechnology and Pollution Control**
Bharti, P.K. and Chauhan, Alka (eds.)
(ISBN: 978-93-5056-887-3).

20. **Biodiversity of Aquatic Ecosystem: *Significance, Threat and Conservation* (2013)**
Bharti, P.K. and Kaoud, H.A.H. (eds.)
(ISBN: 978-93-5056-297-0).

21. **Biological Diversity and Ecology**
Arya, M.K.; Bharti, P.K. and Ritesh Joshi (eds.)
(ISBN: 978-93-5056-785-2).

22. **Bioremediation and Microbial Biotechnology**
Gupta, Sandeep; and Bharti, P.K. (eds.)
(ISBN: 978-93-5056-783-8).

23. **Biotechnological Approaches and Water Ecosystem**
Zaki, M.S.A.; and Bharti, P.K. (eds.)
(ISBN: 978-93-5056-779-1).

24. **Biotechnology, Agro-ecology and Environment**
Chauhan, Avnish and Bharti, P.K. (eds.)
(ISBN: 978-93-5056-757-9).

25. **Biotechnology and Environmental Management**
Arya Arun; Maheswari Raaz K., & Bharti, P.K (eds.)
(ISBN: 978-93-5056-862-0).

26. **Clean Technologies and Environmental Protection**
Chauhan, A.; Sharma, S. and Bharti, P.K. (eds.)
(ISBN: 978-93-5056-731-9).

27. **Climate Change and Agriculture**
Bharti, P.K. and Chauhan, Avnish (eds.)
(ISBN: 978-93-5056-148-5).

28. **Climate Change and Biodiversity**
Bharti, P.K. and Chauhan, Avnish (eds.)
(ISBN: 978-93-5056-360-1).

29. **Climate Change, Disaster Management and Environment**
Chauhan, Alka; Bharti, P.K. (eds.)
(ISBN: 978-93-5056-784-5).

30. **Conservation and Cultivation of Medicinal Plants**
Bharti, P.K. and Singh Narayan (eds.)
(ISBN: 978-93-5056-740-1).

31. **Crop Productivity and Plant Disease Management**
Chauhan, Alka; Bharti, P.K. and Sadana, Deepti (eds.)
(ISBN: 978-93-5056-791-3).

32. **Eco-toxicology and Eco-technology**
Bharti, P.K. and Zaki, M. (eds.)
(ISBN: 978-93-5056-313-7).

33. **Environmental Biotechnology and Application**
Bharti, P.K. and Chauhan, Avnish (eds.)
(ISBN: 978-93-5056-262-8).

34. **Environmental Conservation and Biotechnology**
Chauhan, A. and P.K. Bharti (eds.)
(ISBN: 978-93-5056-512-4).

35. **Environmental Health and Problems**
Bharti, P.K. and Gajananda, Kh. (eds.)
(ISBN: 978-93-5056-263-5).

36. **Environmental Pollution and Biodiversity**
Bharti, P.K.; Chauhan, Avnish and Kumar, P. (eds.)
(ISBN: 978-93-5056-149-2).

37. **E-Waste and Environmental Issues**
Bhalla, Resham and Bharti, P.K. (eds.)
(ISBN: 978-93-5056-886-6).

38. **Farming Techniques and Crop Production**
Chauhan Alka; Sharma Anubhuti; Ray Jaswant and 'Bharti' P.K. (eds.)
(ISBN: 978-93-5056-855-2).

39. **Fisheries and Toxicology**
Zaki, M.S.A.; Bharti, P.K. and Chauhan, A. (eds.)
(ISBN: 978-93-5056-452-3).

40. **Fish Habitat and Aquaculture**
Bharti, P.K.; Gupta Kr. Sanjay (eds.)
(ISBN: 978-93-5056-744-9).

41. **Forest and Biodiversity Conservation**
Chauhan Alka; Bharti, P.K. (eds.)
(ISBN: 978-93-5056-873-6).

42. **Food Processing, Management and Nanotechnology**
Chauhan, Avnish; Bharti, P.K. (eds.)
(ISBN: 978-93-5056-796-8).

43. **Freshwater Ecosystem and Xenobiotics**
Bharti, P.K.; Zaki, M. and Chauhan, A. (eds.)
(ISBN: 978-93-5056-299-4).

44. **Geospatial Technology and Water Management**
Chauhan, Alka; Bharti, P.K. (eds.)
(ISBN: 978-93-5056-885-9).

45. **Heavy Metals and Metalloids in Biosphere:** ***Impacts & Assessment***
Chauhan, Avnish, Gupta, Sandeep; and Bharti, P.K. (eds.)
(ISBN: 978-93-5056-860-6).

46. **Land Reclamation, Soil Quality and Agriculture**
Bharti, P.K. and Chauhan, Alka (eds.)
(ISBN: 978-93-5056-882-8).

47. **Limnology and Aquatic Science**
Sharma, S., and Bharti, P.K. (eds.)
(ISBN: 978-93-5056-735-7).

48. **Medicinal Plants:** ***Distribution, Utilization and Significance***
Sharma, P.; Bharti, P.K. and Narayan Singh (eds.)
(ISBN: 978-93-5056-734-0).

49. **Microbial Applications and Environment**
Bharti, Pawan K. (ed.)
(ISBN: 978-93-5056-515-5).

50. **Microbial Ecology and Habitat**
Bharti, Pawan K. (ed.)
(ISBN: 978-93-5056-514-8).

51. **Microbial Environment and Bioremediation**
Chauhan Alka; K. Rathoure Ashok; and K Maheshwari Raaz (eds.)
(ISBN: 978-93-5056-856-9).

52. **Microbiological and Pharmacological Aspects of Biodiversity**
Sharma Pankaj; Sharma Gautam Neha and Sharma Pankaj (eds.)
(ISBN: 978-93-5056-878-1).

53. **Natural Ecosystem and Climate Change**
Bharti, P.K., and Kh. Gajananda (ed.)
(ISBN: 978-93-5056-745-6).

54. **Pest Management and Agro-Techniques**
Biswas, Asim; Bharti, P.K., Chauhan, Avnish (eds.)
(ISBN: 978-93-5056-794-4).

55. **Plant Biotechnology and Industrial Applications**
Chauhan, Alka; Bharti, P.K. (eds.)
(ISBN: 978-93-5056-884-2).

56. **Prakriti me Aushadhi (*in Hindi*)**
Singh, J.R.; Bharti, P.K. and Bharti, B.
(ISBN: 978-93-5056-200-0).

57. **Seed Technology, Plant Growth and Cropping System**
Tyagi, P.K. and Bharti, P.K. (eds.)
(ISBN: 978-93-5056-738-8).

58. **Seed Treatment, Plant Heath and Agro-technology**
Chauhan, A. and Bharti, P.K. (eds.)
(ISBN: 978-93-5056-810-1).

59. **Soil Characteristics and Agro-ecology**
Avnish Chauhan and Bharti, P.K. (eds.)
(ISBN: 978-93-5056-758-6).

60. **Soil Contamination and Conservation**
Ezeaku, P.I. and Bharti, P.K. (eds.)
(ISBN: 978-93-5056-737-1).

61. **Soil Quality and Contamination**
Bharti, P.K. and Chauhan, Avnish (eds.)
(ISBN: 978-93-5056-361-8).

62. **Sustainable Aquaculture Management**
Gupta, S.K.; Bharti, P.K (eds.)
(ISBN: 978-93-5056-797-5).

63. **Waste Disposal and Management**
Bharti, P.K.; Tabassum, B. and Bajaj, P. (eds.)
(ISBN: 978-93-5056-729-6).

Preface

Plants make many chemical compounds that are for biological functions, including defence against insects, fungi and herbivorous mammals. At least 12,000 such compounds have been isolated so far; a number estimated to be less than 10% of the total. Chemical compounds in plants mediate their effect on the human body through processes identical to those already well understood for the chemical compounds in conventional drugs; thus herbal medicines do not differ greatly from conventional drugs in terms of how they work. This enables herbal medicines to have beneficial pharmacology, but also gives them the same potential as conventional pharmaceutical drugs to cause harmful side effects. Moreover, plant material comes with a variety of compounds which may have undesired effects, though these can be reduced by processing.

The use of plants as medicines pre-dates written human history. Ethnobotany, the study of traditional human uses of plants, is recognized as an effective way to discover future medicines.

Research in the field of nutrition has greatly contributed in finding out the essential facts about how environmental depletion can lead to crucial nutrition-related health problems like contamination, spread of contagious diseases, malnutrition, etc.

The present book updates the subject content of medicinal properties of plants, nutrient content in various parts of floral diversity, ethanobatnical significance of plants available on Earth. Thanks are due to contributors from various prestigious institutions and publishers.

The book will be helpful for the researchers, academia working in the field of medicinal properties of plants, nutrient content in various parts of floral diversity, ethanobatnical significance of plants.

Editors
(envbooks@gmail.com)

Contents

Introduction

Plants in general make a great source of food as they're available, obtainable and can meet most of a person's nutritional needs. But the key point in eating whatever it is you come across consists in identifying the plants first. This is crucial in a survival situation as many of the plants you'll stumble across could easily kill after one bite. Many are edible, many are poisonous, and having nutritional and medicinal values also.

Aside from identifying plants, there are other factors you'll need to consider. Even apparently harmless plants can be life-threatening for various reasons. For example, plants growing near urbanized zones (near houses, along the road) should be avoided. If avoiding them is not an option, washed them carefully before consuming them, as they most like are sprayed with pesticides or contaminated by noxious vehicle fumes. The plants that grow in water should not only be washed, but also boiled properly, due to the fact that the surrounding waters could be contaminated. The boiling process reduces the risk of indigestion or even worse complications (like Giardia lamblia).

Many wild plants are abundant in oxalic acids or oxalate compounds, which can permanently damage the kidneys and cause distress to your throat and mouth. The acid however is usually destroyed during the process of boiling, baking, roasting or frying. So, if it's possible, best prepare the plants before eating them.

Plants uptake essential elements from the soil through their roots and from the air (consisting of mainly nitrogen and oxygen) through their leaves. Green plants obtain their carbohydrate supply from the carbon dioxide in the air by the process of photosynthesis. Carbon and oxygen are absorbed from the air, while other nutrients are absorbed from the soil. Nutrient uptake in the soil is achieved by cation exchange, wherein root hairs pump hydrogen ions (H^+) into the soil through proton pumps. These hydrogen ions displace cations attached to negatively charged soil particles so that the cations are available for uptake by the root. In the leaves, stomata open to take in carbon dioxide and expel oxygen. The carbon dioxide molecules are used as the carbon source in photosynthesis.

Although nitrogen is plentiful in the Earth's atmosphere, very few plants can use this directly. Most plants, therefore, require nitrogen compounds to be present in the soil in which they grow. This is made possible by the fact that largely inert atmospheric nitrogen is changed in a nitrogen fixation process to biologically usable forms in the soil by bacteria.

Plant nutrition is a difficult subject to understand completely, partially because of the variation between different plants and even between different species or individuals of a given clone. Elements present at low levels may cause deficiency symptoms and toxicity is possible at levels that are too high. Furthermore, deficiency of one element may present as symptoms of toxicity from another element and vice versa.

Nutrition

Research in the field of nutrition has greatly contributed in finding out the essential facts about how environmental depletion can lead to crucial nutrition-related health problems like contamination, spread of contagious diseases, malnutrition, etc. Moreover, environmental contamination due to discharge of agricultural as well as industrial chemicals like organocholrines, heavy metal and radionucleotides may adversely affect the human and the ecosystem as a whole. As far as safety of the human health is concerned, then these environmental contaminants can reduce people's nutritional status and health. This could directly or indirectly cause drastic changes in their diet habits. Hence, food-based remedial as well as preventive strategies are essential to address global issues like hunger and malnutrition and to enable the susceptible people to adapt themselves to all these environmental as well as socio-economic alterations.

Medicinal plants have been identified and used throughout human history. Plants make many chemical compounds that are for biological functions, including defence against insects, fungi and herbivorous mammals. At least 12,000 such compounds have been isolated so far; a number estimated to be less than 10% of the total. Chemical compounds in plants mediate their effect on the human body through processes identical to those already well understood for the chemical compounds in conventional drugs; thus herbal medicines do not differ greatly from conventional drugs in terms of how they work. This enables herbal medicines to have beneficial pharmacology, but also gives them the same potential as conventional pharmaceutical drugs to cause harmful side effects. Moreover, plant material comes with a variety of compounds which may have undesired effects, though these can be reduced by processing.

The use of plants as medicines pre-dates written human history. Ethnobotany, the study of traditional human uses of plants, is recognized as an effective way to discover future medicines. In 2001, researchers identified 122 compounds used in modern medicine which were derived from traditional plant sources; 80% of these have had a traditional use identical or related to the current use of the active elements of the plant. Some of the pharmaceuticals currently available to physicians are derived from plants that have a long history of use as herbal remedies, including aspirin, digoxin, quinine and opium.

The use of and search for, drugs and dietary supplements derived from plants have accelerated in recent years. Pharmacologists, microbiologists, botanists and natural-products chemists are combing the Earth for phytochemicals and leads that could be developed for treatment of various diseases. In fact, according to the World Health Organisation, approximately 25% of modern drugs used in the United States have been derived from plants.

Among the 120 active compounds currently isolated from the higher plants and widely used in modern medicine today, 80 percent show a positive correlation between their modern therapeutic use and the traditional use of the plants from which they are derived. More than two thirds of the world's plant species - at least 35,000 of which are estimated to have medicinal value - come from the developing countries.[verification needed] At least 7,000 medical compounds in the modern pharmacopoeia are derived from plants. In many medicinal and aromatic plants (MAPs), significant variations of plants characteristics have been ascertained with varying soil traits, and the selective recovery and subsequent release in food of certain elements have been demonstrated. Great attention must be paid to choose soil and cropping strategies, to obtain satisfactory yields of high quality and best-priced products, respecting their safety and nutritional value.

Phytochemistry

The carotenoids in primroseproduce bright red, yellow and orange shades. People consuming diets rich in carotenoids from natural foods, such as fruits and vegetables, are healthier and have lower mortality from a number ofchronic illnesses.

All plants produce chemical compounds as part of their normal metabolic activities. These phytochemicals are divided into:

1. primary metabolites such as sugars and fats, which are found in all plants; and
2. secondary metabolites—compounds which are found in a smaller range of plants, serving a more specific function.

For example, some secondary metabolites are toxinsused to deter predation and others are pheromones used to attract insects for pollination. It is these secondary metabolites and pigments that can have therapeutic actions in humans and which can be refined to produce drugs—examples are inulin from the roots of dahlias, quinine from the cinchona, morphine and codeine from the poppy and digoxin from the foxglove. Toxic plants even have use in pharmaceutical development.

Healthy herbs have long been held an holistic place in our wellbeing. Prized since ancient times and today, we even more depend upon them to purify our body, mind and soul!

Of course, we all use herbal parts in our daily lives, one way or the other, whether for their rich flavor, for their healing power, or in lovely recipes. Herbal benefits are many; be it for spiritual reasons or to spice up your taste buds, or as a home remedy for ailments like cold, or sore throat... herbs are handy for each need!

Although, the herbs been in use in our diet since antiquity, only recently they have taken the center-stage of nutrition scientific world for their potential health benefiting and detoxification properties.

Humans are dependent upon plants. Directly or indirectly, plants provide food, clothing, fuel, shelter and many other necessities of life. Humankind's dependence on crops such as wheat and corn (maize) is obvious, but without grass and grain the livestock that provide people with food and other animal products could not survive either.

References

Joanna Tatomir (2011): The Nutritional Use of Thai Medicinal Plants and the Etiology of Breast Cancer in Thai Women, Thesis for the degree of Doctor of Philosophy (Anthropology) in The University of Michigan, pp. 185.

http://www.realworldsurvivor.com/2015/10/23/5-plants-nutritional-medicinal-value/

https://en.wikipedia.org/wiki/Plant_nutrition

http://nzic.org.nz/ChemProcesses/soils/2A.pdf

http://www.nutrition-and-you.com/healthy-herbs.html

http://kids.britannica.com/comptons/article-206598/plant

64. **Waste Generation and Utilization**
Bajaj Priya; Tabassum, B., and Bharti, P.K. (eds.)
(ISBN: 978-93-5056-792-0).
65. **Waste Management and Environmental Health**
Tabassum, B., Bajaj Priya, and Bharti, P.K. (eds.)
(ISBN: 978-93-5056-777-7).
66. **Water Resources:** ***Mapping Monitoring and Management***
Tyagi, P.K., Chauhan, Avnish and Bharti, P.K. (eds.)
(ISBN: 978-93-5056-861-3).
67. **Water Resources and Agriculture**
Bharti, P.K. and Ezeaku Peter Ikemefuna (eds.)
(ISBN: 978-93-5056-481-3).
68. **Waste Resources Management:** ***Monitoring and Assessment***
Gupta, Sandeep and Bharti, P.K. (eds.)
(ISBN: 978-93-5056-799-9).

Medicinal and Nutritional Values of Plants
Edited by: Alka Chauhan and Pawan Kumar 'Bharti'
ISBN: 978-93-5056-883-5
Edition: 2017
Published by: Discovery Publishing House Pvt. Ltd., New Delhi (India)

1 Datura as Valuable Medicinal Plant and Pharmacological and Toxicological Aspects of Datura Stramonium L.

[1]Showkat Ahmad Bhat, [2]Sabhiya Majid,
[2]Tehseen Hassan, [2]Hilal Ahmad Wani, [2]N. A. Naikoo

ABSTRACT

Datura is well-known as a medicinal plant and plant hallucinogen all over the world. Datura has a very special place in Ayurveda since all parts of the plant namely leaves, flowers, seeds, roots, have been used for a wide range of medication such as treatment of leprosy, rabies, insanity, etc. The extract of Datura, however, is a potent poison and its indiscriminate use may lead to delirium and acute poisoning that may lead to death. The active constituents in Datura include scopolamine, atropine, hyoscyamine, withanolides (lactones) and other tropanes. Recently, with anolide compounds have shown significant antitumor, cytotoxic, anti-inflammatory, antibacterial, hepatoprotective, sedative, cytostatic and immunosuppressive activity. The present review includes phytochemical investigations and biological activities of various Datura species wherein several novel compounds have been isolated, characterized and screened for their biological activities. Datura stramonium L., is one of the Datura species, a wild-growing plant, widely distributed and easily accessible. It contains a variety of toxic tropane alkaloids such as atropine, hyoscamine, and scopolamine. In Eastern medicine, especially in Ayurvedic medicine, D. stramonium has been used for curing various human ailments, including ulcers, wounds, inflammation, rheumatism and gout, sciatica, bruises and swellings, fever, asthma and bronchitis, and toothache. A few previous studies have reported on the pharmacological effects of D. stramonium; however, complete information regarding the pharmacology, toxicity, ethnobotany and phytochemistry remains unclear. Ethnomedicinally, the frequent recreational abuse of D. stramonium has resulted in toxic syndromes. D. stramonium, in the form of paste or solution to relieve the local pain, may

1 Division of Veterinary Biochemistry, Faculty of Veterinary Sciences & Animal Husbandry, Sheri Kashmir University of Agricultural Science & Technology (SKUAST-K), Srinagar, J&K, India 190006
2 Department of Biochemistry, Government Medical College, Srinagar, J&K India

not have a deleterious effect; however, oral and systemic administration may lead to severe anticholinergic symptoms. For this reason, it is very important for individuals, mainly young people, to be aware of the toxic nature and potential risks associated with the use of this plant. This chapter includes information on botany, phytochemistry, pharmacology, toxicology and ethnomedicinal usesof Datura.

Key Words: Datura, chemical constituents, alkaloids, biological activities, therapeutic usage.

INTRODUCTION

Datura is a wild weed belonging to family Solanaceae, its name derived from Sanskrit word "Dhutra" (divine inebriation) is used for its healing properties. Various species of Datura are known and widely employed for their medicinal and toxic properties that are based upon more than 30 alkaloids. Because of their funnel form, fragrant nocturnal blooms, species such as atura inoxia, Datura metel, Datura stramonium and Datura wrightii are cultivated as ornamental plants with all but D. metel known from wild populations. Navajos chewed dried roots to reduce fever. Zunis made poultice from it to treat inflammation and bruises. In China, it is known as "Yangjinhua" and used for the treatment of asthma, convulsions, pain, and rheumatism. Flos Daturae has an effect on the treatment of psoriasis for clinical use in China. It is used in Italy to remove lice from hen bundles. D. stramonium seeds are used for acne and bronchitis in Sakarya province of North-west Turkey and locally called "Tatala", while the petroleum ether extract is also found to possess antimicrobial activities against Esherichia coli and Trachystemon orientalis. It is also used commonly in ethno veterinary practices in Nepal and by Gujjar community in India. In Ayurveda, Datura plant parts are sed to treat various disorders including asthma, skin disorders, jaundice, piles, and diabetes. Datura seeds have been used as a prophylactic measure to treat animal bites, especially dog bites. Person bitten by mad dog is administered with juice of Datura along with butter milk and jaggery. Also, the site of bite is smeared with a paste of the fruit. Extensive research has been carried out since 1925 for the isolation and characterization of the total alkaloid contents in Datura species. That The total alkaloid content in Datura varies from 0.02 to 0.52% and scopolamine from 0.0029 to 0.32% relative to the dried material, depending on the geographical area, the part of the plant studied and the stage of growth.(Del Pozo, 1966, Pan *et al.*, 2007, Guarrera, 1999, Uzun *et al.*, 2004, Raut and Shreshtha, 2012, Gaur *et al.*, 2010, Dash and Kashyap, 1991, Papadoyannis, 1995, Berkov *et al.*, 2006, Dovelana *et al.*, 2006, Vitale *et al.*, 1995).

Atropine is the racemic form of hyoscyamine. It binds competitively to muscarinic receptors blocking parasympathetic cholinergic neurons. It acts on both peripheral and central muscarinic receptors. In lower doses, it affects cardiovascular system causing bradycardia. Atropine increases acetylcholine release (cholinesterase inhibitors) and hence used as an antidote to treat organophosphate poisoning, to dilate the pupil, decrease the salivation and to reduce the gastrointestinal activity. Hyoscyamine and scopolamine act as anti muscarinic compounds and act on both CNS and peripheral nervous system. Scopolamine is used as CNS depressant in small doses and used to treat motion sickness. Apart from this, other therapeutic implications include antiemetic, antidysmenorrheal, and gastric anti spasmodic. Hyoscyamine is used as an adjunct in Zollinger-Ellison syndrome. Typical findings in Datura poisoning are dryness of the mouth, thirst, flushing, fever, amnesia, urinary retention, decreased salivation, papillary dilation, tachycardia, hallucinations (which are frightening), palpitation, ataxia, delirium leading to coma, cardiac and respiratory arrest and death (Maheshwari *et al.,* 2887, Bliss, 2001 &Barceloux, 2008).

Analgesic Effect

Aqueous extract of D. fastuosa leaves and seeds (10% w/v) were taken to evaluate the analgesic effect on acetic acid induced writhing pain and hot plate reaction in mice. Oral treatment of 400 and 800 mg/kg proved effective and showed significant analgesic effect. Upon naloxone administration, analgesic effect was reduced in leaf extract while the seed extract remained unaffected. Swiss mice under standard environment conditions were subjected to i.p. acetic acid injection (0.6%, 10 ml/kg) and hot plate to check the analgesic effect. Aqueous seed extract of D. metel L. was found not to possess analgesic activity on acetic acid induced model as well as the radiant heat tail-flick model (Abena *et al.,* 2003 & Wannang *et al.,* 2009).

Antiviral

Atropine inhibited only the growth of enveloped viruses independent of the nucleic acid content of the virus. The activity of atropine was checked by plaque reduction test and one step growth experiments. The test viruses included Herpes Simplex Virus, Influenza virus, New Castle Disease Virus, Sindbis, Vaccinia, Adenovirus, Japanese encephaitis Virus. Viruses were cultivated on primary chick embryo (CE), HeLa S3, primary monkey kidney cells (MK). Atropine also blocks the glycosylaton of viral proteins of Herpes virus and hence the production of new infectious virus particles (virions). Virions formed in the presence of atropine are noninfectious (Yamazaki and Tagaya, 1980 &Alarcon *et al.,* 1984).

Anticancer Activity

Chemical investigation of a methanol extract of the flowers of D. metel has led to the isolation of new withanolides I-P, 1-10-seco-withametelin B and 12-hydroxy-1,10-seco-withametelin B together with seven known withanolides. The structures where elucidated using spectroscopic data, while single crystal X-ray analysis was done for structure 9. The compounds where screened against various cancer cell lines including A549 (lung), BGC-823 (gastric) and K562 (leukemia). Compounds 1, 3, 4 and 6 exhibited cytotoxic activities with their IC50 values ranging from 0.05 to 3.5 μM. Sasaki *et al.*, (2002) have found that D. stramonium agglutin (DSA (lectin)) induced irreversible differentiation in C6 glioma cells. The differentiated cells had long processes, a low rate of proliferation and a high content of glial fibrillary acidic protein. Experiments with several other lectins indicated that both recognition of inear Nacetyllactosamine repeats and recognition of multiantennary units of cell-surface glycans were required for the inhibition of C6 proliferation. Proliferation of four human glial tumor cells was also inhibited by DSA, which suggests its usefulness as a new therapy for treating glioma without side effects. Li *et al.*, (2005) isolated endophytic fungi from D. stramonium and tested for the antitumor activities by MTT assay on human gastric tumor cell line BGC-823, which exhibited 100% growth inhibition rate. Iman Ahmad *et al.*, (2009) recently carried out studies on human cancer cell lines in vitro on MDA-MB231 (breast), and FaDu (neck). The treatment with D. stramonium aqueous leaf extract for 24 and 48 h showed increase in GSSG in FaDu cells indicating oxidative stress in treated cells.

Wound Healing Properties

In vivo healing potential of Datura alba alcoholic extract on burn rat wounds were studied (Shanmuga *et al.*, 2002). A 10% w/w ointment was prepared and applied topically on thermal wounds. Complete wound healing was observed within 12 days in treated rats against control rats which required about 30 days for healing. Apart from antimicrobial activity, studies were carried out to check rate of wound contraction and histochemical analysis to examine cellular infiltration. Biochemical assays to check collagen and hexosamine content of tissue on various days were carried out by using gelatin zymography. The antimicrobial assay done by disc diffusion method of the crude extract showed antimicrobial activity on pathogenic organisms obtained from burn patients. Silver sulfadiazine (1 mg/ml), DMSO and solvents used for fractionation were also tested simultaneously. The pathogens isolated from Burn ward unit, Child Trust Hospital, Chennai were Staphylococcus sp., Klebsiella sp., E. coli, Streptococcus sp.

Pseudomonas sp., Salmonella sp. and Vibrio sp. Wound healing was increased due to enhanced epithelialisation. The crude extract has enhanced chemotactic effect which attracted inflammatory cells towards the wound site and cellular proliferation was observed by hematoxylin and eosin staining. Increase in cellular proliferation may be due to mitogenic effect of the plant extract. Increase in hydroxyproline content was observed which indicates the increase in collagen synthesis which is essential for wound healing. Matrix metalloproteases (MMP's) such as MMP 9 were expressed in early days, and MMP 2, a 72 kDa gelatinase were also observed. MMP's are helpful in removal of fibrin and eschar which results in formation of peptides which are known to have angiogenic and chemotactic properties. The presence of gelatinase indicates progression of wound healing process.

Antiperspirant Activity

Anticholinergic compounds have antiperspirant action (Mac Millan *et al.*, 1964). Various compounds have been studied and esters of cholinergic compounds have been found to be more effective. Scopolamine hydrobromide is found to be most effective due to its skin penetration ability.

Anti-quorum Sensing Activity

One of the way to check anti pathogenic effect of medicinal plant is to check anti-quorum sensing activity of the extracts (Adonizio *et al.*, 2006). A wide range of plants were selected of different families for their anti-quorum sensing activity. Plant chosen from Solanaceae was D. metel L. Double purple, c.v. from South Florida. Ethanolic and aqueous extract of flowers and leaves were used to check the activity. Biomonitor organisms used were Chromobacterium violaceum and Agrobacterium tumefaciens NTL4 (pZLR4). Bioassay was done using disk diffusion method where C. violaceum (wt), CV026 supplemented with AHL and A. tumefaciens.

NTL4 supplemented with AHL and X-gal. The plates were incubated overnight and QS was observed by a ring of colourless but viable cells around the disc. D. metel did not show anti-QS activity, but the extracts are known to have anti-microbial activity which indicates other mechanism of inhibition.

Hypoglycemic Effect

In vivo hypoglycemic and anti-hyperglycemic effect of D. metel seeds were studied (Krishnamurthy *et al.*, 2004). Experiments were carried out on normal and alloxan induced diabetic rats. Alloxan is a cytotoxin and induces diabetes chemically through the damage of insulin secreting cells. Seed powder extract were tested on both normoglycemic as well as alloxan induced hyperglycemic rats to compare whether excess hypoglycemic effect is hypoglycemic effect is lethal. Gliclazide was used as control to reduce blood glucose level. Histopathological studies were not performed and hence detail mechanism of action could not be studied. Effect of seed powder showed rapid normalization of blood glucose level. Possible mechanism could be that some of the cells might have survived the damage and secreted insulin when treated with seed extract. Further studies need to be carried out to check the exact mode of action and the active component participating from the seed extract and to check the synergistic action of the components present in the seed extract. Investigation on Insulin release and enzyme inhibition activity also needed to be studied.

Immunomodulatory Activity

Phytochemical investigations of D. quercifolia has led to the isolation and characterization of several Datura lactones, which are of withanolide skeleton by Bhat *et al.*, (2005). Phytochemical investigation yielded a new Datura lactone, 1",5!,12!-trihydroxy-6!,7!, 24!, 25!-diepoxy- 20S, 22R with 2-enolide (5) along with two known compounds, 3 and 4. These compounds were evaluated for their immunomodulatory activity by observing the B and T-cell activation and cytokine production from splenocytes. Of the three compounds isolated, Compound 4 showed dose related increase in primary and secondary antibody production, while Compound 5 act as a suppressor where levamisole was use as standard which increases primary and secondary antibody production. Compound 3 showed higher SRBC induced DTH response at a dose of 0.1 mg/kg p.o. BMS (Betamethasone) was used as standard. Compound 3 was checked for the activation of spleen Tcell sub types, CD4 and CD8, selective release of cytokines, IL-2 and TNF-!. It stimulated and showed increase in CD4+ T-cell count and stimulated increase in IL-2 and TNF-! in dose dependent manner (0.01 mg/kg was found more effective) (figure 1.1).

Anti Ulcer

Investigation was done to evaluate anti ulcer activity and its mechanism on various models on experimentally induced ulcers in rats (Falcao *et al.*, 2008). W.E. (20 mg/kg) reduced the ulcer and ulcer index significantly in rats. It decreased the volume of gastric secretion, acid and peptic output significantly; it did not affect the mucin secretion and total mucosal glycoprotein content in terms of total carbohydrate, protein gastric cell shedding or cell replication. It also augments prostaglandins.

Anti-stress

Withanolides from D. fastuosa possess anti-stress activity (Manickam *et al.*, 1997; Ratan *et al.*, 2011). When administered with diazepam, it exhibited an axiolytic effect effect and inhibited the immobilization stress induced depletion of adrenal cortisone. Adrenal cortisone help organism to overcome annoying stimuli, but such responses can cause stress induced disorders.

Detailed study of varying doses, duration and mode of administration is essential to know the effectiveness as an anti-stress agent.

Anti-microbial Activity

A new antibacterial agent, 5′,7′ dimethyl 6′-hydroxy 3′, phenyl 3 !-amine "-yne sitosterol (28) was isolated by Okwu and Igara (2009) from D. metel leaves. The structure was established using 13C, 1H NMR, IR and MS spectroscopic studies. This compound displayed antibacterial activity against Staphylococcus aureus, Pseudomonas aeruginosa, Proteus mirabilis, Solmonella typhi, Bacillus subtilis and Klebsiella pneumonia but could not inhibit Escherichia coli. In vitro antibacterial activity of aqueous as well as organic extract from various plant parts of D. innoxia was checked. Gram negative bacteria such as P. aeruginosa, E. coli, K. pneumonia, S. typhi, Enterococcus faecalis, Vibrio sp., Proteus vulgaris, while the Gram positive: B. subtilis, S. aureus, Bacillus cereus were evaluated by Kaushik and Goyal (2008). It was found that the organic extracts from leaves are more potent inhibitors and displayed better antibacterial activity as compared to the stems and roots. Methanol extract shows more inhibition. While chloroform extract is found to be active against Aspergillus flavus, Aspergillus niger, Aspergillus fumigatus. Candida albicans (Eftekar *et al.,* 2005). Acetone extracts of D. stramonium plant parts were tested against Vibrio cholerae and Vibrio parahaemolyticus by Sharma and Patel (2009). The crude plant extracts exhibited a MIC of 2.5 to 15 μg/ml. The assays were done by disc diffusion method. Banso and Adeyemo (2006) have also assessed the phytochemical components and antimicrobial activity of D. stramonium ethanolic leaf extract against P. aeruginosa, K. pneumonia and E. coli. It was recorded that higher concentrations of the extracts were required to inhibit growth. Antimicrobial substances may affect the synthesis of peptidoglycan around the bacterial cell, and the cell dies by osmotic shock. The MIC of the plant extracts ranged from 15 to 25% w/v.

Anti-fungal Activity

The hexane, chloroform, acetone and methanolic fractions of D. metel L. were investigated for antifungal properties against three species of Aspergillus, that is, A. fumigates, A. flavus, and A. niger (Rajesh and Sharma, 2002). The MIC of the chloroform extract was found to be 625.0 μg/ml by microbroth dilution method and 12.5 μg/disc by the disc diffusion assay. Although the chloroform extract of D. metel was 9.2 time less active than amphotericin B, it was 117.8 times less cytotoxic than the standard drug. A concoction brewed from D. stramonium, Calotropis gigantean, Azadirachta indica and cow manure was used against floral malformations caused by Fusarium mangiferae (Usha *et al.,* 2009). The study proved that the concoction is effective, inexpensive, easy to prepare and constitutes a sustainable and eco-friendly approach to control floral malformation in mango when it is sprayed at Aqueous extract of D. alba Rees was evaluated against Rumex dentalus L., a problematic weed of wheat. Application of aqueous extracts caused 68% reduction in germination, 62% in shoot length, 96% in root length and 68% in seedling biomass (Jamid *et al.,* 2009). Scopalamine has been shown to attenuate memory task. Grasby *et al.,* (1993) have suggested that the acute blockade of cholinergic neurotransmission effects diverse brain areas, including components of visual and motor systems and in addition modulates memory task activation at distinct points in distributed network for memory function.

Datura Stramonium L

Datura stramonium, the most common species within this family, is native to Asia, but is also found in the United States, Canada, and the West Indies. It is widespread with higher abundance in temperate, tropical and subtropical regions. Traditionally, D. stramonium has been used for mystic and religious purposes, and as an herbal medicine with narcotic effects or to treat asthma. The seed of D. stramonium is smoked to achieve hallucinogenic experiences as well. D. stramonium is toxic when consumed improperly. Accidental poisoning of humans and animals who consumed food sources contaminated with D. stramonium has been reported (Diker *et al.*, 2007 & Naude *et al.*, 2005). In areas where millet, wheat, rye, corn, and bean seeds are used for human consumption, and where D. stramonium is a common weed, the grain sometimes has been contaminated with Datura seeds .In Ayurvedic medicine, D. stramonium is described as a useful remedy for various human ailments including ulcers, wounds, inflammation, rheumatism and gout, sciatica, bruises and swellings, fever, asthma and bronchitis, toothache, etc. Many folk medicine remedies use D. stramonium therapeutically. In the Hindu religion, the seed of D. stramonium is believed to be associated with the God Shiva, which can promote misuse of the plant on religious occasions, such as Shivaratri and Swasthani Pujall In modern medicine, the therapeutic uses of D. stramonium are overshadowed by its toxic effects. The administration of large amounts of D. stramonium affects the central nervous system with symptoms such as confusion, bizarre behavior, hallucinations and subsequent amnesia. Though death by D. stramonium poisoning is rare, recovery may take several days. Therefore, a thorough understanding of the possible pharmacological and toxicological effects of D. stramonium is needed. This review focuses on the botany, phytochemistry, pharmacology, toxicology and ethnomedicinal uses of D. stramonium (Norton *et al.*, 2008, Kirtikar *et al.*, 1999 & Gaire *et al.*, 2008).

BOTANY

Scientific Name and Classification

In Nepal, D. stramonium L. is commonly known as Dhaturo, Seto Dhaturo, Dhattur, and Madak. In Sanskrit language, it has several names such as Dhatturdhurtadhustura Unmatta, Kanakahwaya, Dewatakitawasturi Mahamohi Shivapriya, and Matulo Madanashchasya phale Matulaputraka. Other common names of D. stramonium include, Estramonio (Brazil); Chan K'iue Tse (Chinese); Thorn apple, Jimson weed, Mad Apple (English); Chasse-taupe (French); and Trompetilla (Spanish). D. inermis Juss. ex Jacq., D. chalybea W. D. J. Koch and D. tatula (L.) Torr. are the synonyms of D. stramonium. It can be classified as Kingdom: Plantae - Plants; Subkingdom: Tracheobionta - Vascular plants; Superdivision: Spermatophyta - Seed plants; Division:

Magnoliophyta - Flowering plants; Class: Magnoliopsida - Dicotyledons; Subclass: Asteridae; Order: Solanales; Family: Solanaceae - Potato family; Genus: Datura L.; and Species: D. stramonium L. (figure 1.1).

Fig. 1.1: Different parts of Datura stramonium St: stem; L.f: leaf; Fl: flower; Fr: fruit; Sd: seed.

Distribution

D. stramonium is native to deserts of the North American Southwest, Central and South America, Europe, Asia, and Africa. It is mainly distributed in the Himalaya region from Kashmir to Sikkim up to 2 700 m, in the hilly district of central and south India.

Botanical Description

D. stramonium is a large and coarse shrub of about 3 to 4 feet in height. On rich soil, it may even reach the height of 6 feet. The root is large, whitish in color, with a taproot system giving off many fibers. The stem is green or purple, hairless, cylindrical, erect and leafy, smooth, branching repeatedly in a forked manner. Leaves and a single, erect flower arise through the forks of the branches. The alternate leaves are ovate in outline, but pinnately lobed. These lobes are somewhat shallow and point at their tips; there are usually 2 to 3 of these lobes on each side of the leaf blade. Leaves are cauline and ramal, exstipulate, up to 8 cm long and 6 cm across, petiolate, simple, dissected, acute, glabrous, unicosted, and arranged in reticular venation. The upper surface is dark and grayish- green, generally smooth, whereas the underside is paler, and when dry, minutely wrinkled. Leaves, when bruised, exude a rank, heavy, and somewhat nauseating narcotic odor. The flowers are ebracteate, ebracteolate, pedicellate, actinomorphic, bisexual, complete, regular, pentamerous, except fourth whorl and are hypogynous. They are sweet-scented, and can produce stupor if breathed for a prolonged period of time. Each flower is replaced by a hard fruit that is dry and spiny, and spheroid-ovoid in shape. Underneath, each fruit is a truncated remnant of the calyx that curves sharply down. These fruits are initially green, but become brown with maturity; they divide into four segments to release the seeds. The seeds are dull, irregular, and dark-colored; their surface may be pitted or slightly reticulated (Preissel *et al.*, 2002 & Das *et al.*, 2012).

Propagation

D. stramonium is germinated via seeds. It is essentially a temperate plant but is found growing in the vicinity of cultivation, on rank soil, in all parts of the world. The seed usually germinates in 3 to 6 weeks at 15 °C. Seeds can remain viable for several years in storage.

Ethnomedicinal Uses

In Western Nepal, leaves of Datura along with the leaves of Cannabis sativa and stem of Neopicrorhiza scrofulariflora, are pounded with water and applied to treat headaches. Datura seeds are crushed with grains of rice and taken orally to relieve indigestion. In parts of Central Nepal, fresh leaves are warmed and placed on a sprained body part repeatedly, before going to bed, for the alleged analgesic effect. Juice from the leaves is given with warm milk to expel intestinal worms, specifically tapeworm. In Nigeria, the seeds are mixed with palm oil and applied to severe cases of insect bites and stings. In India, the seeds are used as a tonic and febrifuge; the leaves are roasted and applied locally to relieve pain. Women in Pakistan warm up 5 to 8 leaves in low fire, and then tie onto sagging breasts to bust them up. Two to five seeds are added to a cup of green tea to relieve headache. Native Americans used Datura seed for many years as a euphoric agent. Since the 1800s, it was used as a therapeutic agent in Great Britain (Gorsi *et al.*, 2002 & Hussain *et al.*, 2006).

Phytochemistry

Phytochemical studies of D. stramonium have been conducted since the early 1930s. The major phytochemicals isolated from D. stramonium are tropane alkaloids, atropine and scopolamine. It is reported that the whole plant contains 0.26% alkaloids. Seeds of Datura contain the alkaloid daturine, first isolated, purified and crystallized by Geiger and Hesse, in 1833. Von Planta (1850) pro-nounced daturine to be identical with atropine, the principal belladonna alkaloid; later, Ladenburg differentiated daturine into atropine and hyoscyamine, the latter alkaloid predominating. Schmidt, however, contended that atropine predominates. The seeds contain fatty oil (25%), from which a new fatty acid, daturic acid ($C_{17}H_{34}O_2$), was isolated. Dohme concluded that the stems contain more alkaloids (0.3% to 0.4%, volumetrically) than even the seeds (0.25% to 0.29%), and the seeds contain more alkaloid than the leaves (0.21% to 0.23%, and 0.27% for green leaves). Berkov *et al.*, suggested hyoscyamine as the main alkaloid in both diploid and tetraploid hairy root cultures of D. stramonium.

Iranbakhsh *et al.*, reported the percentage of atropine and scopolamine in different developmental stages and the parts of the Datura. Their study suggested that the root contained lower levels of scopolamine than that of atropine and the same goes for the stem. In stems, atropine was almost three times higher than scopolamine. However, leaves and seeds contained higher level of scopolamine than that of atropine. Recently, Li *et al.*, reported the different alkaloids from D. stramonium seeds such as N-trans-feruloyl tryptamine, hyoscyamilactol, scopoletin, umckalin, daturaolone, daturadiol, N-trans-ferulicacyl-tyramine, cleomiscosin A, fraxetin, 1-acetyl-7-hydrox-beta-carboline, and 7-hydroxy-beta-carboline-propionic acid (Berkov *et al.*, 2003, Iranbakhsh *et al.*, 2006, Li *et al.*, 2012, Charpin *et al.*, 1979 & Pretorius *et al.*, 2006).

D. stramonium contains a variety of alkaloids, including atropine and scopolamine, having anticholinergic and bronchodilating activity. Atropine and scopolamine act on the muscarinic receptors by blocking them (particularly the M2 receptors) on airway smooth muscle and submucosal gland cells, which dilate bronchial smooth muscle and ease asthmatic attacks. Charpin *et al.*, reported that using D. stramonium as an antiasthmatic cigarette is an effective bronchodilator in asthmatic patients with mild airway obstruction. However, the exposure of D. stramonium to the fetus when a mother uses it for asthma will cause a continuous release of acetylcholine, resulting in the desensitizing of nicotinic receptors, which could ultimately result in permanent damage to the fetus.Though the antiepileptic activity of D. stramonium has not been reported yet, combination therapy with other herbs has the protective effect on status epilepticus. An experimental model of status epilepticus was induced in male rats by a single systemic injection of lithium (3 mmol/kg) and pilocarpine (30 g/kg). Rats were then treated with herbal mixture containing D. stramonium. One week after the induction of status epilepticus, the rat group treated with extracts of Scutellaria lateriflora (Skullcap), Gelsemium sempervirens (Gelsemium) and D. stramonium (Jimson Weed) displayed no seizure during treatment. The results of this experiment strongly suggest that the appropriate combination of herbs with D. stramonium may be helpful as adjunctive interventions to treat epilepsy. Since D. stramonium contains atropine and other anticholinergic compounds, it is a useful remedy for the central cholinergic symptoms of organophosphate (OP) poisoning. Bania *et al.*, determined the beneficial effect of Datura seed extracts following a severe OP poisoning. According to their experiment, D. stramonium seeds were heated in water to make 2 mg/mL atropine solution and administered to male rats as a single intraperitoneal injection 5 min before the subcutaneous injection of 25 mg/kg of dichlorvos. Pretreatment with Datura seed extracts significantly increased survival in a rat model of severe OP poisoning. (Peredery *et al.*, 2004 & Bania *et al.*, 2004)

The methanol extracts of aerial parts of D. stramonium showed the bactericidal activity against Gram-positive bacteria in a dose-dependent manner. However, little or no antibacterial activity was found against Escherichia coli and Pseudomonas aeruginosa. Ethanol extract exhibited the highest inhibitory activity against Klebsiella pneumonia followed by Staphylococcus aureus, with the least activity against Salmonella typhi. The aqueous extract showed activity on only S. aureus, while Neisseria gonorrhea was resistant to both extracts. D. stramonium was very effective as vibriocidal against various strains of Vibreo cholera and Vibreo parahaemolyticus. The minimum inhibitory concentration (MIC) value of acetone extracts of D. stramonium was in the range of 2.5 to 15 mg/mL serving as broad-spectrum vibriocidal agents.Acetone extracts of D. stramonium have been reported to have antifungal activity against several fungi including Penicillium expansum, Aspergillus niger, Aspergillus parasiticus, Colletotrichum gloeosporioides, Fusarium oxysporum, Trichoderma harzianum, Phytophthora nicotiana, Pythium ultimum and Rhizoctonia solani. The MIC of D. stramonium extracts ranges from 1.25 to 2.5 mg/mL. The fungicidal effects of the extracts indicate the potential of D. stramonium seeds as a natural source of antifungal agent.The ethanolic extract of D. stramonium leaf showed significant anti-inflammatory activity against carrageenan-induced paw edema in rats. In one experiment, 39.43% inhibition of the edema was observed after 3 h of oral administration of 200 mg/kg extracts. Maximum activity was observed when the extract was administered in doses of 3-hour intervals. Since the extract of D. stramonium inhibited the carrageenan-induced edema that involves the release of histamine and serotonin in the first phase, the inhibitory effect of the extracts could be partly due to inhibition of mast cell mediator release. (Mdee *et al.*, 2009, Sonika *et al.*, 2010 & Kurnal *et al.*, 2010)

Datura plant generates a characteristic odor that acts as repellent for various insects and pests. Kurnal *et al.*, have reported that the ethanol extracts of D. stramonium leaf and seed showed potent acaricidal, repellent, and oviposition deterrent activity against adult two-spotted spider mites (Tetranychus urticae) under laboratory conditions. Leaf and seed extracts, which were applied in 167.25 and 145.75 g/L concentrations (using a Petri leaf disc-spray tower method), caused 98% and 25% mortality among spider mite adults after 48 h, respectively. These results suggest that D. stramonium could be used to manage the two-spotted spider mite. D. stramonium was reported to have anticancer effect against human epidermal carcinoma of the nasopharynx at a therapeutic dose of 0.05 to 0.1 g. However, precaution should be taken while using Datura as an anticancer agent since adverse anticholinergic effects may occur. The half lethal dose (LD50) for ethanolic extracts of D. stramonium leaves showed potential larvicidal and mosquito repellent activities against Aedesaegypti (LD50: 86.25 mg/L), Anopheles stephensi (LD50: 16.07 mg/L) and Culex quinquefasciatus (LD50: 6.25 mg/L). D. stramonium is generally administered at a dose of 60 to 185 mg powder for leaf and 60 to 120 mg powder for seed (Swathi *et al.*, 2012, Hirschmann *et al.*, 1990 & Spina *et al.*, 2007.

D. stramonium is mostly studied for its toxicological properties. Datura poisoning is very common in India, usually involving the seeds. Many cases of unintentional poisoning by D. stramonium species have been reported when taken accidentally, or as decoction prepared from herbal prescription. General symptoms of D. stramonium poisoning include delirium, agitation and seizures, mydriasis, blurred vision, photophobia, dry mouth and mucous membranes, extreme thirst, tachycardia, nausea and vomiting, decreased bowel sounds, difficulty swallowing and speaking, hyperthermia, hypertension, loss of consciousness and coma. Dugan *et al.*, have reported that ingestion of D. stramonium seed at concentrations of 0.5% or more in the diet produced adverse physiological changes in rats. Bouzidi *et al.*, reviewed the acute, subacute and chronic toxicity studies of alkaloids from the seeds of D. stramonium. According to them, single dose acute toxicity of 100 mg/kg D. stramonium includes decreases in the weight of the liver, spleen and brain, and significant increases in the levels of red blood cells (RBC), hematocrit (HCT), hemoglobin (HGB), and white blood cells (WBC). Similarly, RBC, HGB, HCT and platelet levels were increased in 4-week subacute toxicity studies. However, the 120-day chronic toxicity study of D. stramonium alkaloids showed decreased levels of RBC, HCT, HBG and WBC, with a significant increase in liver enzymes. Fatal dosages of D. stramonium toxins occured with amounts exceeding 10 mg for adults, and mg for children. The amount needed to poison an adult is about 20 seeds, and the estimated LD in an adult is >10 mg atropine or >2 to 4 mg scopolamine. Almost all the parts of D. stramonium are reported to have toxic effects, and the toxicity of this plant is mainly due to the tropane alkaloids. Each part varies in the concentrations of alkaloids and other active substances. For this reason, it is very important for individuals, especially young people, to be aware of the toxicity and potential risks associated with the "recreational" use of this plant. D. stramonium in the form of a paste or solution to relieve local pain may not have a deleterious effect; however, oral and systemic administration of the D. stramonium may lead to severe anticholinergic symptoms. Various cases of toxic delirium and psychiatric symptoms have been reported after ingestion of D. stramonium indicating the necessity of extreme precaution while using this plant (Oberndorfer *et al.*, 2002,

Dugan *et al.*, 1989, Bouzidi *et al.*, 2011, Kurzbaum *et al.*, 2001, Karada *et al.*, 2001 & Karada *et al.*, 2011).

Conclusion

Medicinal plants have formed the basis of health care throughout the world since the earliest days of humanity and are still widely used and have considerable importance in international trade. Plants are important for pharmacological research and drug development, not only when bioactive phytocompounds are used directly as therapeutic agents, but also as starting materials or the synthesis of drugs or as models for pharmacologically active compounds. With latest advances in medicinal chemistry and knowledge of biosynthetic route for the development of lead compounds have opened a new perspectives in the field of drug chemistry. There is a need to design new molecules from natural sources to combat lethal diseases. Thus plants are proving as potential source for drug discovery. With anolides have known anticancer activity which needs to be further explored. However, the integration of herbal medicine into modern medicinal practises, including treatments for infections and cancer, must contemplate the related issues of quality, safety and efficacy. This review has been directed towards various interesting findings of the medicinal value of Datura, apart from its toxicity and ornamental importance to prove it as a potent chemotherapeutic agent. Thus concerted efforts in the relevant areas is still necessary to establish rational and sustainable exploitation of the worlds biodiversity. In Ayurveda, different parts of D. stramonium are used for various human ailments when applied both locally and through oral administration, but classic Ayurveda lacks specific knowledge on the toxicity of D. stramonium. The pharmacological effect of D. stramonium described above can be applied through modern or alternative herbal medicine approaches. D. stramonium should only be used therapeutically while under the care of knowledgeable health care professionals. The adverse effects of D. stramonium can be extremely severe and detrimental. Therefore, even in light of its many beneficial effects, the risk benefit ratio should be always taken into consideration before using D. stramonium.

REFERENCES

Abena AA, Miguel LM, Mouanga A, Assah HTH, Diatewa M (2003). Evaluation of Analgesic Effect of Datura Fastuosa Leaves and Seed Extracts. Fitoterapia 74:486-488.

Adonizio AL, Downum K, Bennett BC, Mathee K (2006). Anti-quorum Sensing Activity of Medicinal Plants in Southern Florida. J. Ethnopharmacol. 105:427-435.

Ahmad IM, Abdalla MY, Mustafa NH, Qnais EY, Abdulla FA (2009). Datura Aqueous Leaf Extract Enhances Cytotoxicity via Metabolic Oxidative Stress on Different Human Cancer Cells. Jordan J. Biol.Sci. 2(1):9-14.

Alarcon B, Gonzalez ME, Carrasco L (1984). Antiherpesvirus Action of Atropine. Antimicrob. Agents Chemother. 26(5):702-706.

Bania TC, Chu J, Bailes D, O'Neill M. Jimson Weed Extract as a Protective Agent in Severe Organophosphate Toxicity. Acad Emerg Med. 2004; 11(4): 335-338.

Banso A, Adeyemo S (2006). Phytochemical Screening and Antimicrobial Assessment of Abutilon Mauritianum, Bacopa Monnifera and Datura Stramonium. Biokemistri 18(1):39-44.

Begum SA, Sahai M, Fujimoto Y, Asai K, Schneider K, Nicholson G, Suessmuth R (2006). A New Kaempferol Diglycoside from Datura Suaveolens Humb. & Bonpl. Ex. Willd. Nat. Prod. Res. 20:1231-1236.

Berkov S, Pavlov A, Kovatcheva P, Stanimirova P, Philipov S. Alkaloid Spectrum in Diploid and Tetraploid Hairy Root Cultures of Datura Stramonium. Z Naturforsch C. 2003; 58(1-2): 42-46.

Berkov S, Zayed R, Doncheva T (2006). Alkaloid Pattern in Some Varieties of Datura Stramonium. Fitoterapia 77:179-182.

Bhat BA, Dhar KL, Puri SC, Qurishi MA, Khajuria A, Gupta A, Qazi GN (2005). Isolation, Characterization and Biological Evaluation of Datura Lactones as Potential Immunomodulators, Bio. Med. Chem. 13:6672-6677.

Bliss M (2001). Datura Plant Poisoning. Clin. Toxicol. Rev. 23:6.

Bouzidi A, Mahdeb N, Kara N. Toxicity Studies of Alkaloids of Seeds of Datura Stramonium and Synthesis Alkaloids in Male Rats. J Med Plants Res. 2011; 5(15): 3421-3431.

Broekaert WF, Allen AK, Peunes WJ (1987). Seperation and Characterization of Isolectin with Different Subunits Components from Datura Stramonium Seeds. FEBS Lett. 220:116-120.

Charpin D, Orehek J, Velardocchio JM. Bronchodilator Effects of Antiasthmatic Cigarette Smoke (Datura stramonium). Thorax. 1979; 34(2): 259-261.

Cirigliano A, Velerio AS, Oberti JC, Burton G (1995). A 15!- Hydroxywithanolide from Datura Ferox. Phytochemistry 40:611-613.

D, Markovitz D, Rothman M, Sendovski U. Coma as a Presenting Sign of Datura Stramonium Seed Tea Poisoning. Eur J Intern Med. 2007; 18(4): 336-338.

Das S, Kumar P, Basu SP. Review Article on Phytoconstituents and Therapeutic Potentials of Datura Stramonium Linn. J Drug Deliv Ther. 2012; 2(3): 4-7.

Dash B, Kashyap L (1991). Five Specialized Therapies of Ayurveda, Panchakarma: Based on Ayurveda; Concept Publishing Company New Delhi, .165. (b) Database on Medicinal Plants used in Ayurveda, Vol. 2: Central Council for Research in Ayurveda and Siddha: 200. (c) Satyavati G.V, Rama M.K, Sharma M (1976). Medicinal Plants of India Vol. 1, ICMR: New Delhi, p. 333.

Datura Innoxia and Datura Stramonium, Fitoterapia 76:118-120.

Del Pozo EC (1966). Aztec Pharmacology. Ann. Rev. Pharmacol. 6:9- 18.

Desai NN, Allen AK, Neubergerr A (1981). Some Properties of Lectins from Datura Stramonium (Thorn Apple) and Nature of Its Glycoprotein Linkages. Biochem. J. 187:345-353.

DeWolf GP (1956). Notes on Cultivated Solanaceae 2 Datura. Baileya 4:12-13.

Dhar KL, Kalla AK (1976). A 12-oxowithanolide from Datura Quercifolia Phytochemistry 15:339. Eftekar F, Youxfardi M, Tafakori V (2005). Antimicrobial Activity.

Dugan GM, Gumbmann MR, Friedman M. Toxicological Evaluation of Jimson Weed (Datura Stramonium) Seed. Food Chem Toxicol. 1989; 27(8): 501-510.

Gaire BP. Monograph on Datura Stramonium. Kaski, Nepal: Pokhara University Press. 2008: 1-114.

Gaur RD, Sharma J, Painuli RM (2010). Plants Used in Traditional Healthcare of Livestock by Gorsi MS, Shahzad R. Medicinal Uses of Plants with Particular Reference to the People of Dhirkot, Azad Jammu and Kashmir. Asian J Plant Sci. 2002; 1(3): 222-223.

Grasby PM, Frith CD, Friston KJ, Frackowiak, RJ, Dolan RJ (1993). The Effect of Muscarinic Antagonist Scopolamine on Regional Cerebral Blood Flow during Performance of a Network Task. Exp. Brain Res. 109:337-348.

Guarrera PM (1999). Traditional Antihelmintic, Antiparasitic and Repellent Uses of Plants in Central Italy. J. Ethnopharmacol. 68:183-192. Jamid A, Shafique S, Shafique S (2009). Herbicidal Activity of Withania Somnifera and Datura Alba Against Rumex Dentatus. J. Agric. Res.47:37-45.

Gujjar Community of Sub-Himalayan Tracts, Uttarkhand, India. Ind. J. Nat. Prod. Res. 12:243 248.

Hirschmann GS, De Arias AR.A Survey of Medicinal Plants of Minas Gerais, Brazil. J Ethnopharmacol. 1990; 29(2): 159-172.

Hussain F, Badshah L, Dastagir G. Folk Medicinal Uses of Some Plants of South Waziristan, Pakistan. Pak J Plant Sci. 2006; 12: 27-39.

Iranbakhsh A, Oshaghi MA, Majd A. Distribution of Atropine and Scopolamine in Different Organs and Stages of Development in Datura Stramonium L. (Solanaceae). Structure and Ultrastructure of Biosynthesizing Cells. Acta Biol Crac Ser Bot. 2006; 48(1): 13-18.

Jayaprakasam B, Zhang Y, Seeram NP, Nair MG (2003). Growth Inhibition of Humor Cell Lines by Withanolides from Withania Somnifera Leaves. Life Sci. 74:125-132.

Karada S, Selvi Y, §ahin M, Selvi F, Oncu R, Ozgokfe F. Datura Stramonium Intoxication: Report of a Case with Psychiatric Symptoms. Duunen Adam: J Psychiatry Neuro Sci. 2011; 24(2): 152-154.

Kaushik P, Goyal P (2008). In Vitro Evaluation of Datura Innoxia (Thorn Apple) for Potential Antibacterial Activity. Indian J. Microbiol. 48:353-357.

Kinghorn AD, Su BN, Kang YH, Park EJ, Pizzuta JM (2004). Induction of the Phase II Enzyme, Quinone Reductase, by Withanolides and Norwithanolides from Solanaceous Species. Mini. Rev. Org. Chem. 1:115-123.

Kirtikar KR, Basu BD. Indian Medicinal Plants. 2nd ed. Volume III. Dehradun: International Book Distributors. 1999: 1783-1787.

Kocor M, St. Pyrek J (1973). Triterpenes of Datura Innoxia Mill. Structure of Daturadiol and Daturaolone, J. Org. Chem. 38:3685-3688.

Krishnamurthy B, Nauri S, Kota MK, Krishna Rao RV, Koteswara Rao N, Annapurna A (2004). Evaluation of Hypoglycemic and Antihyperglycemic Effects of Datura Metel (Linn) Seeds in Normal and Alloxan-induced Diabetic rats. J. Ethnopharmacol. 91:95-98.

Kurnal NA, Qobanoglu S, Yalcin C. Acaricidal, Repellent and Oviposition Deterrent Activities of Datura Stramonium L. against Adult Tetranychus Urticae (Koch). J Pest Sci. 2010; 83(2): 173-180.

Kurzbaum A, Simsolo C, Kvasha L, Blum A. Toxic Delirium Due to Datura Stramonium. Isr Med Assoc J. 2001; 3(7): 538-539.

Li H, Qing C, Zhang Y, Zhao Z (2005). Screening for Endophytic Fungi with Antitumor and Antifungal Activities from Chinese Medicinal Plants.World J. Micro Biotechnol. 21:1515-1519.

Li J, Lin B, Wang G, Gao H, Qin M. Chemical Constituents of Datura Stramonium Seeds. Zhongguo Zhong Yao Za Zhi. 2012; 37(3): 319-322. Chinese with Abstract in English.

Mac Millan FSK, Reller HH, Synder FH (1964). The Antiperspirant Action of Topically Applied Anticholinergics. J. Investig. Dermatol.p. 363.

Manickam M, Awasthi SB, Sinha-Bagchi A, Sinha SC, Ray AB (1996). Withanolides from Datura Tatula. Phytochemistry 41:981-983.

Manickam M, Padma P, Chourasia JPN, Ray AB (1997). Evaluation of Antistress Activity of with a Fastuosin D, a Withanolide of Datura Fastuosa. Phytother. Res. 11:384-385.

Manickam M, Srivastava A, Ray AB (1998). Withanolides from the Flowers of Datura Fastuosa. Phytochemistry 47:1427-1429.

Mdee LK, Masoko P, Eloff JN (2009). The Activity of Extracts of Seven Common Invasive Plant Species on Fungal Phytopathogens. South Afr. J. Bot. 75:375-379.

Mdee LK, Masoko P, Eloff JN. The Activity of Extracts of Seven Common Invasive Plant Species on Fungal Phytopathogens. S Afr J Bot. 2009; 75(2): 375-379.

Mohan R, Hammers HJ, Zhan XH, Herbstritt CJ, Ruiz A, Zhang L, Hanson AD, Commer BP, Rougas J, Priblude VS (2004) Withaferin A is a Potent Inhibitor of Angiogenesis. Angiogenesis 7:115.

Naude TW, Gerber R, Smith RJ, Botha CJ. Datura Contamination of Hay as the Suspected Cause of an Extensive Outbreak of Impaction Colic in Horses. J S Afr Vet Assoc. 2005; 76(2): 107-112.

Norton S. Toxic Effects of Plants. In: Klaassen CD. Caserett and Doull's Toxicology, the Basic Science of Poisons. 7th ed. New York: McGraw Hill. 2008: 1110.

Oberndorfer S, Grisold W, Hinterholzer G, Rosner M. Coma with Focal Neurological Signs Caused by Datura Stramonium Intoxication in a Young Man. J Neurol Neurosurg Psychiatr. 2002; 73(4): 458-459.

Okwu DE, Igara EC (2009). Isolation, Characterization and Antibacterial Activity of Alkaloid from Datura Metel Linn Leaves. Afr. J. Pharm. Pharmacol. 3:277-281.

Pan Y, Wang X, Hu X (2007). Cytotoxic Withanolides from the Flowers of Datura metel. J. Nat. Prod. 70:1127-1132.

Papadoyannis IN (1995). Determination of Datura Alkaloids by using Chromatographic Techmiques: Rev. Natl. Tox. 3:310-316.

Peredery O, Persinger MA. Herbal Treatment Following Post-seizure Induction in Rat by Lithium Pilocarpine: Scutellaria Lateriflora (Skullcap), Gelsemium Sempervirens (Gelsemium) and Datura Stramonium (Jimson weed) may Prevent Development of Spontaneous Seizures. Phytother Res. 2004; 18(9): 700-705.

Preissel U, Preissel HG. Brugmansia and Datura: Angel's Trumpets and Thorn Apples. New York: Firefly Books. 2002: 106-129.

Pretorius E, Marx J (2006). Datura Stramonium in Asthma Treatment and Possible Effects on Prenatal Development. Environ. Toxicol. Pharmacol. 21:331.

Pretorius E, Marx J. Datura Stramonium in Asthma Treatment and Possible Effects on Prenatal Development. Environ Toxicol Pharmacol. 2006; 21(3): 331-337.

Rajesh C, Sharma GL (2002). Studies on Antimycotic Properties of Datura metel. J. Ethnopharmacol. 80:193-197.

Raut B, Shreshtha AP (2012). Ethenoveterinary Practices in Western Morang, Nepal. Int. J. Pharm. Sci Res. 3:182-188.

Sasaki T, Yamazaki K, Yamori T, Endo T (2002). Inhibition of Proliferation and Induction of Differentiation of Glioma Cells with Datura Stramonium Agglutinin. Brit. J. Cancer 87:918-923.

Savitharam N, Sulochana C, Rao KA (2007). Ethnobotanical Survey of Plants used to Treat Asthma in AP, India, J. Ehthano. 113:54-61.

Shanmuga PK, Gnanmani A, Radhakrishnan N, Mary B (2002). Healing Potential of Datura Alba on Burn Wounds in Albino Rats. J. Ethnopharmacol. 83:193-199.

Sharma A, Patel VK (2009). In vitro Screening of the Antibacterial Activity and Identification of Bioactive Compounds from Plants against Selected Vibrio spp. Pathogens Turk. J. Biol. 33:137-144.

Sharma N, Trivedi PC (2002). Screening of Leaf Extracts of Some Plants for their Nematicidal and Fungicidal Properties against Meloidogyne Incognita and Fusarium Oxysporum. Asian J. Exp. Sci. 16:21-28.

Siddiqui S, Sultana N, Ahmed SS, Haider SI (1986). Isolation and Structure of a New Alkaloid Datumetin from the Leaves of Datura metel. J. Natural Prod. 49:511-513.

Sonika G, Manubala R, Deepak J. Comparative Studies on Anti-inflammatory Activity of Coriandrum Sativum, Datura Stramonium and Azadirachta Indica. Asian J Exp Biol Sci. 2010; 1(1): 151-154.

Spina SP, Taddei A. Teenagers with Jimson weed (Datura stramonium) Poisoning. CJEM. 2007; 9(6): 467-468.

Swathi S, Murugananthan G, Ghosh SK, Pradeep AS. Larvicidal and Repellent Activities of Ethanolic Extract of Datura Stramonium Leaves against Mosquitoes. Inter J Pharmacogn Phytochem Res. 2012; 4(1): 25-27.

Tosun F, Akyüz KC, Sener B, Vural M, Palittapogarnpim P (2004). Antimycobacterial Screening of Some Turkish Plants. J. Ethnopharmacol. 95:273-275.

Usha K, Singh B, Praseetha P, Deepa N, Agarwal DK, Agarwal R, Nagaraja A (2009). Antifungal Activity of Datura Stramonium, Calotropis Gigantean and Azadirachta indica against Fusarium Mangiferae and Floral Malformation in Mango. Eur. J. Plant Pathol. 124:637-657.

Uzun E, Sariyara G, Adsersenb A, Karakocc B, Ötük G, Oktayoglua E, Pirildara S (2004). Traditional Medicine in Sakarya Province (Turkey) and Antimicrobial Activities of Selected Species. J. Ethnopharmacol. 95:287.

Vitale AA, Acher A, Pomilio AB (1995).Alkaloids of Datura Ferox from Argentina. J. Ethanopharmacol. 49:81-89.

Wannang NN, Ndukwe HC, Nnabuife C (2009). Evaluation of the Analgesic Properties of the Datura Metel Seeds Aqueous Extract. J. Med. Plants Res. 3:192-195.

Wollenweber E, Dorsam M, Dörr M, Roitman JN, Valant-Vetschera KM (2005). Chemodiversity of Surface Flavanoids in Solanaceae. Z. Naturforsch. 60c:661-670.

Yamazaki Z, Tagaya I (1980). Antiviral Effects of Atropine and Caffeine. J. Gen. Virol. 50:429-431.

Medicinal and Nutritional Values of Plants
Edited by: Alka Chauhan and Pawan Kumar 'Bharti'
ISBN: 978-93-5056-883-5
Edition: 2017
Published by: Discovery Publishing House Pvt. Ltd., New Delhi (India)

2

Rauvolfia Serpintina
Pharmacological and Therapeutic Aspects

[1]Showkat Ahmad Bhat, [1]Bilal Ahmad Mir, [1]Muneeb U Rahman, [1]Insha Amin, [1]Bilal Ahmad Sheikh, [1]Ishraq Husain, [1]Manzoor R Mir

ABSTRACT

Plants as a medicine for the prevention and treatment of various metabolic and infectious disorders have been used since time immemorial.Their medicinal properties are due to their rich phytochemistry. The currently available drugs used for the disease treatment are full of side effects, ineffective and heavy costly, because of this trend is changing and blind dependence on allopatheic drugs is over and move towards plant based medicine is going on at high speed. 80% of world populations have strong belief in herbal medicine.The plants having therapeutic properties often have rich phytocompounds with strong antioxidant and anti-inflammatory properties. Rauwolfia Serpintina is one of the commonly known medicinal plant with rich pharmacologically active constituents used traditionally for the treatment of various diseases. Reserpine, Rescinnamine, Reserpiline, Ajmaline e.t.c are its principle phytocompound responsible for its pharmacological properties. This plant is having a full potential against infectious diseases and metabolic diseases like Hypertension,diabetes cancer and obesity.Due to all of its health promoting properties the current review is going to evaluate the various pharmacological and therapeutic properties of Rauvolfia serpintina.

Key words: Reserpine, Rauwolfia serpentine, Drug, Hypotension.

INTRODUCTION

Plants as a medicine have been used dates back from the Ebres papyrus about 1550 B.C (Kesari *et al.*, 2005). Before the introduction of pharmaceutical preparations medicinal plants had been used for the treatment of diseases. Uses of herbs has been practiced for centuries in all parts of the world in different systems of medicine like Ayruveda, Siddha, Unani, Naturopathy and others (Kameswara Rao and Appa Rao, 2001). Herbal remedies and plant derived compounds has gathered a lot of interest since the 1980s and the use

1 Division of Veterinary Biochemistry, Faculty of Veterinary Sciences & Animal Husbandry, Sheri Kashmir University of Agricultural Science & Technology (SKUAST-K), Srinagar, J&K, India 190006

of complementary and alternative medicine has grown in many countries around the world. 80% of world population rely on herbal based medicine. In India people use plants to prevent and cure many diseases. Medicinal plant contain certain bioactive compounds like oxygen, carbon, hydrogen alkaloids, tannins, glycosides, resins, essential oils, fatty acids, which are responsible for its pharmacological action. The active compounds in plants differ due to their biodiversity. Ijeh *et al.*, (2004) noted the growing interest on the medicinal properties of a number of common plants. Edeoga *et al.*, (2003) have explored the importance of medicinal plants and their importance in the pharmaceutical industry. *Rauvolfia serpintina* (Family: Apocynaceae) commonly known as sarpagandha in India. It is extensively used in traditional medicine for the treatment of various commonly occurring diseases like insomnia, hypochondriasis, and irritable conditions of the central nervous system and high blood, insanity and gastrointestinal disorders.

Rauvolfia is threatened with extinction in India due to indiscriminate collection, over exploitation and limited cultivation for commercial purposes to meet the requirements of pharmaceutical industry. It has been included in the Appendix II of The Convention on International Trade in Endangered Species of Wild Fauna and Flora (CITES) and in the negative list of exportsplants by the Government of India (Notification no. 24(RE-98)/1977-2002 the plant has gained universal acclamation as a useful therapeutic weapon in high blood pressure states. (Vakil, 1955).

Common Name

Hindi	Chandrabhaga, Chota-chand, Sarpagandha
English	Rauvolfia/Indiansnakeroot
Latin	*Rauvolfia serpentine*
Sanskrit	Sarpaghandha
Tamil	Chevanamalpodi, Sarpagandha
Kannada	Keramaddinagaddi
Telgu	Patalaguni, Patalagandha, Sarpagandha
Malayalam	Churannavilpori, Suvapavalporiyam. Amalpori

Distribution: Sarpagndha medicinal plant is widely distributed in the foot hills of Himalyan range, and almost all over the India. It is used as a natural and traditional medicine in India, China, Africa and many other countries. It is commonly occurring in moist deciduous forests up to the elevation of 1200-1300 m high from the sea level. It grows not only in India but also in Pakistan, Sri Lanka, Burma and Thailand.

Morphological Features

Rauvolfia serpentina is a perennial evergreen erect under shrub. The height of the plant is up to 60 cm maximum. Its roots are tuberous with pale brown cork. The Leaves of the plant are large, darkgreen above and pale green below, simple in whorls of three, elliptic to lanceolate or obovate, reticulate venation, tapering base and slender.

Flowers: Its flowers are pantamerous and found in umbellate or corymbose cymes. A cup shaped or annular disk is found. White or pale colored flowers often have violet coloured tinge. Calyx glabrous, lanceolate and bright red. The diameter of flower is 0.2-0.6 and the flowering time is from March to May in Indian conditions.

Fruit: Its fruits are single Drupe, or dumbbell shaped, glabrous, semi-apocarpous shining black, the average weight of single seeded fruit is 0.0192 gms inflorescence is with red pedicels and calyx and white corolla.

Seeds: Its seeds are subolongoid, one side flat and other bullate, the color of seed is creamy yellow. Texture is rugose, reticulate and alveolate, its micropyle is constricted and rounded and shape of embryo is straight.

Root: Its roots are long and tuberous with pale brown cork. The root is crooked in shape and branched its diameter is usually 0.2 to 2.9 diameter goes 40 to 75 cm.

Cultivation

Land preparation: Acidic to neutral soil is quite favorable for optimum growth of the plant with medium to deep drained fertile soils also soils rich in organic matter like clay–loam are suitable. It grows well in frost-free tropical to sub-tropical situations under irrigation.

Planting: Propagation of the plant can be done by various methods like seed, stem cutting and root cuttings. For commercial plantation seed propagation is ideal method. In root cutting: Nearly 5 cm long root cutting are planted during spring season closely in nursery beds containing well matured FYM, sand and saw-dust. The beds are kept moist through watering of beds. The cuttings of the plant begin to sprout within 3 weeks. These can be planted in field during rainy season after 8 to 10 cm rains are received; the seedlings are transplanted at 45 cm row to row and 30 cm plant to plant distance. In this manner, an estimated 100 kg of root cuttings are found sufficient for planting one hectare area. (*ii*) By stem cuttings: Hard wooded stem cutting measuring 15 to 22 cm are closely planted during June in the nursery beds where continuous moisture is maintained. After sprouting and giving.

Chemical constituents: Chemically it contains alkaloids (1.24 to 1.48 mg/ 100 g), saponins (1.46 to 1.72 mg/100 g), flavonoids (1.46 to 1.86 mg/100 g), phenols (0.06 mg/100 g) and tannins (0.04 to 0.5 mg/100 g). Rauwolfia contains ascorbic acid (26.42 to 44.03 mg/100 g), riboflavin (0.20 to 0.42 mg/100 g), thiamine (0.11 to 0.18 mg/100 g) and niacin (0.02-0.09 mg/100g). Among alkaloids Reserpine isa major alkaloid present in root, stem and leaves of plant and its concentration 1.7 to 3%. Alaloids present in Rauwolfia serpintina have been divided into three major classes. Three types of alkaloids are present in *Rauwolfia serpentina.*

1. Weakly basic indole alkaloids

The principal alkaloids are Reserpine, Rescinnamine.

2. Indoline alkaloids of intermediate basicity

Reserpiline, Ajmaline, Iso-Ajmaline, rauwolfinineare tertiary Indoline alkaloids.

3. Strong anhydronium bases

Serpentine, serpentinine and alsotonine are stronglybasic anhydronium alkaloids (Tyler *et al.*, 1988). While Ajmalinine, Ajmalicine, Chandrine, renoxidine, reserpinine, Sarpagine, Tetraphyllicine, Yohimbine, 3-epi-ayohimbineare the other alkaloids present in *Rauwolfiaserpentina* (Herbal monograph).

The concentration of alkaloids in plant varies with geographical positions and seaseons. Generally samples from Assam in India have higher percentage of alkaloids (2.57%) and December is the ideal month for collection of samples containing higher percentage of alkaloids.

The chemical composition of *Rauvolfia serpentine*was evaluated by *Harisaranraj R. et al.*, which are presented in table no. 2.1, 2.2 & 2.3.

Rauwolfia Serpentine

It contain high content of saponins it shows that its extract has potential to stop bleeding and to be used for treating wounds Flavinoid is, on the other hand are potent water-soluble antioxidants and free radical scavengers, which prevent oxidative cell damage, have strong anticancer activity (Salah *et al.*, 1995). Flavonoids in intestinal tract lower the risk of heart disease. As antioxidants, flavonoids from this plant provide anti-inflammatory activity (Okowo, 2004) used for the treatment of diseases in herbal medicine. The zinc present in plant reveals that it can play an important role in management of diabetes which results from malfunction of insulin. This plant is also a significant source of ascorbic acids, thiamine, Riboflavin and niacin. Natural ascorbic acid is very significant for the vital body performance. Deficiency of ascorbic acid results impairment of the normal formation of intercellular substances throughout the body, including collagen, bone matrix and tooth dentine. The weakening of endothelial walls of capillaries occur due to reduction in the content of intercellular matrix which in turn leads to scurvy hemorrhage of mouth and gastrointestinal tract finally manifested in the form of anemia.Tanins also play an important role in hastening the healing of wounds and inflamed mucus membranes. There is lower content of sodium present in this plant which in turn might be beneficial for Hypertensive patients. As a result of availability of Flavinoidis, Ascorbic acid, Zinc*in Rauwolfia serpentina* this plant is used in herbal medicine for the treatment of many diseases (Okowo 2004).

Table 2.1: Phytochemical Composition of *Rauwolfia serpentina* and Expressed as mg/100 g dry Weight

Phytochemicals	*Rauwolfia serpentina*
Alkaloids	1.48 + 0.02
Flavonoids	1.72 + 0.11
Phenols	1.86 + 0.11
Tannins	0.51 + 0.20

Results are mean of triplicate determinations on a dry weight basis ± Standard Deviation

Table 2.2: Mineral Composition of *Rauwolfia serpentina* and on m g/100 g dry Weight

Minerals Macroelements	*Rauwolfia serpentine*
Magnesium	0.10 + 0.20
Calcium	0.32 + 0.10
Potassium	0.04 V 0.11
Phosphorus	0.18 + 0.22
Sodium	0.02 + 0.10
Iron and Zinc	1.85 + 0.20 5.38 + 0.11

The Pure extracted alkaloids and their synthetic derivatives have been used as basic medicinal agents due to their analgesic, antispasmodic and bactericidal effects [Stary 1998, Okowo 2004]. They exhibit marked physiological activity when administered to animals.

Pharmacology: Reserpine has broad spectrum of activity. Its effects include respiratory inhibition, stimulation of peristalsis, myosis, relaxation of nictating membranes, and influence on the temperature regulating centre. It increases the gastric secretions. Reserpine also improves glycemic index and antioxidant status.Reserpine can be used as moderate hypotensive agent. It is most valuable in young patients with mild labile hypertension associated with tachycardia. The response to reserpine varies in patients and the dosage of reserpine should be adjusted to individual requirements. In severe hypertension, it might be given by intravenous or intramuscular injection when the effect begins within a few hours.

Deserpidine is almost as active as reserpine in its hypotensive and sedative activity, it is responsible for reduction of hypertension and intestinal movements. It also possesses anti-fibrillar activity. Serpentineleads to the marked inhibition of succinate dehydrogenasein brain and liver tissues. It produces hypotension both systemic and pulmonary due to its ability of causing decrease in cardiac output; Ajmaline has been revealed to stimulate respiration and intestinal movements. Ajmaline produces same action on systemic and pulmonary blood pressure as is produced by serpentine.

Reserpine Mechanism of Action

Chopra, Gupta and Mukherjee reported that the alkaloids present in the plant produce a marked hypotensive effect which might be due to depression of central nervous system mechanisms (Chopra *et al.,* 1933). They found Reserpine injection in the systemic circulation of rabbit produce an immediate fall in systemic blood pressure which is accompanied by immediate rise in limb perfusion pressure instead of a fall and which was been expected were fall of blood pressure mediated through the nervous system. Furthermore, injection of Reserpine directly in to the artery of the perfused hind-limb causes immediate diminution in vasomotor tone. So according to this Chopra, Gupta and Mukherjee reported that, a feature of all this reactions is their remarkably prolonged duration, suggesting binding of the drug by the musculature. They had also obtained evidence that such a direct peripheral effect may play some part in hypotensive action of Reserpine in man. Mc Queen, Doyle and Smirke have been reported that, direct peripheral effect may play some part in the hypotensiveaction of Reserpine in Man.

Ajmalicine

It is derived from tryptophan which in turn is converted to tryptampine through an intermediate product of cathenamine. Cathenamine is reduced into ajmalicine by NADPH and tryptophan decraboxylase enzyme. Decarboxylase is key enzyme involved in synthesis of ajmalicine in rauvolfia (Liu *et al.,* 2006). Ajmalicine has broad range of therapeutic applications. It provides smooth cerebral blood flow, prevents strokes, maintains normal blood flow and facilitates reduction in blood pressure (Srivastav *et al.,* 2006).

Rescinnamine

Rescinnamine is chemically and pharmacologically similar to reserpine. Its potency is less as antihypertensive alkaloid as compared to reserpine and is not much effective in reducing blood pressure (Klohs, 1954). It inhibits angiotensin conveting enxyme (ACE) that converts angiotensin I to angiotensin II and in turn leads to lowering of blood pressure.

Serpentine

Ajmalicine is transformed into serpentine by the peroxidase enzyme by catalizing bisindol alkaloid (Conner *et al.,* 2006). The beuty of serpentine is that it inhbits Topoisomerase type II enzyme and exhibits antipsychotic properties (Costa *et al.,* 2004).

Ajamaline

In 1931 Ajmaline was first isolated by Salimuzzaman Siddiqui from the roots of R. serpentine (COMSATAS, 2013). Burgada syndrome is highly diagnosed by ajmaline and helps in differentiating subtypes of this disease. Ajmaline is quite ideal for its diagnostic purpose because of its ability in inhibiting sodium ion channels when given intravenously (Rolf *et al.,* 2003). The administration of ajmaline in patients with arrhythmia is known as ajmaline test. It has been reported to inhibit intestinal and respiratory movements.

Yohimbine

It is well characterized pharmacologically active constituent alkaloid in Rauvolfia. It is used for the treatment of erectile dysfunction due to its strong alpha adrenergic inhibiting property. It increases blood flow and maintains the firmness of penis (Morales, 2000). It dilates pupil of eye by facilitating certain chemicals.

PREPARATIONS AND DOSAGE

Powdered Rauwolfia is *Rauwolfia serpentina* root reduced to a fine powder to confirm to the official requirements for Reserpine-rescinnamine group alkaloids. It contains not less than 0.15% and not more than 0.20% of Reserpinerescinnamine group alkaloid calculated as Reserpine.

Dosage: The usual dose of Reserpine is initially 500 mg once a day for 1-2 weeks, maintenance 100 to 250 mg once a day. The patient should be advised to notify his physician if a change in mood occurs.

Action of Rauwolfia on Different Systems of Body

Rauwolfia serpentina is said to have the following pharmacologic attributes (Rustom, 949):

1. it leads to generalized vasodilatation, with a lowering of blood Pressure bythe action on vasomotor tone.
2. it soothes the general nervous system By its depressant action on the cerebral centers (Werner 1953).
3. It stimulates the bronchial musculature.

Siddiqui and Siddiqui reveled in 1931 that Ajmaline group acts as a general depressant to the heart while serpentine group causes paralysis of respiration, depression of the nerves and stimulation of the heart on the experiment on frog (Siddiqi S.S and Siddiqi R.H 1931). Ajmaline has been reported to stimulate respiration and intestinal movements. The action of Ajmaline on systemic and pulmonary blood pressure is similar to that of Serpentine; Rauwolfinine has hypotensive properties on the autolysis of rat brain and liver tissue, but to a lesser extent than Reserpine (Herbal monograph).

Medicinal Uses

Rauwalfia roots are commonly used in medicine for the treatment of various nervous disorders including schizophrenia, psychosis, insanity and epilepsy, intestinal disorders including diarrohea, dysentery can be treated by the extract of the roots of *Rauvolfia*. The roots of Rauwalfia also leads to the contaction of uterine muscles and recommended for the use in parturition in dystocia cases. the juice of its leaves can be used for the treatment of opacity of cornea.

Anidiabetic Activity

It has been revealed that extract of Rauwalfia improves glycemic index in alloxan induced diabetic mice by significantly upgrading the antioxidant status in diabetes. It scavenges the Reactive Oxyen Species (ROS) which are responsible for the major complications in diabetes (Bilal Azmi and A. Qureshi, 2013).

Lipolytic activity therapeutic uses of commercially available lipid lowering drugs are associated with side effects. The root powder of *R. serpentina* is a potent hypolipidaemic agent especially having hypotriglyceridemic and hypocholesterolemic effects with undetectable side effects on liver and cardiac functions. And can be used as potent lipolytic agent (shami *et al.*, 2009).

Hypotensive activity: Rauwalfia exhibits potent hypotensive activity in patients suffering from hypertension.it reduces both systemic and pulmonary bllod pressure by decreasing crdiac out put. Half a teaspoon of its powder taken thrice a day is effective in relieving hypertension.

Sedatitve activity: Rauwalfia is used for the treatment of insominia and insanity because of its highly sedative properties. The very first dose of *Rauwolfia* enables the patient of a phlegmatic and gouty nature to go to sleep. About 0.6 to 1.25 grams of the powder of its root is mixed with some scented vehicle and taken. It is non-stimulating and should be given in doses of 0.25 grams to the patient at bedtime for sound sleep.

Antidiarroheal activity: Rauwalfia extracts has been reported to have antidiarroheal action, which may be due to inhibition of prostaglandin biosynthesis with resultant decrease in secretion of fluid into the lumen or may be due to promotion of absorption of water and electrolytes in the gut. Suppression of intestinal fluid accumulation by extracts (Ezijibo *et al.*, 2012).

Antibiotic Activity

The extract of Rauwolfia is highly effective against *staphylococcus aureus bacteria* so it can be used as antibiotic against the infectious diseases like respiratory tract infections, urinary tract infections etc caused by staphylococcus aureus (Vishal and kavita, 2012).

Anticancer Activity

Cancer is a lethal disease and causing tremendous mortality in allover the world the transformation of normal dividing cell to uncontrolled cancerous cell is caused by so many factors including genetic, environmental and lifestyle changes. Prostate cancer is leading cause of death among males. Modern therapeutic techniques including chemotherapy and radiotherapy have not proven to be effective against prostate cancer (American C.A.S. 2006). Plant phytocompounds with anticancer propery is need of hour because of their effectiveness, minimum side effects and economical. β-carboline alkaloid present in Rauvolfia have been reported to tumor cell growth in mice (Beljanski, 1986). This plant exhibits its anticancer activity against prostate cancer both invitro and invivo models by its cell control signaling pathway. (*Bemis et al.*, 2006). It also shows strong anticancer activity against breast cancer (Stanford *et al.*, 1986).

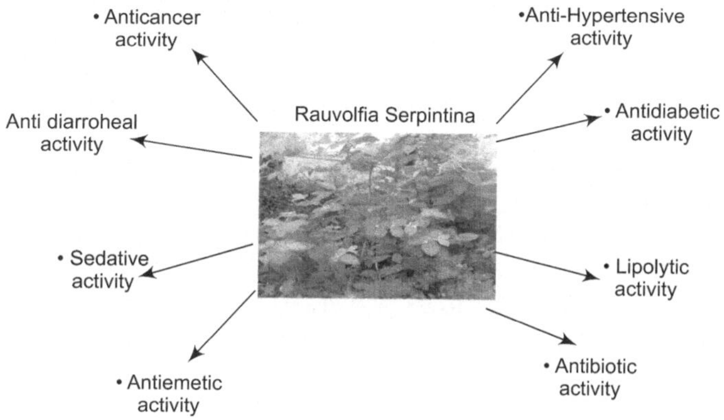

Summary of pharmacological properties of *Rauvolfia serpintina.*

Side Effects

Although there are very less side effects of the plant as a medicine but the overdose of it produces few side effects but none of serious consequence like over dose of Rauwolfia leads to bradycardia, hypotension, drowsiness.

CONCLUSION

The currently used Allopatheic drugs are full of side effects. Plants used in tradional medicine represent valuable alternative for the treatment of various diseases. Among these plants Rauwolfia serpintina is quite superior in its effect on high blood pressure, besides it has been proved to be used a antilipolytic, antidiabetic, antidiarroheal and antibiotic. The drug is useful in releving various nervous symptoms such as headache, insomnia, vertigo etc. The effect of drug is long lasting and is effective in small doses. Due to its abundance avilability, low cost and safety in consumption, Rauwolfia has been the subject of intensive scientific research over the past two decades. Due to antioxidant properties of this herbal plant, it can be widely used in the treatment of many diseases like in diabetes. Besides, this plant also has anti lipolytic properties. It also has immense role against hypertension and helps in reduction of blood pressure. There are ill effects of this plant as well if ever taken in excess. Sedation is the main ill effect of this plant. Bradycardia may occur which may lead to shock. In my opinion it is safe and beneficial in small doses in hypertensive cases.

REFERENCES

American Cancer Society, Cancer Facts and Figures 2006, Atlanta: American Cancer Society, 2006.

Beljanski, M. and Beljanski, M.S. 1986. Three Alkaloids as Selective Destroyers of Cancer Cells in Mice, Synergy with Classic Anticancer Drugs, *Oncology*, 43: 198-203.

Bemis, D.L., Capodice, J.L., Gorroochurn, P., Katz, A.E., Buttyan, R. 2006. Antiprostate Cancer Activity of a Beta-carboline Alkaloid Enriched Extract from *Rauvolfia vomitoria. International Journal of Oncology*, 29(5):1065-1073.

Bhatia, B.B., M.D., M.R.C.P. (Lond.), 2004. Head of the Department of Pharmacology, K.E.M. Medical College, Lucknow, India. 10. Okwu, D.E., Phytochemicals and VITAMIN Content of Indigenous Spices of Southeastern Nsigeria. *J. Sustain. Agric. Environ* 6(1): 30-37.

C OMSATS Newsletter: Biographies of Eminent Scientists. 2013. Dr. Salimuzzamman Siddiqui, COMSATS Secretariat, Islamabad–Pakistan 5(3).

Chopra, R.N., Gupta, J.C. and Mukherjee, B. 1933. The Pharmacological Action of an Alkaloid Obtained from Rauvolfia Serpentina. A preliminary Note, *Ind., J. Med. Res.* 21: 261-71.

Connor, S.E., Maresh, J. 2006. Chemistry and Biology of Monoterpene Indole Alkaloid Biosynthesis, *Natural Product Reports*, 23:532-547.

Costa-Campos, L., Dassoler, S.C., Rigo, A.P., Iwu, M., Elisabetsky, E. 2004. Anxiolytic Properties of the Antipsychotic Alkaloid Alstonine, *Pharmacology Biochemistry & Behaviour*, 77: 481-489.

Del-Rio, A., Obdululio, B.G., Casfillo, J., Marin, F.G. and Ortuno, A. 1997. Uses an Properties of Citrus Flavonoids. *J. Agric Food Chem* 45: 4505-4515.

Edeoga, H.O., Okwu, D.E. and Mbaebie, B.O. 2003. Minerals and Nutritive Values of Some Nigerian Medical Plants. *J. Med. Aromatic Plants Sci.* 25: 1010-1015.

Edeoga, H.O., Okwu, D.E. and Mbaebre, B.O. 2005. Phytochemical Constituent of Some Nigerian Medicinal Plants. *Afr. J. Biotechnol* 4(7): 685-688.

Ezeigbo II., Ezeja, M.I., Madubuike, K.G., Ifenkwe, D.C., Ukweni, I.A., Udeh, N.E., Akomas S.C. 2012. Antidiarrhoeal Activity of Leaf Methanolic Extract of Rauwolfia Serpentine. *Asian Pac J Trop Biomed* 2(6): 430-432.

Harisaranraj, R., Suresh, K and Saravanababu, S. 2009. Evaluation of the Chemical Composition Rauwolfia Serpentina and Ephedra Vulgeris. Advances in Biological Research 3(5-6): 174-178.

Herbal Monograph, The Himalaya Drug Company,http://www. himalayahealthcare.com/ herbfinder/h_ber ber.htm.

Ijeh, I.I., O.U. Njoku and E.C. Ekenze, 2004. Medicinal Evaluation of Extracts of *Xylopia aethiopica* and *Ocimumgratissimum. J. Med. Aromatic Plant Sci* 26: 44-47.

Kesari, A.N., Gupta, R.K., and Watal, G. (2005). Hypoglycemic Effect of *Murray koenigii* on Normal and Alloxan Diabetic Rabbits. *Journal of Ethnopharmacology* 97:247-255.

Klohs, M.W., Draper, M.D., Keller, F. 1954. Alkaloids of *Rauvolfia serpentine* Benth III. Rescinnamine, A New Hypotensive and Sedativeprinciple, *Journal of American Chemical Society*, 76(10):28-43.

Liu, W., Chen, R., Chen, M., Zhang, H., Peng, M., Yang, C., Ming, X., Lan, X., Liao, Z. 2012. Tryptophan Decarboxylase Plays an Important Role in Ajmalicine Biosynthesis in *Rauvolfia verticillata, Planta* 236(1): 239-250.

Mc Queen, E.G., Doyle, A.E., *et al.*, 1954: "Mechanism of Hypotensive Action of Reserpine, an Alkaloid of *Rauwolfia serpentina*", *Nature*, 174: 1015-1021.

Ministry of Health & Family Welfare Regional Research Laboratory Journal of Indian Medical Association (1942): (XI), 9, 262] Available at www.ecoplanet.in/Herbs and Plants/ Rauwolfiaserpentina.htm.

Morales, A., Yohimbine in Erectile Dysfunction: The Facts, *International Journal of Impotence Research,* 12(1): 70-74.

Muhammad Bilal, Azmi and Shamim Qureshi, A. 2013. *Rauwolfia Serpentina* Ameliorates Hyperglycemic, Haematinic and Antioxidant Status in Alloxan-Induced Diabetic Mice. *Journal of Applied Pharmaceutical Science,* 3: 136-141.

Okwu, D.E. and Okwu, M.E. 2004. Chemical Composition of *Spondias mombin* Linn Plant Parts. *J. Sustain Agric. Environ* 6(2): 140-147.

Ray, G.K., Roy, P.K., Dasgupta, S.R., *et al.,* 1953. Action of Rauwolfia Serpentina on Vasomotor Reflexes, *Arch. Exp. Path. U. Pharmakol* 219 310-14.

Rolf, S., Bruns, H.J., Wichter, T., Kirchhof, P., Ribbing, M., Wasmer, K., Paul, M., Breithardt, G., Haverkamp, W., Eckardt, L. 2003. The Ajmaline Challenge in Brugada Syndrome: Diagnostic Impact, Safety, and Recommended Protocol, *European Heart Journal,* 24(12):1104-1112.

Rustom Jal, Vakil. 1949. "A Clinical Trial of *Rauwolfia Serpentina* in Essential Hypertension", *British Heart Journal,* 11(4):350-355.

Salah, N., Miller, N.J., Pagangeg, G., Tijburg, L., Bolwellg, P., Rice, E. and Evans, C. 1995. Polyphenolic Flavonoils as Seavenger of Aqueous Phase Radicals as Chain Breaking Antioxidant. *Arch Biochem. Broph* 2: 339-346.

Sen, G., Bose, K.C. 1931. Rauwolfia Serpentina, A New Indian Drug for Insanity and High Blood Pressure,–*Indian Med. World* 2: 194-201.

Shamim, A., Qureshi and Shamsa, K. 2009. Udani Hypolipidaemic Activity of *Rauwolfia Serpentina Pakistan Journal of Nutrition* 8(7): 1103-1106.

Siddiqui, S.S. and Siddiqui, R.H. 1931. "The alkaloid of *Rauwolfia serpentina,* Benth", *J. Indian Chem. Soc,* 8:667-674.

Sihag, R.C and Nidhi, Wadhwa. 2011. Floral and Reproductive Biology of Sarpagandha Rauvolfia Serpentina (Gentianales: Apocynaceae) in Semi-arid Environment of India. *J. Threatened Taxa (JoTT) Short Commun.* 3(1):1432-1436.

Srivastava, A., Tripathi, A.K, Pandey, R., Verma, R.K, Gupta, M. 2006. Quantitative Determination of Reserpine, Ajmaline and Ajmalicine in *Rauvolfia serpentina* by Reversed-phase High-performance Liquid Chromatography. *Journal of Chromatographic Science,* 44: 557-560.

Stanford, J.L., Martin, E.J., Brintin, L.A., Hoover, R.N. 1986. Rauvolfia Use and Breast Cancer: A Case-control Study, Journal of the National Cancer Institute, 76: 817-822.

Stary, F., 1998. The Naturalguide to Medicinal Herbs Sand Plants. Tiger Books International, London, pp. 12-16.

Tyler, V.E., Brady, L.R., Robbers, J.E. 1988. Pharmacognosy, 9th edition, Lea and Febiger, Philiadelphia 222-224.

Vakil, R.J. 1955. Rauwolfia Serpentina in the Treatment of High Blood Pressure. American Heart Association, Inc Available at circ.ahajournals.org/content/12/2/220.abstract.

Vishal kumar, Deshwal* and Kavita. 2012. Study on the Antibacterial Effect of *Rauwolfia Serpentina* on *Staphylococcus Aureus* International Journal of Pharmaceutical Invention August, Volume 2(7): 4265-4268.

Medicinal and Nutritional Values of Plants
Edited by: Alka Chauhan and Pawan Kumar 'Bharti'
ISBN: 978-93-5056-883-5
Edition: 2017
Published by: Discovery Publishing House Pvt. Ltd., New Delhi (India)

3

Anti-malarial Medicinal Plants

[1]Prasann Kumar

ABSTRACT

The importance of medicinal plants has been addressed from ancient time. Medicinal plants have been extensively used for diseases cure during the human evolution. Evidence have been found in the grave of a Neanderthal man buried 60,000 years ago which buried several pollen of plants with corpse. About, 4000 year old Sumerian clay tablet was used for various illnesses. In India, it is recorded that several sacred plants used as Ayurvedic medicine maintained in 'Rig Veda'. WHO (1995) reported that approximately 80% of the world's population use medicinal plants for illness. It is known that most of the countries of the world established own system for use of medicine (e.g., Napralert database; Dr. Duke's-Phytochemical and Ethnobotanical database, Tramil). Therefore, plants to be a major source for treatment of number of disease management like malaria, cancer, diabetes and high blood pressure.

Key words: Anti, Base, Cure, Database, Evidence, WHO

INTRODUCTION

Malaria is the spread worldwide and about 1-2 million people kills every year. Young once below the age of 5 years are mostly affected. Malaria is a classical example of a disease that affects whole the society. Most of the poor people and less developed countries of the world suffer from malaria. In the world, Africa faces greatest effects followed by tropical area include East Asia, China and India. In India, 40% cases of malaria are caused by *Plasmodium falciparum*. In 1820, first anti-malarial drug was isolated from the bark of Cinchona species belonging to family Rubiaceae. Quinine is oldest and mostly use drug for treatment as anti-malarial. Later, in 1940 another drug was synthesize like chloroquine and until recently, this was the only drug, used for the treatment of malaria. Unfortunately, *P. falciparum* became resistant to chloroquine, therefore it work with other drug combinations, which were rather expensive and sometimes toxic. Since, combinations were not always working. Hence

[1] Department of Plant Physiology Institute of Agricultural Sciences Banaras Hindu University, Varanasi-221005, U.P., India

several research groups are now continuous working to develop new active compounds as an alternative to chloroquine and artemisin. Moreover, between 1975 and 1999, about 1,400 new drugs were developed worldwide. Major participation in this is pharmaceutical industry and development of new drugs for malaria. Therefore, agencies tend to continued works basic science in development of new drug by such international health organisation like the U.S. National Institutes of Health, the European Commission, Walter Reed Army Institute of Research (WRAIR) in the United States. Apart from that World Health Organization (WHO) every year organizes a special programme on research and training for tropical diseases (TDR). Encourage of peoples about herbal product in medical practice is increasing worldwide. Problems solving of various diseases through herbal remedies has led to global imports by various pharmaceutical agencies in worldwide for cost effective relief from. Before 1820, treatment of ague was solved the use of suspension of finely powdered Cinchona bark in wine (Meshnick, 1997). Opium and Cinchona were first medicinal plants identified among them and their alkaloids prepared from crude extract were very effective for treatment of malaria initially. But later 150 years, second most important medicinal plant Artemisia was discovered by Chinese traditional remedy. They were characterizations and studied to isolate Quinghaosu by Quinghaosu Anti-malaria Coordinating Research Group in 1979. The afford always being in between 1925 and 1955, several synthetic drug were discovered that exhibited several potent anti-malarial activity (Greenwood 1995).

PROPERTIES OF MEDICINAL PLANTS AS CURE FOR MALARIAL TREATMENTS

Anti-malarial drug resistance defined as the ability of a parasite strain to survive and/or multiply despite using a drug given in doses equal to or higher than those usually recommended but within tolerance of the subject. Several reason may be possible to resistance to anti-malarial drugs can cause treatment failure like incorrect dosing, poor quality drug or drug interactions, poor diagnosis, non compliance to the dosing regimen etc. It has been demonstrated that this is major problem throughout the world. In 1960, *P. falciparum* strains has developed resistance to chloroquine, has made the treatment of malaria increasingly problematic in virtually all malarious regions of the world (Winter, R. W. *et al.*, 2008). Extensive use of chloroquine, a cost effective treatment for malaria resulted in resistance to *P. falciparum* parasites everywhere in the world and this was transmitted to various malarious areas like Central America, the island of Hispaniola, and limited areas of the Middle East and Central Asia as well as Indian subcontinents (Bloland, 2001). Mefloquine resistance is also found in some part of South-East Asia and Amazon region of South America and sporadically in Africa (Mockenhaupt, 1995). In India, it is widely spread; about 1,502,742 cases were reported and out of which 1,274 deaths in 2007, were recorded by Indian National Vector-borne Disease Control Programme (NVBDCP). Reasons for under-reporting include management of 2/3rd of the patients by the private sector, absence of routine death certification in rural areas and poor infrastructure for malaria diagnosis in public health care facilities (table 3.1 & table 3.2).

Table 3.1: Lists of Medicinal Plants Derived Crude Extracts and Showing their *in vitro* and *in vivo* Anti-plasmodia Activities Against Different Species and Strains of Plasmodia

Plant species & family	Part used	Extract/ fraction	Dose efficiency	*Plasmodium* sp. & strain	Reference
Ailanthus excelsa	Leaves, Stem bark	80 % methanol 80 % methanol	IC_{50} (μg/mL) 16 & 18027& 50	*P. falciparum*3D7 & Dd2	Tahir *et al.*, 1999
Annona muricata	Leaf	95% ethanol	IC_{50} (μg/mL) 20 & > 63	*P. falciparum* W-2 & D-6	Antoun *et al.*, 1993
Andrographis paniculata	Leaf,	80 % methanol 80 % methanol	IC_{50} (μg/mL) 2& 308.5 & 120	*P. falciparum*3D7 & Dd2	Tahir *et al.*, 1999
Andrographis paniculata	Whole plant	Methanol Chloroform	1 00% inhibition 2.5 mg/ml 0.025 mg/ml	*P. falciparum* FCR-3	Rahman *et al.*, 1997
Aphanamixis	Wood	Ethanol	IC50 (μg/mL) 16.8 & >20	P. falciparum D6 & W2	Mackinnon *et al.*, 1997
Artemisia indica	Stem	Methanol	EC_{50} (g/mL) 6.60 x 10^{-6}	*P. falciparum* K1	Chanphen *et al.*, 1998
Azadirachta indica (Meliaceae)		80 % methanol 80 % methanol	IC_{50} (μg/mL) 5.8 & 1.78.5 & 40	*P. falciparum* 3D7 & Dd2	Tahir *et al.*, 1999
Azadirachta indica (Meliaceae)	Leaves	Ethanol	IC_{50} (μg/mL) 2.5 & 2.45	*P. falciparum* D6 & W2	Mackinnon *et al.*, 1997
Bourreria succulent	Stem	95% ethanol	IC_{50} (μg/mL)> 63 & 21	*P. falciparum* D6 & W2	Antoun *et al.*, 1993
Castilla elastic (Moraceae)	Stem	95% ethanol	IC_{50} (μg/mL) 3 & > 63	*P. falciparum* D6 & W2	Antoun *et al.*, 1993
Cedrela odorata (Meliaceae)	Wood	Ethanol	IC_{50} (μg/mL) 1.20 & 1.11	*P. falciparum* D6 & W2	Mackinnon *et al.*, 1997

Ceiba pentandra (Bombaceae)	Stem	95% ethanol	IC_{50} (µg/mL) 13 & > 63	*P. falciparum* W2 & D6	Antoun *et al.*, 1993
Chukrasia tabularis (Meliaceae)	Leaves	Ethanol	IC_{50} (µg/mL) 6.36 & 3.39	*P. falciparum* D6 & W2	Mackinnon *et al.*, 1997
Cryptolepis	Root bar	Aqueous 80% Ethanol Aqueous 80% Ethanol	IC_{50} (ng/ml) 122, 93 & 16872,56 &	*P. falciparum* 0-6, K-1, W-2*P. berghei yoeli* & *P. berghei berghei*	Cimanga *et al.*, 1997
Hannoa klaineana	Stem bark		IC_{50} (µg/	*P. falciparum*NF 54,clone A1A9	Francois *et al.*, 1998
Kaya senegalensis (Meliaceae)	Leaves, Stem bark	80% methanol 80% methanol 80%	IC_{50} (µg/mL) 5.5 & 4.3150 & 254.3 & 3830 & 31.5	*P. falciparum* 3D7 & Dd2	Tahir *et al.*, 1999
Mangifera indica	Stem bark	Methanol	% suppre-ssion at 50, 100, 200 and 400 mg/kg/day	*P. yoelii nigeriensis*	Awe *et al.*, 1998
Nauclea latifolia (Rubiaceae)		Infusion Decoction Infusion Decoction	IC_{50} (µg/mL) 6.9.& 7.57.3 & 7.05.9 & 6.04.0 & 3.8	*P. falciparum Nigerian* & FcB1	Benoit-Vical *et al.*, 1998
Piper sarmentosum (Piperaceae)	Leaves	Methanol chloroform	1 00% inhibition 0.8 mg/ml 0.05 mg/ml	*P. falciparum* FCR-3 (after 48 h.)	Rahman *et al.*, 1999
Streblus asper (Moraceae)	Stem bark	Aqueous	% complete recovery & survival of mice 30	*P. berghei* NK65	Das and Beuria, 1991
Tinospora paniculata	Stem	Methanol	100% inhibition 2.5 mg/ml	*P. falciparum* FCR-3(after 72 h.)	Rahman *et al.*, 1999
Trichilia emetica	Leaves, Stem bark	80 % methanol 80 % methanol	IC_{50} (µg/mL) 17.5 & 2.58.5 & 200	*P. falciparum* 3D7 & Dd2	Tahir *et al.*, 1999

(**Source:** Sharma and Sharma, 1998)

Table 3.2: Lists of Different Compound Purified from Anti-malarial Plants Showing their dose and Effects Against Different Species and Strains of Plasmodia

Plant species & family	Part used	Extract/fraction	Extract/fraction	Dose efficiency	*Plasmodium* sp. & strain	References
Ancistrocladus	Roots	Triterpene	Betulic acid	IC_{50} (μg/mL) 10.46	*P. falciparum* NF, clone A1A2	Bringmann *et al.*, 1997
Ancistrocladus korupensis (Ancistrocladaceae)	Leaves Twigs	Naphtyltetra	Korupensamine	IC_{50} (μg/mL) 0.31 & 0.56 0.18 & 0.41	*P. falciparum* & *P. berghei*	Hallock *et al.*, 1994
Ancistrocladus korupensis (Ancistrocladaceae	Leaves		Korupensamine E	IC_{50} (μg/mL) 2	*P. falciparum*	Hallock *et al.*, 1997
Artemisia indica (Asteraceae)	Stem	Hydroxy flavanones	Exiguaflavanone A Exiguaflavanone BMaackiain	EC_{50} (μg/mL) 4.6×10^{-6} 7.05×10^{-6} 4.70×10^{-5} 2.70×10^{-5}	*P. falciparum* K1	Chanphen *et al.*, 1998
Asparagus africanus (Liliaceae)	Roots	Steroid Sapogenin Colourless Oil	Muzanzagenin (+)-nyasol	IC_{50} (μM) 61, 163, 23 & 16, 12 & 12	*P. falciparum* K39, VI/Sd, 307 & Od2	Oketch-Rabah *et al.*, 1997
Brunsvigia littoralis (Amaryllidaceae)	Bulb	Alkaloids	Lycorine1,2-Di-0-	IC_{50} (μg/mL) 0.62 & 0.71 &1>20 & 20>20 & 20>20 & 20>20 & 20	*P. falciparum* D10 & FAC8	Campbell *et al.*, 1998
Cryptolepis sanguinolenta (Asclepiadaceae)	Root bark	Alkaloids	Cryptolepine Cryptolepine HCl 11-hydroxy cryptolepine Quindoline Neo	IC_{50} (μ g/ml) 27,33 & 41 41, 62 & 5231, 45 & 59, 63, 87 & 108, 35, 51 & 6513.7 & 45.510.8 & 15.6Not done & 43.242.1 & 48.2 Not done	*P. falciparum* 0-6, K-1 & W-2 *P. berhei yoeli* & *P. berghe berghei*	Cimanga *et al.*, 1997

Eurycoma longifolia (Simarou-baceae)	Roots	Quassinoid â- carboline alkaloid	Eurycomanone 7- methoxy-β carboline-1-propionoic acid	IC_{50} (μg/ml) 47.7 & 48.13144 & 2978	*P. falciparum* D6 & W2	Kardono *et al.*, 1991
Fagara rhetza (Rutaceae)	Bark	Acid amide	Hazaleamide	IC_{50} (μM)43	*P. falciparum*	Shibuya *et al.*, 1992
Hannoa chlorantha	Seeds& Roots	Quassinoids	Chaparrinone	IC_{50} (μ g/	*P. falclparum* NF 54, clone A1A9*P. berghe* Anka	Francois *et al.*, 1998
Nepenthes thorelii	Roots	Naphthaquino-nes	Plumbagin2-	IC_{50} (μM) 0.25.7911.7 622.060.892 .7532.11123 .03.8856.82 168.07	*P. falciparum* T9/94	
Phyllanthus fratemus	Whole plant	Alkamides	E,E-2,4-octadienamide E,Z-2,4-decadienamide	IC_{50} (μM) 192.8 & 20087.1 & 91.3	*P. falciparum* 307 & Dd2	Sittie *et al.*, 1998
Terminalia bellerica (Rubiaceae)	Stem bark	Alkaloid	Harman	IC_{50} (μ g/ml) 0.97	*P. falciparum*	Castaneda *et al.*, 1991

(**Source:** Sharma and Sharma, 1998)

TARGET POINTS FOR MEDICINES IN PLASMODIUM PARASITE

Most important targets for several medicines is β-hematin (BH), are probably lipids. Several experiments were reported that lipids extracted from parasites or infected plasma which is initiator of BH formation put as a screening of new anti-malarial compounds (Fitch *et al.*, 1999; Tripathi *et al.*, 2001). But it is tedious to lipids extraction from parasites or infected plasma is laborious and requires several steps for preparation.

EFFECTS OF MEDICINAL DRUG ISOLATED FROM PLANTS AS AN ANTI-MALARIAL

There is a consensus among the scientific community that natural products have been playing a important role in the development of new drug for the treatment of human diseases (Newman, 2003). Indeed, large amount of anti-malarial chemotherapeutic agents are known; based on natural products. Mostly these drugs isolated from the tropical plant sources. Therefore, chemical obtain from biological diversity is to be an important source of molecular templates in the search for anti-malarial drugs (Portet, B. *et al.*, 2007).

(A) Irridoids: Irridoids phenylpropanoid conjugated compound are obtained from *Morinda morindoides* (Rubiaceae) and inhibit proliferation of parasite (Tamura, S. *et al.*, 2010). However, iridoid swertiamarin had been obtained from *Enicostemma littorale* (Gentianaceae) and inhibit schizont maturation (Soni and Gupta, 2009).

(B) Flavonoids: Flavonoids are low molecular weight, polyphenolic in nature and found nearly all the plant kingdom as secondary metabolites. Among flavonoids; flavonol quercetin, flavones luteolin have growth inhibitory properties on the protozoan parasite genera Toxoplasma, Trypanosoma and Leishmania (Kirmizibekmez, H. *et al.*, 2004).

(C) Quercetin: Quercetin is belonging to a group of flavonoids and bioflavonoids; present in fruits and vegetables like onions, tea, apple and berries. It has several properties like anticarcinogenic, anti-inflammatory, antioxidative, vasodilating and antiaggregatory effect (Hayek, T. *et al.*, 1997, Chopra, M. *et al.*, 2000; Verma, A. K. *et al.*, 1988; Deschner, E. E. *et al.*, 1991; Pereira, M. A. *et al.*, 1996; Ferry, D. R. *et al.*, 1996; Pignatelli, F. M. et., al., 2000; Perez-Vizcaino, F. *et al.*, 2002). It is most abundant polyphenolic compound in diet. Once intake of quercetin in dietary, it will lead to accumulate in plasma. Choi and Han (2004) reported that quercetin act as bioenhancer for calcium channel blocker agents like verapamil.

(D) Hesperidin: Hesperidin is another flavonoid, abundant present in sweet orange and lemon and up to present 15% in immature fruits. It has many medicinal important like chronic venous insufficiency, decreasing in capillary permeability, anti-hypercholesterolemic, anti-inflammatory, analgesic activities, antifertility, anti-oxidant, antiallergic, anticarcinogenic, anti ulcer and antihaemmorhoidal activities (Bisset, N. G. *et al.*, 1991; Struckmann, J. R. *et al.*, 1994; Son, H. S. *et al.*, 1991; Galati, E. M. *et al.*, 1996). It causes some allergic but once it phosphorylate; no express toxic activity in both male and female human being, easily assimilated without accumulated in tissue and organisms (Sieve, 1952).

THE DISCOVERY OF NEW MEDICINAL DRUGS

Several approaches are being made for the selection of plants but four are basic; that may contain new biological agents: (1) ethanopharmacological (2) taxonomical (3) phytochemical and (4) random. In the ethanopharmacological approach, primary information is more important to collection and evaluation of plants. In taxonomical, selection and evaluation of plants depend on either genus or family present in different locations. In phytochemical approaches, plants are collected and evaluated on the basis of chemical nature of secondary metabolite present in plant such alkaloids (Cordel *et al.*, 1991). In the random approach, without any prior information all the species are collected. Apart from that several new antimalarial drug can be found in research papers.

But discovery of new compound from these researches is rarely occurring. Due to chemical complexity, screenings of compounds are being difficult to identifying new drug. Several compounds are present in the crude extract such as tannins and lipids may cause problem in pharmacological assay (Grabley *et al.*, 1999). Therefore, the discovery of these compounds always needs to preliminary chemical analysis and separation of compounds (figure 3.1).

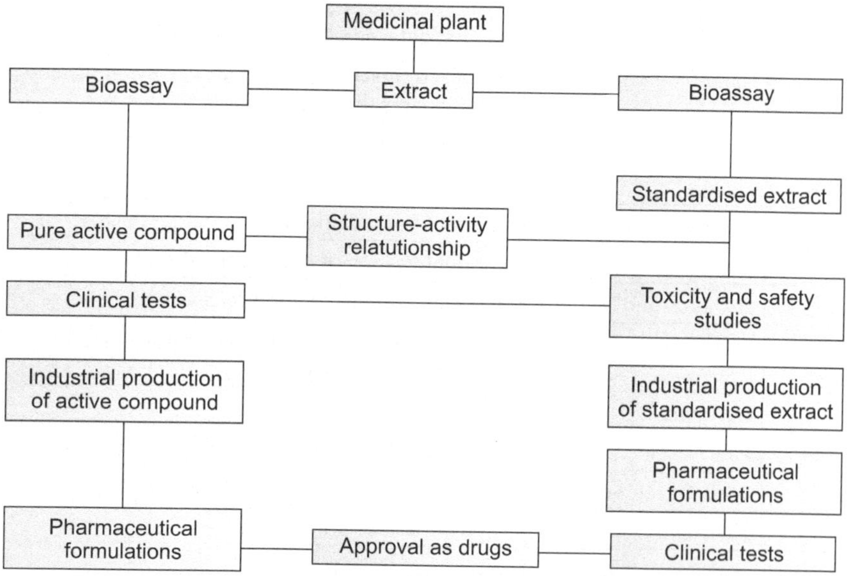

Fig. 1.1: Procedure of medicinal drug isolation from medicinal plants

(**Source:** Houghton, P.J. and Mukharjee and P.K., Evaluation of Herbal Medicinal Product-perspectives on quality, safety and efficacy)++++

MALARIA ACCORDING TO AYURVEDA

On the basis of Ayurveda, Malaria term is use for a type of fever; attended with debility, trembling, headache, caught and yellowness. Due to seasonal variation it has endemic and/or epidemic. The epidemics mostly occurred in summer then the rainy season, and autumn. However, only some part of the Indian continent region endemic malaria severity occur includes continent of India, Munjvan, Mahavrsa, Gandhara, Anga, and Magandha. It was reported that in severe cases patients suffering from malaria was died and assumed that the mortality rate was high. In a classical text, Ayurveda describe in the following way: *"Sukshma Sukshma tarasyesu doso raktadi margesu sanairapla cirena yat kramoyam tena vicchhina santapo laksyate jvara visamo visamarabha kriya anusangavan"*. Vitiated dosha spreads slowly through blood and spread to all parts of body but not simultaneously in all parts. This is the way in which fever is seen in interrupted or irregular onset and relief; known as visama jvara. The patients suffering from this kind of symptoms exhibited fever vary according to stages dependent manner. According to Ayurvedic theory these stages as being due to the involvement of particular body tissues (table 3.3 and 3.4).

Table 3.3: Malaria Milestones

Year	Scientist	Contributions area
400	Hippocrates	Description of malaria
1640	A.D. Huan del Vego	Cinchona bark for malaria treatment
1696	Morton	First detailed picture of malaria
1717	Lanicsi	Linked malaria to bad air in swamps and thus originates the name malaria
1816	Gize	Extraction of quinine from cinchona bark
1820	Pelletier and Caventou	Extraction of pure quinine alkaloids
1880	Laveran	Identifies malarial parasite under microscope
1895	Golgi	Identification of *P. vivax* and *P. malariae*
1889-90	Sakharov and Marchiafava	Celli-identification of *P. falciparum*
1897	Ronald Ross	Demonstration on malarial oocysts in gut of female anopheles mosquito
1934	Germans	Chloroquine synthesized
1939	Paul Miller	Insecticidal properties of DDT
1944	Curd, Davey, Rose	Synthesis of proguanil for treatment
1950	Elderfield	Synthesis of primaquine

(**Source:** National framework for malaria elimination in India (2016–2030))

Table 3.4: Milestones in the Malaria Control Programme in India

Prior to 1940	No organized national malaria control programme
1953	Launching of National Malaria Control Programme (NMCP)
1958	Launching of National Malaria Eradication Programme (NMEP)
1965	Cases reduced to 0.1 million
Early 1970's	Resurgence of malaria
1971	Urban Malaria Scheme launched
1976	Malaria cases 6.46 million; highest in post DDT era
1977	Modified Plan of Operations (MPO) implemented
1984–1998	Annual incidence of malaria restricted to 2 to3 million cases
1995	Modified Action Plan for malaria control implemented
1997	World Bank assisted Enhanced Malaria Control Project (EMCP) launched
1999	Renaming of programme to National Anti-Malaria Programme (NAMP)
2002	Integration of malaria control programme into the National Vector Borne Disease Control Programme (NVBDCP)
2005	RDT (monovalent) introduced in the programme

2005	Global Fund assisted Intensified Malaria Control Project (IMCP)
2006	ACT introduced in areas showing chloroquine resistance in falciparum malaria
2008	Revised NVBDCP Drug Policy, ACT introduced in high *Plasmodium falciparum* predominant districts
2008	World Bank assisted National Vector Borne Disease Control Support Project
2009	LLIN introduced, oral artemisinin monotherapy banned in the country
2010	Revised NVBDCP Drug Policy 2010 extending ACT for all *Plasmodium falciparum* cases. Global Fund (Round 9) assisted Intensified Malaria Control Project (IMCP-II)
2013	RDT (bi-valent) introduced in the programme, National Drug Policy for Malaria Cases introduced ACT-AL in north-eastern states
2014–2015	Newer insecticides and larvicides introduced

(**Source:** National framework for malaria elimination in India (2016–2030))

CAUSE AND CLINICAL MANIFESTATION

Malaria is a serious, sometimes fatal, spread by the bite of an infected Anopheles mosquito. It is caused by the protozoan parasite i.e. Plasmodium that requires two hosts, one is vertebrate (birds, reptiles, rodents, primates, humans) and another invertebrate (Anopheles mosquito); to complete their life cycle. Human malaria may also be transmitted by contaminated blood transfusion, and/or contaminated syringes (Perimann and Troye-Blomberg, 2000). It can be affected by five species of plasmodium like *P. falciparum, P. vivax, P. malarae and P. ovalae*. Among them, *P. falciparum* is the most dangerous human malaria parasite. They cause serious problem due to asexual reproduction in the host, and it have ability to sequester in small blood vessels (Winstanley, 2000). It has 14 chromosomes, encoding about 5,300 protein and almost two thirds of which appear to be unique to the organism. Out of total, 208 genes are involved in the evasion of the host immune system. This information is to be use in development of new chemotherapeutic targets and antigens for potential vaccines. Some promising targets are listed for the control malaria parasite. Therefore, phytomedicine research is an emerging area which anticipates in development of new drugs for combating and solving the malaria (Pizzorno and Murray, 1999). Newly identifying compounds that binds to step involved in biological disease developmental processes have to efforts to develop new drug discovery against malaria and to establish the probable mechanism of action. However, other three species of Plasmodium, not causes severe disease. *P. vivax* and *P. ovale* have hepatic 'hypnozoites' can cause relapse up to 40 weeks after infection. Which, if not killed using primaquine or malariae have lacks hypnozoites property, but can persist in the blood for many years if inadequately treated?

EPIDEMIOLOGY

The severity of falciparum malaria is mainly occurring in tropical Africa. Most of people become infected during childhood stage up to 5 year. Due to partial develop of immunity, mortality is seen in children under the age of five years (Snow *et al.*, 1997). According to the latest WHO estimates, about 214 million peoples are affected due to malaria in December 2015, and out of which 438000 were dead. Between 2000 and 2015, mortality rates due to malaria were decreased by 60%. However, risk about it fell by 37% globally. In Sub-Saharan African continues to share high proportion of the global malaria. In latest estimation, in some countries of sub-Saharan Africa – about 80% of malaria cases were reported and 78% deaths globally. However, the incidence was decline about 32% in these countries since 2000. Indian subcontinent, South America, Southeast Asia and China are less affected by Falciparum malaria. Therefore, due to low transmission rate, partial immunity does not develop as rapidly. *Plasmodium vivax* is spread in both temperate and tropical regions and is relatively uncommon in tropical Africa. While *P. ovale* is found mainly in tropical Africa, whereas *P. malariae* has a widespread distribution throughout the tropics and subtropics. However, *P. falciparum* and *P. vivax* most common malaria parasite occur in India. While *P. vivax* in the plains and *P. falciparum* predominates in forested and peripheral areas are prevalent occurs. Recently, WHO has decided to develop the Global Technical Strategy for Malaria 2016–2030 which have aim to eliminate malaria globally. Today, India is a member of Asia pacific Leaders Malaria Alliance (APLMA), has decide to eliminate malaria by 2030 as per own national and global strategies on the same timelines. In India, central as well as state government have been spending (30-35%) share budget approximately equal in health on malaria control, except by the north eastern states (Sharma, 1998) (figure 3.2).

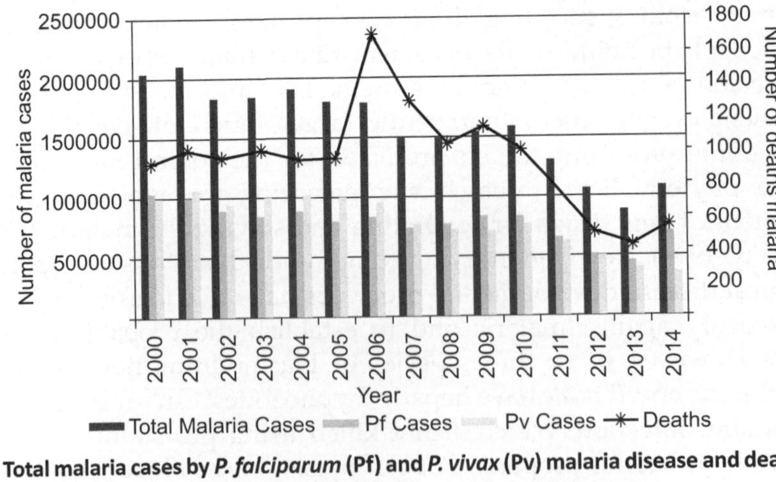

Fig. 3.2: Total malaria cases by *P. falciparum* (Pf) and *P. vivax* (Pv) malaria disease and death in India. (Source: National framework for malaria elimination in India (2016–2030))

LIFE CYCLE OF COMMON MALARIA CAUSED BY P. FALCIPARUM

Intra-erythrocytic schizogony

Intra-erythrocytic schizogony stage also known as asexual reproduction, occurs within the host erythrocytes, and is the indicator of clinical manifestation. Malaria parasite take amino acids as a nitrogen source for development and proliferation in the host erythrocytes mainly depend on degradation of hemoglobin (Slomianny *et al.,* 1982). Sequential metabolism of hemoglobin of take place in an acidic compartment of intra-erythrocytecyte stage by the malaria parasite, result heam (ferriprotoporphyrin IX) is a by-product after digestion (Gluzman *et al.,* 1994; Coombs *et al.,* 2001). Due to acidic in nature, it toxic to both the host cells as well as malaria parasite refers as parasite death. Mainly membrane and different enzymes are affected, and heme oxygenase is play key role to convert heme into an open-chain tetrapyrrole, which is necessary for cellular excretion (Eckman *et al.,* 1997). To protect itself, the malaria parasite take place several solution to detoxifies free heme either by histidine-rich protein (HRP-2) and degradation with reduced glutathione or converts into a water insoluble crystelized form known as hemozoin (β-hematin) (Atamna *et al.,* 1995; Huy *et al.,* 2003). Hemozoin formation is a complex processes which occurs by coordination of one carboxylic oxygen of the propionate side chain to the central iron of an adjacent haem subunit to form oxygen-iron bonds (Lambros and Vanderberg JP, 1979) (figure 3.3).

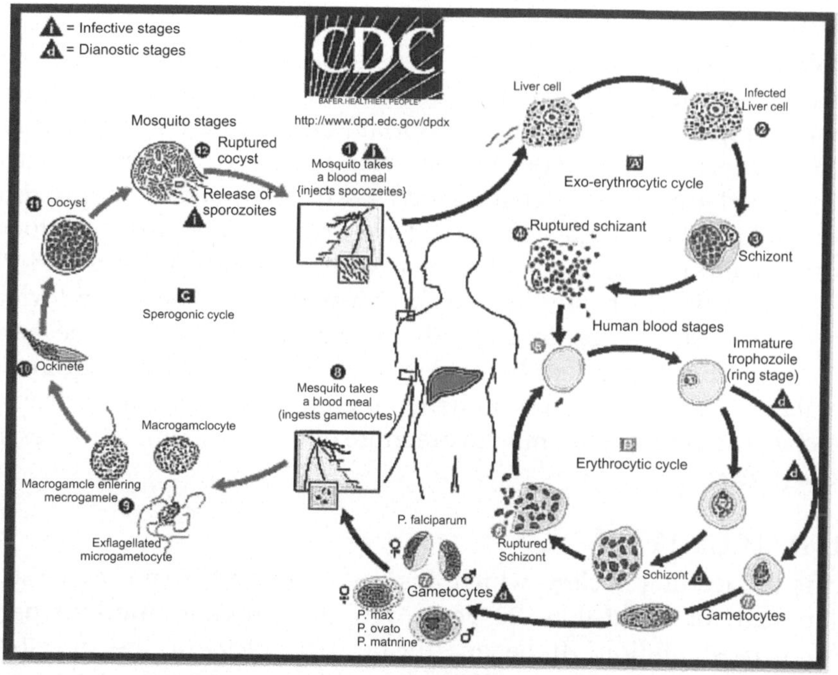

Fig. 3.3: Life cycle of *P. falciparum* in two hosts

(Source: http://www.cdc.gov/malaria/about/biology)

Whereas the figure 3.3 indicate that, Life cycle of *P. falciparum* in two hosts. During a blood intake, a malaria-infected female Anopheles mosquito transfer sporozoites into the human host; (1) Sporozoites infect liver cells; (2) mature into schizonts; (3) which rupture and release merozoites; (4) After this initial replication in the liver (exo-erythrocytic schizogony A), the parasites undergo asexual multiplication in the erythrocytes (erythrocytic schizogony B). Merozoites infect red blood cells; (5) The ring stage trophozoites mature into schizonts, which rupture releasing merozoites; (6) Some parasites differentiate into sexual erythrocytic stages (gametocytes); (7) Blood stage parasites are responsible for the clinical manifestations of the disease. The gametocytes, male (microgametocytes) and female (macrogametocytes), are ingested by an Anopheles mosquito during a blood meal; (8) The parasites' multiplication in the mosquito is known as the sporogonic cycle C. While in the mosquito's stomach, the microgametes penetrate the macrogametes generating zygotes; (9) The zygotes in turn become motile and elongated (ookinetes); (10) which invade the midgut wall of the mosquito where they develop into oocysts; (11) The oocysts grow, rupture, and release sporozoites; (12) which make their way to the mosquito's salivary glands. Inoculation of the sporozoites 1into a new human host perpetuates the malaria life cycle.

KEY TARGET TO PREVENT MALARIA PARASITE (PLASMODIUM FALCIPARUM)

Mutational study to be most effective targets for development of resistance for malaria parasite and establishment of new drugs has been noted. So binding of newer compounds acting on appropriate targets site for *P. falciparum* are likely to be effective. Several biochemical compounds are known to control the invasion of malaria during infection processes. It is assumed that approximately 80% degrade malaria parasite after release from an infected erythrocyte in the host cell and release heme which is toxic to parasite (Wellems and Plowe, 2001). In-activation of heme depends on formation of haemozoin formation, and inhibition of haemozoin depends on binding of drug to the heme or inhibition of GSH dependent heme degradation. Since action of quinoline as anti-malarial are less response on heme, therefore several others drugs such as vasicine, vasicinone and embelin are more effective treatment for resistance purpose (figure 3.4).

HEALTH SECURITY

WHO is the leading society which has been engaged in anti-malarial drug development for more than 20 years ago and provides funding per year around US$2-4 million? It began during 1998-1999 for the development of initial portfolio for the Medicines for Malaria Venture. This was one of the most successful public-private partnerships involved in diseases

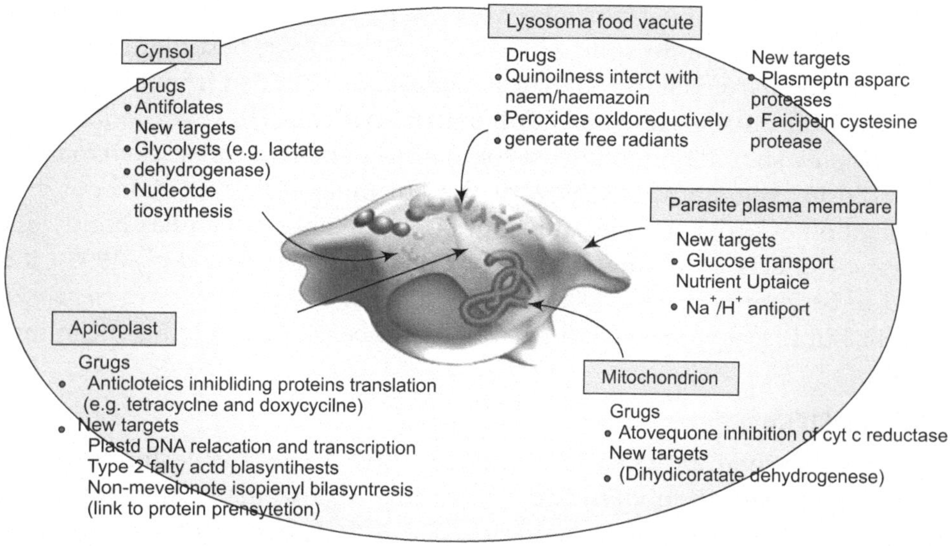

Fig. 3.4: New drug targets and site of anti-malarial drug action.

(Source: Ridley, 2002**).**

management. In that time, WHO worked with other agencies (WRAIR) and many pharmaceutical companies to develop for development of anti-malarial drug such as mefloquine and halofantrine. Presently, it has expanded own work and collaborated with several pharmaceutical company to develop injectable artemether and arteether, which has broad spectrum for severe malaria for treatment. Other recent ongoing work with other agencies (the Bill & Melinda Gates Foundation, Rockefeller Foundation, The Welcome Trust, Swiss Government, U.K. Government, Dutch Government, World Bank via the Global Forum for Health Research, and Exxon Mobil) which have some mandate includes:

1. Gaining regulatory approval of chlorproguanil-dapsone;
2. Developing a fixed-dose combination of chlorproguanil-dapsone plus artesunate;
3. To expand use of Coartem in children which have low weight below the 5 kg and to develop appropriate, user-friendly, and informative packaging?

MARKETING OF ANTIMALARIA DRUG

Malaria is a not much serious disorder if promptly diagnosed at right time. A number of medicinal drugs are commercially available today. Quinine is an alkaloid obtained from bark of the *Chinchona* tree; widely used by people for treatment of malaria suffering patients. Another antimalarial drug such as Mefloquine, work similar to quinine, is effective against all malarial species.

But it has some toxic effects like vertigo, nausea, abdominal discomfort, malaise and insomnia. In spite, chloroquine is low toxic and highly effective against all species of malaria parasites. *Artemisinin*, obtained from the *Artimisia annua* have effective in child and adult malaria patients. However, *Sulfadoxine–pyrimethamine* should preferably use for malaria patients as prescribed manner; but avoid in pregnant cases. Now at present time, Malarone is a new drug combination of proguanil and atovaquone is available, which has highly and synergistic effects as antimalarial treatment (Looareesuwan *et al.*, 1999). It is found to be approximately 95% effective against drug resistant *P. falciparum* malaria; but it cost value is high and could not be easily available to common people.

CONCLUSION

Now days, several antimalarials suitable drugs are available for treatment of malaria disease in modern therapy. In this review, many approaches are mentioned for discovery of new anti-malarial drug. The study of new medicinal plants has been considered for the discovery of new drugs. The primary aims are to evaluate the use of medicinal plants; not only by ethnopharmacological investigators but also by local people. This review provides land mark for identification and isolation of new active molecules through basic step and understanding the appropriate toxicological studies and clinical trials. In modern time, a number of medicinal plants have been identified and tested for their antiplasmodial activity at different doses, belonging to different molecular classes. Most of drugs have show dual activity and have very low side effects. From the above information, it is clear that ethnopharmacology is a rich source of medicinal plants for development of new antimalarial therapeutic agents.

REFERENCES

Atamna, H and ginsburg, H. (1995). Heme Degradation in the Presence of Glutathione. J Biol. Chem., 270: 24876-24883.

Bisset, N.G., Houghton, P.J. and Hylands, P.J. (1991). In the Medicial Plant Industry. Medicinal Plant Industry, CRC Press: Boca Raton, FL.

Bloland, P.B. (2001). Drug Resistance in Malaria. World Health Organization, Geneva, Switzerland.

Chopra, M., Fitzsimons, P.E.E., Strain, J.J., Thurnham, D.I. and Howard, A.N. (2000). Non Alcoholic Red Wine Extract and Quercetin Inhibit LDL Oxidation without Affecting Plasma Antioxidant Vitamin and Carotenoid Concentrations. Clinical Chem., 46(8): 1162–1170.

Chopra, M., Fitzsimons, P.E., Strain, J.J., Thurnham, D.I. and Howard, A.N. (2000). Non-alcoholic Red Wine Extract and Quercetin Inhibit LDL Oxidation without Affecting Plasma Antioxidant Vitamin and Carotenoid Concen. Clin. Chem., 46: 1162–1170.

Cordell, G.A., Beecherer, C.W.W. and Pezzuto, J.M. (1991). Can Ethnopharmacology Contribute to the Development of New Anticancer Drugs? J Ethnopharmacol, 32: 117–133

Deschner, E.E., Ruperto, J., Wong, G. and Newmark, H.L. (1991). Quercetin and Rutin as Inhibitors of Azoxymethanol-induced Colonic Neoplasia. Carcinogen, 12: 1193–1196.

Dr. Duke's (1983). Phytochemical and Ethnobotanical Database. www.ars-grin.gov/duke Phillips.

Ferry, D.R., Smith, A., Malkhandi, J., Fyfe, D.W., de Takats, P.G. and Anderson, D. (1996). Phase I Clinical Trial of the Flavonoid Quercetin: Pharmacokinetics and Evidence for in vivo Tyrosine Kinase Inhibition, Clin. Cancer Res., 2: 659–668.

Fitch, C.D. (2004). Ferriprotoporphyrin IX, Phospholipids, and the Antimalarial Actions of Quinoline Drugs. Life Sci., 74: 1957–1972.

Fitch, C.D., Cai G.Z., Chen, Y.F. and Shoemaker, J.D. (1999). Involvement of Lipids in Ferriprotoporphyrin IX Polymerization in Malaria. Biochim Biophys Acta, 1454: 31-37.

Galati, E.M., Trovato, A., Kirjavainen, S., Forestieri, A.M. and Monforte, M.T. (1996). Biological Effects of Hesperidin, a Citrus Flavonoid Part 1, Anti Inflammatory and Analgesic Activity, Farmaco, 51: 219-221.

Gluzman, I.Y., Francis, S.E., Oksman, A., Smith, C.E., Duffin, K.L. and Goldberg, D.E. (1994). Order and Specificity of the *Plasmodium falciparum* Hemoglobin Degradation Pathway. J Clin Invest., 93: 1602–1608.

Grabley, S., Thiericke, R., Zeeck, A. (1999). The Chemical Screening Approach. In: Drug Discovery from Nature, Grabley, S., Thiericke, Eds., Springer-Verlag, Berlin.

Greenwood, D. (1995). Conflicts of Interest: The Genesis of Synthetic Antimalarial Agents in Peace and War. J Antimicrob. Chemother, 36 (5): 857-872.

Choi, J.S. and Han, H.K. (2004). The Effect of Quercetin on the Pharmacokinetics of Verapamil and Its Major Metabolite, Norverapamil, in Rabbits, J Pharm. Pharmacol, 56: 1537-1542.

Hayek, T., Fuhrman, B., Vaya, J., Rosenblat, M., Belinky, P. and Coleman, R. (1997). Reduced Progression of Atherosclerosis in Apolipoprotein E-deficient Mice Following Consumption of Red Wine, or Its Polyphenols Quercetin or Catechin, is Associated with Reduced Susceptibility of LDL to Oxidation and Aggregation, Arterioscler. Thromb. Vasc. Biol., 17: 2744–2752.

Huy, N.T., Kamei, K., Yamamoto, T., Kondo, Y., Kanaori, K., Takano, R., Tajima, K., Hara, S. (2003). Clotrimazole Binds to Heme and Enhances Heme-dependent Hemolysis: Proposed Anti-malarial Mechanism of Clotrimazole. J Biol. Chem., 277: 4152–4158.

Kirmizibekmez, H., Çalis, I., Perozzo, R. 2004. "Inhibiting Activities of the Secondary Metabolites of Phlomis Brunneogaleata against Parasitic Protozoa and Plasmodial Enoyl-ACP Reductase, A Crucial Enzyme in Fatty Acid Biosynthesis," Planta Medica, 70(8): 711–717.

Looareesuwan, S., Chulay, J.D., Canfield, C.J. and Hutchinson, D.B.A. (1999). Malarone (Atovaquone and Proguanil hydrochloride): A Review of Its Clinical Development for Treatment of Malaria. Am. J. Trop. Med. Hyg., 60: 533–541.

Meshnick SR. (1997). Why Does Quinine Work After 350 Years of Use? Parasitol Today. 13: 89–90.

Mockenhaupt, F.P. (1995). Mefloquine Resistance in Plasmodium Falciparum, Parasitology Today, 11: 248– 253.

Newman DJ, Cragg GM, Snader KM (2003). Natural Products as Sources of New Drugs Over the Period 1981-2002. J Nat. Prod., 66: 1022-1037.

Oliveira, A.B., Dolabela, M.F., Braga, F.C., Jácome, R.L.R.P., Varotti, F.P., Povoa, M.M. (2009). Plant-derived Antimalarial Agents: New Leads and Efficient Phythomedicines. Part I. Alkaloids. An Acad Bras Cienc, 81: 715-740.

Pizzorno Jr, J.E., Murray, M. T. (1999). The Textbook of Natural Medicine, Churchill Livinstone: Edinburgh; 79.

Pereira, M.A., Grubbs, C.J., Barnes, L.H., Li, H., Olson G.R. and Eto, I. (1996). Effects of the Phytochemicals, Curcumin and Quercetin, Upon Azoxymethane-induced Colon Cancer and 7,12-dimethylbenz [a] Anthracene-induced Mammary Cancer in Rats., Carcinogenesis, 17: 1305–1311.

Perez-Vizcaino, F., Ibarra, M., Cogolludo, A.L, Duarte, J., Zaragoza-Arnaez, F. and Moreno, L. (2002). Endothelium-independent Vasodilator Effects of the Flavonoid Quercetin and Its Methylated Metabolites in Rat Conductance Resistance Arteries. J Pharmacol. Exp. Ther., 302: 66–72.

Peter, B. and Bloland. (2014). Drug Resistance in Malaria. WHO/CDS/CSR/DRS/2014.

Perimann, P. and Troye-Blomberg, M. (2000). Malaria Blood-stage Infection and Its Control by Immune System. Folia. Biol. (Praha), 46(6): 210–218.

Piantelli, M., Ranelletti, F.O., Maggiano, N., Serra, F.G., Ricci, R. and Larocca, L.M. (2000). Quercetin Inhibits p21-RAS Expression in Human Colon Cancer Cell Lines and in Primary Colorectal Tumors., Intl. J Can., 85: 438–444.

Portet, B., Fabre, N., Roumy, V., Gornitzka, H., Bourdy, G. 2007. Activity-guided Isolation of Antiplasmodial Dihydrochalcones and Flavanones from *Piper hostmannianum* Var. Berbicense. Phytochem., 68: 1312-1320.

Ridley, R.G. (2002). Medical Need, Scientific Opportunity and the Drive for Antimalarial Drugs. Nature, 415: 686–693.

Sanket S. and Gupta S. 2009. In vitro Anti Plasmodial Activity of *Enicostemma littorale*. Amer. J Infec. Dise., 5(3): 259-262.

Sharma, P.K. and Sharma. J.D. (1998). Plants Showing Antiplasmodial Activity-from Crude Extracts to Isolated Compounds. Ind. J Malarial., 35(2): 57-110.

Sieve, B.J. (1952). Simple Colorimetric Inhibition Assay of Heme Crystallization for High-through Put Screening of Antimalarial Compounds. Antimicrob. Agents Chemother, 51: 335–350.

Lambro, C. and Vanderberg, J.P. (1979). Synchronisatton of *Plasmodlum falciparum* Erythrocytlc Stages in Culture. J Parasitolo, 65: 418-420.

Slomianny, C., Charet, P. and Prensier, G. (1983). Ultrastructural Localization of Enzymes Involved in the Feeding Process in *Plasmodium chabaudi* and *Babesia hylomysci*. J Parasitol., 30: 376-382.

Snow, R.W., Omumbo, J.A., Lowe, B., Molyneaux, C.S. and Obiero, J.O. (1997). Relation between Severe Malaria Morbidity in Children and Level of *Plasmodium falciparum* Transmission in Africa. Lancet, 349: 1650-1654.

Son, H.S., Kim, H.S. and Ju, J.S. (1991). Effects of Rutin and Hesperidin on Total Cholesterol Concentration, Transaminase and Alkaline Phosphatase Activity in Carbon Tetrachloride Treated Rats., Hanguk Nonghwa Hakhoe Chi., 34: 318-326.

Soni, S. and Gupta, S. (2009). In vitro Anti Plasmodial Activity of Enicostemma Littorale., American Journal of Infectious Diseases, 5(3): 259-262.

Struckmann, J.R. and Nicolaides, A.N. (1994). Flavinoids: A Review of the Pharmacology and Therapeutic Efficacy of Daflon-500 mg in Patients with Chronic Venous Insufficiency and Related Disorders, Angiologon, 45: 419-428.

Tamura, S., Kubata, B.K., Syamsurizal, Itagaki, S., Horii, T., Taba, M. K. and Murakami, N. (2010). New Anti-malarial Phenylpropanoid Conjugated Iridoids from Morinda Morindoides. Bioorg. Med. Chem. Lett., 20: 1520-1523.

Tripathi, A.K., Gupta, A., Garg, S.K., Tekwani, B.L. (2001). In vitro β-hematin Formation Assays with Plasma of Mice Infected with Plasmodium Yoelii and Other Parasite Preparations Comparative Inhibition with Quinoline and Endoperoxide Antimalarials. Life Sci., 69: 2725-33.

Verma, A.K., Johnson, J.A., Gould M.N. and Tanner, M.A. (1988). Inhibition of 7, 12-dimethylbenz (a) Anthracene and N-nitrosomethyl Urea Induced Mammary Cancer by Dietary *flavonol quercetin,* Cancer Res., 48: 5754–5788.

Wellems, T., Plowe, C (2001). Chloroquine-resistant Malaria. J Infec. Disea., 184: 770–776.

WHO (1995). Traditional Practioners as Primary Health Care Workers. WHO/SHS/DHS/TRM/95.6. Geneva.

Winstanley, P.A. 2000. Chemotherapy for Falciparum Malaria: The Armoury, the Problems and the Prospects. Parasitology Today, 16: 146–153.

Winter, R.W., Kelly, J.X., Smilkstein, M.J., Dodean, R., Hinrichs, D. and Riscoe M.K. 2008. Antimalarial Quinolones: Synthesis, Potency, and Mechanistic Studies. Exp. Parasitol., 118(4): 487–497.

Yougesh, S., Biradar L., Rajani M. and Padh H. 2009. Evaluation of Antimalarial Activity of Selected Plants of Indian Systems of Medicine and Study the Synergistic Activity of the Compounds Present Therein.

Medicinal and Nutritional Values of Plants
Edited by: Alka Chauhan and Pawan Kumar 'Bharti'
ISBN: 978-93-5056-883-5
Edition: 2017
Published by: Discovery Publishing House Pvt. Ltd., New Delhi (India)

4

An Important Medicinal Plant-Safed Musli (Indian Ginseng)

[1]Archana Rani, [2]Stuti Mishra and [3]Sanjeev Kumar

INTRODUCTION

Nature has been a source of medicinal treatment for thousands of years, and plant-based system maintains to take part in an vital role in primary health care of 80% at universal level (Gupta 2001; Samant, 2011; Bordia, 1995). Wild plant species form the foundation of health care practices throughout much of Asia. This is particularly true in the case of traditional medicine practices, including codified systems such as traditional Chinese medicine, Ayurveyda, Siddha, Unani and Tibetan medicines, and more localised healthcare traditions (Bordia, 1995). Among the various diseases, cancer is one of the most dangerous diseases and can be depicted as a disease in cell proliferation and differentiation becomes uncoupled and damage to numerous regulatory genes ultimately results in the development of invasive and metastatic cancer, which is the culmination of the chronic disease process, carcinogenesis. Natural products have long been a fertile source of cure for cancer, which is projected to become the major causes of death in this century (Puri., 2003). However, there is a continuing need for development of new anticancer drugs, drug combinations and chemotherapy strategies, by methodical and scientific exploration of enormous pool of synthetic, biological, and natural products (Mukherjee *et al.*, 2001; Haque *et al.*, 2011).

Asia's wild plants also form a critical component of 'modern' healthcare practices. India is blessed with very rich biodiversity largely because of highly divergent ecosystem and great altitudinal variations. Medicinal plant constitute one of the major part of the plant diversity. There are around 30,000 species of medicinal plants in the world, out of which about 8000 species belong to India. They constitute about 50% of all higher flowering plant species. The growing demand of medicinal plant is putting a heavy strain on the existing natural resources causing a number of species to be either threatened or endangered

[1,2]Department of Plant Breeding & Genetics, College of Agriculture, Jawaharlal Nehru Krishi Vishwa Vidyalaya, Jabalpur-482 004, Madhya Pradesh (India).

[3] Department of Plant Pathology, College of Agriculture, Jawaharlal Nehru Krishi Vishwa Vidyalaya, Jabalpur-482 004, Madhya Pradesh (India).

(Maiti, 2006). Further medicinal plants constitute more than 80% of the raw material used in various systems of medicine practiced throughout the world. About 90% of the medicinal plants are collected from the wild populations and over 70% of the plant collections involve destructive harvesting mainly because of the use of plant parts like root, bud, wood and even full plant (Trivedi, P.C. (2009; Verma *et al.*, 2004). A recent report of International Union for conservation of nature and natural resources (IUCN) revealed that India ranked 5th in case of threatened plant species and among medicinal plants about 112 species in South India 74 species in North and Central India and 42 species in higher altitude of Himalaya are threatened in wild (Maiti, 2006).

Chlorophytum is a genus of about 250 species of evergreen perennial flowering plants of the Liliaceae family, many of which are greatly valued as medicinal plant. It is native of the tropical and sub tropical regions of Africa and Asia. The plant has a rosette of long slender leaves growing from a thick fleshy rhizome. A total of 17 species of *Chlorophytum* have been reported in India. Most of these *Chlorophytum* species have medicinal properties but *Chlorophytum borivilianum* Santpau and Fernandes is the most important (Ram and Pandey, 2004). *Chlorophytum borivilianum* Santpau and Fernandes is one medicinal plant whose natural availability is continuously decreasing due to heavy demand of useful parts (Kothari, 2004). It is commonly known as Safed musli, because it yields milky white tubers on processing. Safed musli is considered as one of the most important drugs in Indian systems of medicine namely Ayurveda, Unani and Siddha due to its aphrodisiac and sex tonic properties. This is the reason that it is an integral part of more than 100 Ayurvedic formulations (Singh *et al.*, 2004).

VERNICULAR NAME

Arabic	:	Shaqaqule
English	:	India spider plant, Spider plant
French	:	Chlorophytum medicinal
Gujrati	:	Ujlimusli, Dholi musali
Garhwal	:	Jhirna
Hindi	:	Safed musli, Hazarmuli, Satmuli
Kannada	:	Dravanti
Malyalam	:	Shedeveli, Shedheveli.
Marathi	:	Safed musli, Sufed Musli, Kuli
Sanskrit	:	Swetha musli., Musali
Sinhalese	:	Hirtha-wariya, Mushali
Tamil	:	Tannirvittang, Vipurutti, Taniravi thang
Telgu	:	Tsallogadda, Swetha musli
U.P.	:	Khairuwa

DISTRIBUTIONS

C. borivilianum is native of the tropical and sub tropical regions of Africa and Asia.*C. borivilianum* is cultivated in most states of our country, the prominent amongst them being Madhya Pradesh, Maharashtra, Punjab, Andhra Pradesh etc. Based on agro climatic suitability, Safed Musli can be cultivated in Eastern, Western, Central and Southern Plateau and Hill regions, East and West Coast Plains and Hill regions and Gujarat Plains and Hill regions comprising the states of Bihar, Orissa, Madhya Pradesh, Uttar Pradesh, Rajasthan, Maharashtra, Andhra Pradesh, Karnataka, Kerala, Tamilnadu and Gujarat.

There are about 256 species of *Chlorophytum*, out of which 17 are found in India. *Chlorophytum barivilianum* and other species of *Chlorophytum*, *C. arundinaceum*, *C. atteneuatum*, *C. laxum*, *C. tuberosum* and *C. breviscapum* are commonly known as Safed musli because of their white tuberous roots. Out of these 6 species *Chlorophytum borivilianum* and *C. arundinaceum* are the two most important species of medicinal value. Out of these two species *Chlorophytum borivilianum* is superior and with reference to the reputed books of Ayurveda, it is the plant mentioned as safed musli.

The different species of *Chlorophytum* and their specific areas of distribution are:

Species	Distribution
C. arundinaceum	All districts of Jharkhand, Vindhya, Satpura and Aravali Hills, parts of Central India, Tarai region of N-E Himalayas in Assam, West Bengal and Bihar.
C. altenuatum	Western Ghats southwards to Coimbatore, West Peninsula.
C. laxum	Katki Hills, Belgaum, Dharwar, North and South Kanara, Decan Peninsula in India.
C. tuberosum Baker	Parts of Konkan to Travancore in Kerala, Eastern Himalaya, Bihar and West Bengal.
C. hreviscapum	Sikkim, Himalaya, Belgaum and South Peninsula.
C. borivilianum	Bastar forest (Madhya Pradesh), Dangs forest (Gujrat), Mount Abu, Mahi, Aravalli Hills (Rajasthan).

TAXONOMIC CLASSIFICATION

Arabic : Shaqaqule

Phylum : Phenarograms

Class : Monocotyledon

Series : Coronarieae

Family : Liliaceae

Genus : *Chlorophutum*

Species : *Borivilianum*

Habit : A small perennial herb with a full crown of radical leaves appearing over the ground with the advent of summer rain.

Root : Root tubers are fleshy, fascicled, directly originates from the stem disc, devoid of any fibrous structure, cylindrical, 9-16 in number, outer skin is straw coloured and white on peeling; the tubers are 2-14 cms × 0.2-1.0 cms in dimension.

Leaves : Radical, 6-15 in number, 13-23 cms × 1.0-1.7 cm in size, spirally imbricate at the base, sessile, linear of ovate, acute apex, slightly narrowed at the base. The leaves spread horizontally, both surfaces are smooth, margins are wavy; parallel venation.

Inflorescence : Scape solitary, terete, 15-30 cms long; Terminal; unbranched, it bears flowers on above upper ¾ th of its length.

Flowers : Small, white, bracteate, pedicillate, zygomorphic, usually arranged in alternate clusters, each cluster comprising of 3 flowers; the flower clusters are dense on the upper part of the scape; bracts are linear, papery and purplish, 1.0-10.5 cms long, pedicle whitish, jointed and kneed at the joint, 6-10 mm long.

Perianth : Tepals white, 6 in number arranged in two whorls of 3 each, linear, membranous, acute, 3-5 nerved; imbricate aestivation.

Androecium : Stamens 6, arranged in two whorls situated opposite to tepals, united to the perianths, as long as perianth, dithecus, filments are glabrous, anthers are yellow, linear, dehisces by longitudinal slits.

Gynoecium : Tricarpellary, syncarpous; ovary superior, adnate at the base of the perianth, triocular with axile placentation, angles obtuse, green, glabose; ovules numerous in each locule, style single, slightly longer than the stamens, swollen at the apex.

Fruit : Alocilucidal capsule, green to yellow coloured, triquertous to 3-sulcate, almost equal in length and breadth.

Seeds	:	Endospermic, onion-like, black coloured, angular, each capsule bearing 14-16 seeds.
Chromosome	:	$2n = 16$ (Kumar and Subramanium, 1986)
Floral Formula	:	+ P (3 + 3), A (3 + 3) G (3)

MICROSCOPY DESCRIPTION

Epidermis is present without cuticle & stomata, many unicellular root hairs. Cortex shows round parenchymaatous cells with intercellularr spaces. Starch is absent. Endodermis (50 μm thick) shows barrel shaped closely arranged parenchymatous cell lies below the cortex & forms a ring. Single layered pericyclic cells are present below the endodermis which are Uniseriate & composed of thin walled parenchymatous cells. Phloem Composed of companion cells and phloem parenchyma. Numerous Xylem composed of a single layered round metaxylem towards the pith, protoxylem towards the periphery. Powdered microscopy shows raphides of calcium oxalate, isolated single stone cells with simple pits on their walls and isolated and combined reticulate vessels.

CYTOLOGY

The chromosome number as diploid ($2n$ ¼ $2x$ ¼ 16) of *C. borivilianum* was firstly reported (Raghavan *et al.,* 1977). Though, extensive examinations of chromosomes in various accessions by Geetha and Maiti (2004) revealed that the chromosome number in the species is $2n$ ¼ $4x$ ¼ 28, indicating the species as tetraploid with basic number x ¼ 7, but an octaploid number ($2n$ ¼ $8x$ ¼ 56) is also observed in a few somatic cells of some plant samples. Lavania *et al.,* (2005) reconfirmed the chromosome number $2n$ ¼ $4x$ ¼ 28 by applied the fluorescence in situ hybridization (FISH) technique to elucidate physical localization and measurement of the rDNA sites using two rRNA multigene families homologous to 45S and 5S rDNA in *C. borivilianum.*

PHYTOCHEMISTRY

The main components of *C. borivilianum* are:

carbohydrates-42%, fibres 20-30%, protein-10%, saponins 2-17% and alkaloids 15-25%. Primarily saponins and alkaloids impart medicinal value. It is a rich source of over 25 alkaloids, vitamins, proteins, carbohydrates, steroids, saponins, calcium, magnesium, phenol, potassium, resins, polysaccharides and mucilage and also contains high quantity of simple sugars, mainly sucrose, glucose, fructose, galactose, mannose and xylose(Deore and Khadabadi, 2010; Thakur *et al.,* 2009). Recently Stigmasterol and saponin named as furostanol and Chlorophytoside-I (3b, 5a, 22R, 25R)-26-(β-Dglucopyranosyloxy)-22-hydroxy-furostan-12-one-3yl O-β-D-galacto-pyranosyl (1-4) glucopyranoside has been isolated 15 ((Singh *et al.,* 2012).

PHARMACOLOGICAL ACTIVITIES AND USES

Different plant parts of Safed musli possess herbal medication for: bettering immune entire body, curing tiredness, stamina and vigor, blood movement to all areas of the physique, vital amino acid supplementation (Haque *et al.*, 2011; Chakraborthy and Aeri., 2011). Saponin extract of *C. borivilianum has* anthelmintic property. Alcoholic extract of *C. borivilianum* show ulcer healing property. The roots of *C. borivilianum* contain cytotoxic steroidal glycoside saponinchloromaloside-A and spirostanolpentaglycosides embracing beta-Dapiofuranose which are responsible chemicals for anticancer property. Polysaccharide fraction (CBP) of *C. borivilianum* has immunostimulating properties (Thakur *et al.*, 2009; Singh *et al.*, 2012). The tuber roots of the plant of safed musli are utilised to make a tonic to treat all kinds of weakness and male impotency given that historic instances. In ayurveda, it has been referred as 'Divya Aushadh' which indicates divine medication for its curative properties not only for male impotence but enhancement in general wellness for curing other sexual weakness (Chakraborthy and Aeri., 2011; Kenjale *et al.*, 2007). It operates in the direction of hormonal stability by enhancing working of adrenal gland and advertising manufacturing of testosterone, an important hormone to enhance blood movement to genitals which ultimately brings tougher. More powerful and lengthier erections.

Applications for Male

- Controls erectile dysfunction due to any reason whether psychological reason or health problems.
- Stops and cures premature ejaculation.
- Increases sexual desire and overcome frustration and embarrassment over a sexual dysfunction, especially erectile problems.
- Provides ability to maintain the erection throughout the sexual act.
- Improves physical power and stamina, semen quality.
- Increases sperm count substantially (Plays a vital role in Fertility), frequency of orgasm and the volume of ejaculation.
- Used for faster recovery for second orgasm.
- Provides extra time, extra pleasure, and extra satisfaction in sexual act.
- Controls premature ejaculation.
- Improves and promotes general well being and vitality.
- Increases libido.
- Yearlong action with the same intensity.

Applications for Female

- Controls Erectile dysfunction due to any reason whether psychological reasons or health problems.

- Increases sexual desire and overcome frustration and embarrassment over a sexual dysfunction.
- Improves energy and youthfulness.
- Checks veganism's (tightness of Vagina).
- Improves physical power and stamina and vaginal lubrication.
- Increases frequency of desire.
- Checks the menopause, excessive menstrual bleeding, loss of sensation in sexual organs and urinary tract infections.
- Checks hormonal shifts and imbalances.
- Provides full sexual satisfaction throughout the sexual act.
- Improves and promotes general well being and vitality.
- Develops curiosity towards the sexual act.

CULTIVATION

Soil Suitability

- Safed Musli is a tuber species and for better quantity of yield sandy loamy soil, neutral pH with organic matter are required.
- Hard and acidic soils are to be avoided for cultivation of Musli.

Climate

- The vegetative growth and fleshy root development is facilitated by warm.
- Humid weather with sufficient amount of moisture during the growing period.

Propagation Material

- Fingers or tubers are used as planting material.
- Before planting, the fingers are separated in such a way that each finger has a portion of crown disk attached to it.
- Fingers gives better result than seeds. So, fingers are preferred.
- Tissue culture plantlets can also be used for planting.

Planting

- Kharif crop, sowing starts with the onset of monsoon.
- Planting of fingers is done in beds or ridges depending on the slope and drainage of the soil.
- Generally fingers are planted at a distance of 35 to 40 cm.
- Qty of the seed needed for sowing is 450 kgs (30,000 – 35,000 fingers are required per acre).

- The seed to be sown has to be treated with growth promoter and fungicide to avoid possible diseases after transplanting.
- Seed should be treated with Humicil @ 5ml/Lt water. & Dithane-M 45@ 5 gm/Lt water.

Irrigation

- Safed Musli is cultivated during the rainy season, because of continuous necessity of water.
- It needs a regular supply of water even after the stage of fall of leaves.
- A good drainage system is essential to avoid waterlogging.
- Drip irrigation is ideal for cultivation of Musli.

Manuring

- *Bone Meal:* For a tuber species like Musli, application of bone meal provides the necessary micronutrients.
- *Cow Dung:* Well dried, decomposed cow dung is to be provided over the soil in large quantities because of its vital role to increase the richness level of soil.
- *Green Manure:* Green manuring is vital to develop the fertility of the soil. Sesbania, Crotalaria or Jammu are used as ideal sources of green manure.

Plouging

- Plough the field upto 1 to 1.5 ft depth & draw the cultivator.
- Broadcast green manure seeds and irrigate the crop if needed.
- Incorporate into field at peak flowering stage.
- Spread well decomposed or compost evenly over the field, along with 50 kgs of single super phosphate and apply post-emergence weedicide (Glyphosate group) 7 days after emergence of weeds.
- Leave the land for 20 days for sowing.

Preparation of Beds

- Cultivation of musli is good on raised beds and beds are to be prepared along the slope of the land for proper surface water run-off.
- The beds are automatically raised with the implement to a height of 1½ ft at the center, tapering to sides with a width of 3½ ft and two beds are separated with 1½ ft width of trench.
- When beds are raised, half way through, add 100 kgs of single super phosphate, 50 kg of Murate of Potash, Bone meal 100 Kgs.
- Micro Nutrients as per requirement are to be applied per acre.
- Then, the beds are to be raised to fullest height.

- Drip-lines are to be placed at the middle of each of the raised beds.
- The inline drippers are of 3 litres per hour capacity and placed 1.5 ft apart so as to wet the bed evenly.
- Irrigation to be given to beds before sowing of tubers.

Sowing

- It should be made sure that the crown is at the upper side of the tuber and noncrown part at the down side (Tuber should be in slanting position).
- The seed is to be sown ½ inch deep in the soil and be covered by soil by hand so as not to cause any damage to it.

Inter-Cropping

- Musli could be cultivated as an inter-crop with Mango, Teak, Neem, paulownia etc with remarkable results.

Growth of Seed

- Monsoon, starting with thunders, is responsible for sprouting of the tubers.
- The plant emerges in about 10-12 days.
- Flowering begins on 15th day and the leafy part grows to its maximum by 65-70 days.

- It matures by 120 days as the leaf-fall starts.
- In 4-5 months, the tuber gets the cuticle layer on the fingers and there is an intake of material through soil to the tuber till 9 months.

Plant Protection

- Musli, being in the form of tubers underneath the ground, is intrinsically strong to survive disasters like heavy showers.
- Care should, be provided in form of proper drainage to avoid damage to tubers by water-logging.

Disease Management

- To control leaf eating caterpillars, spray 0.2 per cent metacid aqueous solution fortnightly intervals.
- White grub can be easily controlled by the application of Aldrin @ 25 kg per hectare at the time of last ploughing during land preparation.
- Spray Bavistin solution @ 1 g/l at 25 days interval (2 times) to control the diseases.
- Diseases like leaf spot, anthracnose and wilt affect this crop. Spraying of neem or chrysanthemum or tobacco extracts (upto permitted levels) or application of*Trichoderma* etc., are adopted under organic growing.
- Plant extracts and biological agents are also used for pest control.

Harvesting

- At maturity (about three months after planting), the leaves become yellowish and ultimately dry.
- Thus, the crop should be harvested in the month of September-October.

Post Leaf Fall

- After the leaf fall, the tubers should continue to be in the ground and should not be plucked, as changes occur internally in the tuber that will increase its value.
- At the time of the leaf fall, the tubers are light in colour and, and after maturity by time, they turn deep black.
- Each tuber is to be delicately lifted with the prescribed implements, to obtain maximum quantity of the tuber and to avoid any damage to the crown or disc of the tuber.
- Harvesting should be carried out in the month of March/April.

Cleaning of Tuber

- As the tuber is dug out from the soil, naturally it contains a lot of mud.
- As such, the tuber has to be cleaned properly before it is peeled.

Peeling

- After the separation of the material to be resown, only tubers without a crown are to be peeled.
- Peeling helps the tuber dry easily and various methods are in vogue for peeling.
- Peeling is no specialized task.
- It can easily be done with a knife without any loss of quality or quantity. A person can peel up to 5 kg per day.

Drying

- Once peeled, Musli should be dried of the moisture content. It takes 7 days for Musli to dry.

Packing

- After drying, Musli must be packed in poly bags to prevent entry of moisture. Shorter and stouter the tuber, lesser is the loss of weight.

Yield

- On an average, 2000 kg of fleshy roots per hectare can be obtained, which may yield up to 400 kg of dry safed musli.

Economics

- The global markets of Safed Musli are U.S.A Britain, European countries, Australia, Japan and even China. Japan and China have the highest per capita consumption of botanical medicines in the world.
- Safed Musli have annual demand ar und 35000 MT while only 15000 MT is produced Safed musli (Chlorophytum borivillianum) root powder is in great demand for power and sexual energy capsules.
- The world is demand of Safed Musli is over 50,000 Tons. And is much higher than present production, which is less than 5,000 Tons in various farmlands in India.
- Best Nutrition Products U.S.A is seriously looking for farmers who would like to growthese medicinal plants especially in Orissa.
- Nearly ten quintals of fleshy root (wet) per hectare collected is reduced to 200 kg (about 20% of wet root wt) after processing and drying.
- In the domestic market, the rates rangers between Rs. 800 to Rs. 1800 per kg depending on the quality of the product The Medicinal Plants Board.
- Government of India has recognized Safed Musli as 6th important herb to be protected and promoted. The Board encourages mainstream cultivation of Safed Musli by farmers by extending a subsidy of 20% through National Horticultural Board on project cost.

VARIETY IMPROVEMENT

Crop improvement realized in this species is mainly due to direct introductions from the wild habitat. A number of clonal selections have been made that are under different stages of testing for their yield performance. Recently, a variety, 'Jawahar Safed musli 405', identified by clonal selection under the All India Networking Project on Medicinal and Aromatic Plants, has been released at the state level by Jawaharlal Nehru Krishi Vishwa Vidalia (JNKVV), Mandsaur, Madhya Pradesh. Other important superior lines in the pipeline are MCB 402 and MCB 412 (developed by AINPMAP, Jawaharlal Nehru Krishi Vishwa Vidyalaya, Mandsaur, Madhya Pradesh), CBI 8, CBI 12 and CBI 22 (developed by AINPMAP, Jawaharlal Nehru Krishi Vishwa Vidyalaya, Indore, Madhya Pradesh), and RC 5 (developed by AINPMAP, Maha Rana Pratap University of Agriculture and Technology, Udaipur, Rajasthan).

TISSUE CULTURE IN *CHLOROPHYTUM BORIVILIANUM*

The unsustainable practice of exploitation of natural wild collections of medicinal plants should be discouraged in under to save the plant from the threat of extinction. There is an urgent need of development of agro-techniques for the large-scale cultivation of medicinal plants. Unprecedented increase in demand of Safed musli and a consequent rise in its prices necessitated its systematic cultivation about a decade ago (Gaikwad *et al.,* 2012). Safed musli cultivation has been initiated in many areas of Maharastra, Madhya Pradesh, Chattisgarh, Rajasthan, Uttar Pradesh, Bihar and many other states. The further increase in its cultivation will help in reducing pressure on natural forest resources and ultimately help in saving the plant from being extinct.

Expansion of Safed musli cultivation will require substantial amount of quality propagules. Safed musli (*Chlorophytum borivilianum*) is generally propagated by seeds as well as vegetative propagules. Seed propagation has not become popular due to the poor seed germination (Bardia *et al.,* 1995). poor tuber development in the seed raised plant and higher period taken for maturity and harvesting of these plants. Vegetative propagation through stem disc is better than seed propagation, but the method is costly. The cost of planting material through such vegetative propagules alone contributes more than 50% of the cost of the cultivation. Therefore, the immediate need is the development of an alternative propagation technique that can provide very large amount of quality propagules at lower cost. This will facilitate expansion of Safed musli cultivation and conservation of Natural Forest Resources.

The demand of this unique medicinal plant is increasing very fastly in Indian and International markets which has created a pressure on Indian forest for its supply. The over exploitation of natural forest resources has dwindled the natural population and habitats of Safed musli bringing it on the verge of extinction. To overcome this problem its systematic cultivation was started about a decade ago. Expansion of Safed musli cultivation will require substantial amount of quality propagules. Safed musli (*Chlorophytum borivilianum)* is generally propagates by seeds as well as vegetative propagules. Seed propagation has not become popular due to the poor seed germination, poor tuber development in the seed raised plant and higher period taken for maturity and harvesting of these plants. Vegetative propagation through stem disc is better than seed propagation, but the method is costly. Tissue culture or *in vitro* techniques provide an alternative vegetative propagation method known as microproapgation. Micro propagation can lead to production of a very large number of plants in relatively short time and space from a single mother plant. Tissue cultured medicinal plants have been reported to exhibit higher medicinal value(Singh *et al.,* 2004). *Chlorophytum borivilianum* was cultivated in pots to study its botanical aspects as well as for its multiplication for a continuous supply of its explant to be used in tissue culture experiment. Micropropagation can lead to production of a very large number of plants in relatively short time and space from a single mother plant. They are normally disease free, genetically uniform and show more many vigour and higher yield. Tissue cultured medicinal plants have been reported to exhibit higher medicinal value. Micropropagation would also help in ensuring the production of uniform plants, thereby restricting the variation in commercial population and quality of roots, which at present, is a major problem encountered with seed and stem disc propagating materials.

Micropropagation has been successfully used for multiplication of many medicinal plants and several other members of Liliaceae (Jha *et al.,* 1987; Nair,1989;). Though, multiple bud shoot formation was observed in

Chlorophytum borivilianum from cultured stem discs (Purohit *et al.*, 1994; Suri *et al.*, 1999 and Pudake and Dhumale, 2003) and callus formation and regeneration of shoots and roots from four different explants namely seedling, root, stem disc and leaf base (Gaikwad *et al.*, 2003), no work has been reported on enhanced axillary bud formation in tissue culture for the micropropagation of the species. Except for the callus mediated regeneration of *Chlorophytum borivilianum* (Joshi *et al.*, 1999) and variation in chromosome number and structure in the plants regenerated through long term callus culture (Arora *et al.*, 1999). Arora *et al.*, (1999) obtained somatic embryogenesis in the species. Germination of somatic embryos was highest (48%) on MS medium supplemented with 17.6M BA. However, somatic embryos developed from long-term cultures were abnormal due to chromosomal abnormalities. Callus produced from shoot cultures derived from stem disc explants on modified B5 medium produced cytologically stable embryogenic cultures. Plantlets produced from in vitro embryo germination gave 90% survival on transfer to the field. Development of tissue culture techniques for micropropagation and for further improvement of *Chlorophytum borivilianum* is greatly desired.

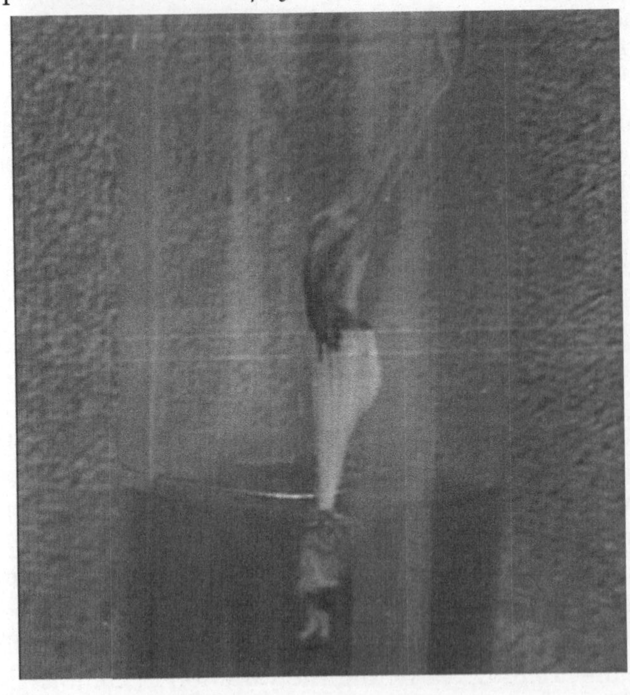

LEGAL ASPECTS

Safed Musli is an economically valuable and endangered herb and hence its preservation and conservation bears lot of importance. As per the provisions embodied in the Indian Forest Act 1927 *Chlorophytum borivilianum* and its derived products come under the purview of definition of forest produce.

Therefore its transit need be covered by a transit pass. This will ensure to check illegal transportation of the herb. The produce of the cultivators can be allowed to be transported after they have procured a legal procurement certificate from forest authorities. The existing laws can be amended so as to check the illegal transportation of Safed Musli.

CONCLUSION

It would not be an exaggeration to call Safed Musli a unique gift of nature to mankind since the time immemorial. Safed Musli is celebrated as a Divya Aushad with unparalleled medicinal properties as the preparation of *C. borivilianum* is a very popular herb in traditional Indian medicine, chief ingredient in over a hundred Ayurvedic formulations. The increased commercial exploitation and low productivity of this endangered plant has raised the concern over its conservation. It has been predicted that efforts should be made to standardize, encourage and popularize the cultivation of *Chlorophytum borivilianum* as a commercial crop. The analysis of pharmacological and genetic enhancement investigations suggested lack of substantial scientific evidences in various studies and do not stand the test of critical assessment. Due to high economic value, *Chlorophytum borivilianum* has also encountered a problem of adulteration with closely resembling medicinally inferior species. The studies available on toxicity, safety and quality of *Chlorophytum borivilianum* are inadequate for providing information on commercial utilization. Thus, the present review summarizes comprehensive information on *Chlorophytum borivilianum* and possible scope for future research to fill the existing lacunae on its different aspects of the study. Therefore, required steps for the for this important medicinal plants are:

(*a*) The wide range of phenotypic variability present within the germplasm (on the basis of biochemical constitutions) for prioritizing selection criteria with an ultimate aim to select superior genotypes in terms of chemical quality and yield.

(*b*) Price of cultivation can be drastically reduced if commercial cultivation through true seeds could be made possible. Perfect environmental and geographic locations need to be identified for true seed production meeting commercial feasibility.

(*c*) The crop improvement programme should use the cross-pollinated and self compatibility nature of the crop to harness hybrid vigour which can be fixed easily through its vegetative propagating route.

(*d*) Molecular characterization of the germplasm is another field for molecular marker-assisted breeding as well as to protect our germplasm under the new Intellectual Property Rights regimes.

(*e*) Isolation and structure elucidation of active principles responsible for effectiveness of the raw drug need to be suitably worked out.

REFERENCES

Acharya, D., Claire, A., Kaushik, N., Miyamoto, T., Paululat, T., Mirjolet, J.F., Duchamp, O., and Lacaille-Duboi, M.A. 2010. Steroidal Saponins from *Chlorophytum orchidastrum,* 2010. *J. Nat. Prod.* 73. 7–11.

Arora DK, Suri SS, Ramawat KG and Merillon JK. 1999. Factors Affecting Somatic Embryogenesis in Long Term Callus Cultures of 'Safed Musli' an Endangered Wonder Herb. *Indian Journal of Experimental Biology,* 37(1): 75-82.

Bordia, P.C., Joshi, A. and Simlot, M.M. 1995. Safed Musli. In: Medicinal and Aromatic Plants, (Eds, K.L. Chadha and R. Gupta). Advances in Horticulture, Malhotra Publishing House. New Delhi, 429-451.

Chakraborthy GS and Aeri V. 2011. Pharacognostical Studies of Potential Herb-*Chlorophytum borivilianum.* IJPSR. 2010. 1(4):89-95.

Deore SL and Khadabadi SS. 2010. *In-vitro* Anthelmintic Studies of *Chlorophytum borivilianum. Ind jou of Nat Prod and Resources* 1(1):53-56.

Deore SL and Khadabadi SS.2010. Isolation and Characterization of Phytoconstituents from *Chlorophytum borivilianum.* Phcog Res. 2:343-9.

Dwivedi, Rashmi. 2013. High Performance Liquid Chromatographic Analysis of Derivatized Saponin Content of *Chlorophytum borivilianum. International Journal of Advanced Research.* 1(7). 285-291.

Gaikwad PD, John SC and Billore M. 2003. Callus Induction and Regeneration Studies in Safed Musli (*Chlorophytum borivilianum* Sant and Fern). *Research on Crops,* 4(2):249-253.

Gaikwad, V., Patel, D. H., Shelk, A.2012. Safed Musali (*Chlorophytum borivillianum*): An Endangered Medicinal Plant with High Demand. Lambert Academic Publisher.

Gupta SK. 2001. *Pharmacology and Therapeutics in the New Millennium.* New Delhi: Narosa Publishing House.

Handa, S.S. 1996. Rasayana Drugs. In: Handa SS, Kaul MK (eds). Supplement Cultivation and Utilization of Medicinal Plants, Jammu Tawi: Regional Research Laboratory 1:509-12.

Haque R, Saha, S and Bera T.2011. Peer Reviewed Literature on Medicinal Activity of *Chlorophytum borivilianum* Commercial Medicinal Plant. *Int J Drug Dev & Res.* 3(1):1116-1130.

Jha S. Gupta JS and Sen S. 1987. Tissue Culture of *Smila zevlanica L. Acta Hort.,* 208:273-279.

Joshi A, Ganesh R, Sharma A and Sharma GS. 1999. Plant Regeneration from Stem-disc Derived Callus Cultures of *Chlorophytum borivilianum* L. *Annals of Plant Physiology,* 13(1):79-83.

Kenjale RD, Shah RK and Sathaye SS. 2007. Anti-stress and Anti-oxidant Effects of Roots of *Chlorophytum borivilianum* (Santa Pau & Fernandes). Indian J Exp Biol. 45(11): 974-9.

Kothari, S.K. 2004. Safed Musli (*Chlorophytum borivilianum*) Revisited. J. Med. Arom. Plant. Sci., 26: 60-69.

Maiti S. 2006. Inventary and Documentation of Medicinal Plants in India. *Medicinal Plants Research in Asia.* 1: 50-52.

Lavania UC, Basu S, Srivastava S, Mukai Y and Lavania S .2005. In situ Chromosomal Localization of rDNA Sites in 'Safed musli' Chlorophytum Ker-Gawl and their Physical Measurement by Fiber FISH. *Journal of Heredity* 96: 155–160.

Mukherjee AK, Basu S, Sarkar N and Ghosh AC 2001. Advances in Cancer Therapy with Plant Based Natural Products. *Current Medicinal Chemistry*, 8(12): 1467-1486.

Nair AS. 1989. Micropropagation of *Scilla hycinthiana* (Rath) Macbrid *Proceeding of Indian. National Science Academy (Biol. Sci.)*, 55(2):121-123.

Pudake RN and Dhumale DB. 2003. *In vitro* Multiplication of *Chlorophytum borivilianum* Sant. and Fern. *Journal of Maharashtra Agricultural Universities*, 28(3):265-267.

Puri, H.S. 2003. Rasayana , Ayurvedic Herbs for Longevity and Rejuvenation. London: Taylor and Francis, pp. 212-24.

Raghavan SR, Ansari MY and Kamble SY.1977. Cytotaxaonomic studies in *Chlorophytum* Ker-Gawl. (Liliaceae). *Current Science* 46: 534–535.

Samant, S.S., Vidyarthi, Shalini., Pant, S., Sharma, P., Marpa, S. and Sharma, P. 2011. Diversity, Distribution, Indigenous Uses and Conservation of the Medicinal Plants of Indian Himalayan Region Used in Cancer. *Journal of Biodiversity*. 2(2): 117-125.

Singh, BD. 2006. Plant Tissue Culture and Micropropagation. *Plant Biotechnology.* Kalyani Publishers. Ist Edition. India. 22-82.

Singh, Devendra, Pokhriyal, Bhagirath, Joshi, YM. and Kadam, Vilasrao 2012.Phytopharmacological Aspects of *Chlorophytum Borivilianum* (Safed musli): A Review. *International Journal of Research in Pharmacy and Chemistry* 2(3):853-859.

Suri SS, Jain S, Arora DK and Ranawat KG. 1999. In vitro High Frequency Regeneration of Plantlets and Tuberous Root Formation in *Chlorophytum borivilianum. Gartenbauwissen schaft*, 64(3):106-110.

Tandon, M. and Shukla, Y.N. 1993. A Bibenzyle Xyloside from *C. arundinaceum. Phytochemistry.* 32: 1624-1625.

Thakur GS, Bag M, Sanodiya BS, Debnath M, Zacharia A, Bhadauriya P, Prasad GB and Bisen PS. 2009. *Chlorophytum borivilianum*: A White Gold for Biopharmaceuticals and Neutraceuticals. *Curr Pharm Biotechnol.* 10(7):650-66.

Trivedi, P.C. (2009) Medicinal Plant: Utilization and Conservation. Aavishkar Publisher. Ed. 1,303.

Verma, SK; Sharma, SK; Singh, C and Mehta, H. 2004. Breeding, Improvement and Germplasm Conservation of Medicinal and Aromatic Plants—A Review. *Indian Forester*. 130(3):291-303.

Medicinal and Nutritional Values of Plants
Edited by: Alka Chauhan and Pawan Kumar 'Bharti'
ISBN: 978-93-5056-883-5
Edition: 2017
Published by: Discovery Publishing House Pvt. Ltd., New Delhi (India)

5 The Antimicrobial Properties of Herbal Skin Cream Against Skin Infection

[1]Deepika Chauhan and [2]Abhishek Swami

INTRODUCTION

The history of medicinal plants can be traced back to Vedic periods about 4500-1600 BC. Ayurveda has an extensive medical formulations based on products of plant, animal kingdom. Medicinal plants constitute the dominant part of drug substances. There are some 1250 Ayurvedic medicinal plants (Dev, 2012), which go into formulating therapeutic preparation as per Ayurvedic and other traditional systems. If folklore medicinal herbs are added to these the total number of plants with medicinal applications used throughout India will exceed 2000. Therefore India has often been referred to as the Medicinal Garden of the World.

Plants produce a diverse range of bioactive molecules, making them rich source of different types of medicines. Most of the drugs today are obtained from natural sources or semi synthetic derivatives of natural products used in the traditional systems of medicine (Sukanya *et al.,* 2009). Thus, it is a logical approach in drug discovery to screen traditional natural products. Approximately 20% of the plants found in the world have been submitted to pharmaceutical or biological test and a sustainable number of new antibiotics introduced in the market are obtained from natural or semi synthetic resources (Mothana *et al.,* 2005). Medicinal plants are finding their way into pharmaceuticals, cosmetics, and neutraceuticals. In Pharmaceutical field medicinal plants are mostly used for the wide range of substances present in plants which have been used to treat chronic as well as infectious diseases (Okigbo *et al.,* 2009). Long before mankind discovered the existence of microbes, the idea that certain plants had healing potential, indeed, that they contained what we would currently characterize as antimicrobial principles, was well accepted. Since antiquity, man has used plants to treat common infectious diseases and some of these traditional medicines are still included as part of the habitual treatment of various maladies (Rios *et al.,* 2005). The drugs already

1 Department of Botany, Samrat Prithviraj Chauhan Degree College, Haridwar, U.K., India.
2 Department of Applied Science, Dronacharya Group of Institutions, Greater Noida, U.P., India.

in use to treat infectious disease are of concern because drug safety remains an enormous global issue. Most of the synthetic drugs cause side effects and also most of the microbes developed resistant against the synthetic drugs (Chanda *et al.*, 2005). To alleviate this problem, antimicrobial compounds from potential plants should be explored. These drugs from plants are less toxic, side effects are scanty and also Cost effective. They are effective in the treatment of infectious diseases while simultaneously mitigating many of the side effects that are often associated with Synthetic antimicrobials (Harishchandra *et al.*, 2012).

According to World Health Organization (WHO) medicinal plants would be the best source to obtain a variety of drugs (Nascimento *et al.*, 2000). Several plant species are used by many ethnic groups for the treatment of various ailments ranging from minor infections to dysentery, skin diseases, asthma, malaria and a horde of other indications (Dahanukar *et al.*, 2000). Plant based antimicrobials represent a vast untapped source of medicines and further exploration of plant antimicrobials is the need of the hour. Antimicrobials of plant origin have enormous therapeutic potential. Plant-derived antimicrobials have a long history of providing the much needed novel therapeutics (Silwa *et el.*, 2012). Plants constantly interact with the rapidly changing and potentially damaging external environmental factors. Being organisms devoid of mobility, plants have evolved elaborate alternative defense strategies, which involve an enormous variety of chemical metabolites as tools to overcome stress Conditions.

Using plant based drugs as preventive and curative medicines is a rich heritage in India. In recent years, numbers of studies have been reported which screened the extracts of medicinal plants against pathogenic microbes (Kannan *et al.*, 2007). This made applications in pharmaceuticals, alternative medicines and natural treatment (Kannan, 2010). Some of the active principles of bioactive compounds are preferred for therapy either singly or in combination to inhibit microbes (Dheeba *et al.*, 2010; Kannan, 2010).

In developing countries, low income people such as farmers, people of small isolate villages use folk medicine for treating common infections. They ingest plants as decoctions, teas, juice preparations to treat respiratory tract infections (Kannan *et al.*, 2009). They are also made into a practice and applied directly on the infected wounds or burns (Aburjai *et al.*, 2001). Many plants have been used due to their antimicrobial nature, which are due to the compounds synthesized during the secondary metabolism of the plant. The active substances include phenolic compounds which are part of the essential oils (Ahmad *et al.*, 2001) as well as in tannin (Ahmad *et al.*, 1994).

The whole human body is covered by the protective covering called skin (Kowt, 1998). Our skin serves many functions like thermo regulation, absorption, secretion etc. But the most important function of skin is protection. As a primary interface between the body and the external environment, our skin provides the first line of defence against the injuries caused by microbes and chemical agents (Jawetz *et al.*, 1978), but there are several pathogens like bacteria, fungi that impact on our skin. Skin disease is a major problem which may be caused due to bacteria, virus, fungi or other microscopic organisms. Bacteria like *Staphylococcus aureus, Streptococcus pyogenes, Enterobacter aerogenes, Pseudomonas aeruginosa, Klebsiella pneumonia* and *Escherichia coli* may also be a reason for so many skin infections. *Staphylococcus aureus* can cause a range of illness from minor skin infections such as pimples, impetigo, boils, cellulitis, folliculitis and carbuncles to life-threatening diseases such as pneumonia, meningitis, osteomyelitis, endocarditis, toxic shock syndrome, bacteremia and sepsis (Chomnawang *et al.*, 2005).

Pseudomonas aeruginosa is the most common cause of burn injury infections and otitis externa. It may also cause "hot-tub dermatitis or rash" which is due to lack of proper, periodic attention to water quality. It is frequently associated with osteomyelitis involving puncture wounds of the foot, believed to result from direct inoculation with *Pseudomonas aeruginosa* through in the foam padding found in tennis shoes. *Enterobacter aerogenes* cause various community acquired infection, wound infection, skin and soft tissue infections. *Klebsiella* cause vaginitis, nasal mucosa atrophy and rhinoscleroma which are the mucosal skin infection (Crops, Agriculture, & Republic, n.d.).

Skin Infections

Skin infections are caused by many Fungi, Bacteria, and viruses etc., some common types of skin infections are as follows:

1. Bacterial skin infections

Leprosy: Leprosy is caused by a slow-growing type of bacteria called *Mycobacteriumleprae* (*M. leprae*). Leprosy is also known as Hansen's disease, after the scientist who discovered *M. leprae* in 1873.

Carbuncles: A carbuncle is a red, swollen, and painful cluster of boils that are connected to each other under the skin.

Staph infection: The infection often begins with a little cut, which gets infected with bacteria. These staph infections range from a simple boil to antibiotic-resistant infections to flesh-eating infections.

Cellulitis: Cellulitis is a common infection of the skin and the soft tissues underneath. It happens when bacteria enter a break in the skin and spread.

Impetigo: Impetigo is a highly contagious bacterial skin infection. It can appear anywhere on the body but usually attacks exposed areas.

Boils: A boil is a skin infection that starts in a hair follicle or oil gland. At first, the skin turns red in the area of the infection, and a tender lump develops.

After four to seven days, the lump starts turning white as pus collects under the skin.

Pilonidal cyst and abscess: A pilonidal cyst occurs at the bottom of the tailbone and can become infected and filled with pus. Once infected, the technical term is pilonidal abscess.

2. Fungal skin infections

Fungal infections of the skin are very common and include athlete's foot, jock itch, ringworm, and yeast infections.

Ringworm: Worms don't cause ringworm. Rather, this superficial skin infection, also known as tinea, is caused by fungi called dermatophytes.

Athlete's foot: Athlete's foot is a common fungal infection and you don't have to be an athlete to get it. This annoying ailment occurs in boys, girls, men, and women of all ages.

Candidiasis (Yeast Infection): Candidiasis is an infection caused by a group of yeast. There are more than 20 species of *Candida,* the most common being *Candida albicans*. These fungi live on all surfaces of our bodies.

Sporotrichosis: This fungus is related more closely to the mold on stale bread or the yeast used to brew beer than to bacteria that usually cause infections. The mold is found on rose thorns, hay, sphagnum moss, twigs, and soil. Therefore, the infection is more common among gardeners who work with roses, moss, hay, and soil.

Fungal nail infections: A fungal nail infection occurs when a fungus attacks a fingernail, a toenail, or the skin under the nail, called the nail bed.

3. Viral skin infections

Viral skin infection is as follows:

Molluscum contagiosum: Molluscum contagiosum is a viral skin infection that causes either single or multiple raised, pearl-like bumps (papules) on the skin.

Shingles: Shingles (herpes zoster) results from a reactivation of the virus that also causes chickenpox.

Chickenpox: Chickenpox (varicella), a viral illness characterized by a very itchy red rash, is one of the most common infectious diseases of childhood.

Herbal medicine can be broadly classified into various basic systems. Traditional and Chinese verbalism, which is a part of traditional oriental medicine. Ayurvedic Herbalism which is derived from Ayurveda, and Western Herbalism, which originally come from Greece and Rome to Europe and then spread to North and South America. Chinese and Ayurveda Herbalism have developed into highly sophisticated systems of diagnosis and treatment over the centuries . Western Herbalism is today primarily a system on folk medicine interest in the united States had been growing in the recent years from the reported success stories related with the use of Herbs. Plants are very complex in their compositions and their therapeutic activity depends on their major active chemical constituents. Also, improper authentication of herbs, adulterations by microorganism, and pesticide residue, has made standardization of herbal drug of primary importance. Thus, before using these medicinal herbs in any formulation, their authentication is necessary.

Skin cream should aid the skin in carrying out its normal functions that is, restoring moisture to dry skin, allowing the elimination of waste matter through the pores, and the cooling of the body by evaporation of water (perspiration) and radiation, thus aiding in the maintenance of the normal body temperature. If the cream clogs the pores of the skin with heavy, insoluble, inert material, it results in a thick sticky coating on the skin and prevents sufficient normal skin function, being detrimental to health. Skin creams contain a variety of ingredients that range from common, such as mineral oil, to the exotic, such as placenta extract. Some skin creams may contain small amounts of vitamins or other nutrients.

The compositions of some Herbal Creams formulation are as follows:

Table 5.1: Ingredient of Boro Plus Antiseptic Cream

S.No.	Name	Botanical Name	Family	Part used
1.	Shati	*Hedychium Spicatum*	Zingiberaceae	root/shoot
2.	Chandan	*Santalum album*	Santalaceae	stem
3.	Dhritumari	*Aloe barbadensis*	Xanthorrhoeaceae	leaves
4.	Neem	*Azadirachta indica*	Maliaceae	leaves/bark
5.	Swampmallows	*Paonia odorata*	Malvaceae	leaves
6.	Tulsi	*Ocimum sanctum*	Lamiaceae	leaves
7.	Haldi	*Curcuma longa*	Zinziberaceae	rhizome/leaves
8.	Kattha	*Acacia catechu*	Fabaceae	stem/bark

Table 5.2: Ingredient of Thuja Cream

S.No.	Name	Botanical Name	Family	Part used
1	White cedar	*Thuja occidentalis*	Cupressaceae	leaves/stem

Table 5.3: Ingredient of Nourishing Skin Cream

S.No.	Name	Botanical Name	Family	Part used
1	Dhritumari	*Aloe barbadensis*	Xanthorrhoeaceae	*leaves*
2	Ashwagandha	*Withania somnifera*	Solanaceae	bark/stem
3	Vijayasar	*Pterocarpus marsupium*	Fabaceae	stem
4	Gotu kola	*Centella asiatica*	Apiaceae	stem

Table 5.4: Ingredient of Patanjali Tejus Cream

S.No.	Name	Botanical Name	Family	Part used
1	Dhritumari	*Aloe barbadensis*	Xanthorrhoeaceae	leaves
2	Kutaj	*Hemidesmus indicus*	Apocynaceae	stem/leaves
3	Manjishtha	*Rubia cordifolia*	Rubiaceae	Stem
4	Chandan	*Santalum album*	Santalaceae	stem
5	Haldi	*Curcuma longa*	Zinziberaceae	rhizome/leaves
6	Tulsi	*Ocimum tenuiflorum*	Lamiaceae	stem/leaves

Table 5.5: Ingredient of Himalaya Antiseptic Cream

S.No.	Name	Botanical Name	Family	Part used
1	Nirgundi	*Vetex negundo*	Lamiaceae	leaves
2	Indian Madder	*Rubia cordifolia*	Rubiaceae	leaves /stem
3	Dhritumari	*Aloe barbadensis*	Xanthorrhoeaceae	leaves
4	Almond	*Prunus dulcis*	Rosaceae	Seed

Table 5.6: Ingredient of Himalaya Foot Care

S.No.	Name	Botanical Name	Family	Part used
1	Haldi	*Curcuma longa*	Zinziberaceae	rhizome/leaves
2	Salasara	*Shorea robusta*	dipterocarpaceae	Stem
3	Suthi	*Zingibera officinale*	Zingiberaceae	rhizome/leaves
4	Methi	*Trigonella foenum-graeceum*	Fabaceae	Seed

Table 5.7: Ingredient of Patanjali Boro Safe Antiseptic Cream

S.No.	Name	Botanical Name	Family	Part used
1	Dhritumari	*Aloe barbadensis*	Xanthorrhoeaceae	leaves
2	Wheat oil	*Triticum sativum*	Poaceae	oil
3	Kutuj	*Holarrhena pubescens*	Apocynaceae	whole plant
4	Manjishtha	*Rubia cordifolia*	Rubiaceae	stem/flower
5	Tulsi	*Ocimum tenuiflorum*	Lamiaceae	stem/leaves

Table 5.8: Ingredient of Nomarks Skin Cream

S.No.	Name	Botanical Name	Family	Part used
1	Amla	*Emblica officinalis*	Phyllanthaceae	whole plant
2	Dhritumari	*Aloe barbadensis*	Xanthorrhoeaceae	leaves
3	Nimbu	*Citrus limon*	Rutaceae	whole plant
4	Gulab	*Rosa Damascus*	Rosaceae	flower
5	pudina	*Menthe arvensis*	Lamiaceae	leaves
6	Kayaputri	*Cinnamomum camphora*	lauraceae	root

Table 5.9: Ingredient of Eraser Antimarks Cream

S.No.	Name	Botanical Name	Family	Part used
1	Nimbu	*Citrus limon*	Rutaceae	whole plant
2	Haldi	*Curcuma longa*	Zinziberaceae	rhizome/leaves
3	Tulsi	*Ocimum tenuiflorum*	Lamiaceae	stem/leaves
4	Chandan	*Santaluma lbum*	Santalaceae	stem
5	Manjishtha	*Rubia cordifolia*	Rubiaceae	stem/flower
6	Saffron	*Crocus sativus*	Iridaceae	whole plant

Table 5.11: Ingredient of Vicco Turmeric Cream

S.No.	Name	Botanical Name	Family	Part used
1	Haldi	Curcuma longa	Zinziberaceae	rhizome
2	Chandan	Santalum album	Santalaceae	Stem

Antimicrobial Activity of Medicinal Plant

The antimicrobial activity medicinal plant used in herbal skin cream against skin infection in given below:

Hibiscus rosa-sinensis (Gurhal)

Hibiscus rosa-sinensis was named by Carl Linnaeus.belonges to the family malvaceae. The Latin term *rosa-sinensis* literally means "rose of China", though it is not closely related to the true rosesIt is native to East Asia and a species of tropics Hibiscus.

Description

Hibiscus rosa-sinensis is bushy, evergreen shrub or small tree growing 2.5–5 m tall and 1.5–3 m wide, with glossy leaves and solitary, brilliant red flowers in summer and autumn. The 5-petaled flowers are 10 cm in diameter, with prominent orange-tipped red anthers. The root is a branched tap root. The stem is aerial, erect, green, cylindrical and branched. The leaf is simple, with alternate phyllotaxy and is petiolate. The leaf shape is ovate, the tip is acute and margin is serrated. The flower is complete (bisexual), actinomorphic, bracteate or ebracteate, bracteolate or ebracteolate, pedicellate,dichlamydeous, regular, pentamerous, hypogynous, and solitary.

Antimicrobial Activity

Antibacterial activity for methanolic extract of *Hibiscus rosasinensis* was screened against the seven isolated skin pathogens *Pseudomonas aeruginosa, Escherichia coli, Enterobacter aerogenes, Staphylococcus aureus, Streptococcus pyogenes, Candida albicans* and *Aspergillus niger shown* varied zone of inhibition *(Hemarana et al., 2014)*. The maximum zone of inhibition 13 mm was observed against *Escherichia coli* followed by 12 mm against *Enterobacter aerogenes* and *Staphylococcus aureus* at 80 μl concentration. Of the two fungi obtained, the maximum activity of 9 mm was observed against *Aspergillus niger* and 7 mm against *Candida albicans.* The most inhibited *Escherichia coli* was tested by the extract for identifying the minimum inhibitory concentration which was found to be 80 μl. The activity may be due to the presence of tannins, saponins, flavanoids, alkaloids and terpenoids in the extract.

The methanolic extract of various parts of *Hibiscus rosasinensis* was most effective against various skin infection causing microorganisms like *Escherichia coli, Staphylococcus aureus, Streptococcus pyogenes, Candida albicans* and *Pseudomonas aeruginosa* (Chandrasekaran *et al.*, 2004).

Lawsonia inermis (Henna)

Lawsonia inermis, also known as hina, belonges to the family Lythraceae. Historically, henna was used for cosmetic purposes primarily in Ancient India. It was also found to be used in the Arabian Peninsula, South Asia, Carthage and other parts of North Africa, and the Horn of Africa. Bridal henna nights remain an important custom in many of these areas, particularly among traditional families.

Description

Henna is a tall shrub or small tree, standing 1.8 to 7.6 m tall. It is glabrous and multi-branched, with spine-tipped branchlets. The leaves grow opposite each other on the stem. They are glabrous, sub-sessile, elliptical, and lanceolate. Henna flowers have four sepals and a 2 mm calyx tube, with 3 mm spread lobes. Its petals are obvate, with white or red stamens found in pairs on the rim of the calyx tube. Henna fruits are small, brownish capsules, 4–8 mm in diameter, with 32–49 seeds per fruit, and open irregularly into four splits.

Antimicrobial Activity

In the previous studies has been found to be a best solvent for extraction of the active ingredient (asarone) from leaves. Though, solvents such as methanol, ethanol and aqueous used the most of the previous studies studies were also found to be suitable for extraction of active ingredients. It is well established that the β-asarones found in leaf, roots and rhizomes tissues are responsible for almost all of the antimicrobial activities of the *Lawsonia inermis* (MacGaw *et al.*, 2002). The ethanol and water extract of the back of *Lawsonia inermis* showed antimicrobial activity against gram positive and gram negative bacteria Diacyl heptenoid and its Fyrosdia crosyenin were identified at the constituent responsible for this activity. Aqueous extracts of *Lawsonia inermis* inhibits the skin pathogens *Staphylococcus aureus, Streptococcus mutans* and *pseudomonas aeruginosa*potentially at 100% concentration. This extracts control the bacterial and fungal pathogen which cause skin disease. The antibacterial activity may be attributed to not only a single active principle but to a cocktain of a variety of active principles or alkaloid (Eassawi *at el.*, 2000). The activity of methanol extracts of *Lawsonia inermis* leaves by Disc diffusion method against *Staphylococcus aureus* showed minimum activity (2.3±2.01 mm) at 25 % concentration and maximum activity (9.3±8.9 mm) at 100% level. The activity of methanol extracts of *Lawsonia inermis* against *Streptococcus mutans* showedminimum activity (2.3±1.516 mm) at 25%followed by 50% (3.6±3.23 mm), 75% (5±5.12 mm) and 100% 17±16.04 mm). The activity of methanol extracts of *Lawsonia inermis* against *pseudomonas aeruginosa,* showed maximum activity was obtained at 75% (4.6±3.16 mm) followed by 100% (3.3±2.16 mm), 50% (2.8±2.4 mm) and 25% (2.6±2.1 mm). The ethanol extracts of *Lawsonia inermis* leaves against *Staphylococcus aureus* showed minimum activity (3.1±3.21 mm) at 25% concentration and maximum activity (8.1±6.2 mm) at 100% level. The ethanol extracts of *Lawsonia inermis* leaves *Streptococcus mutans* showed minimum activity (2.0±4.31 mm) at 25 %concentration maximum activity (9.1±5.1mm) at 100%. The ethanolextracts of *Lawsonia inermis* leaves against *pseudomonas aeruginosa* showed minimum activity (9.1±8.61 mm) an 25% concentration and maximum activity (7.6±6.41 mm) at 100%. There was noactivity showed by aqueous extracts of *Lawsonia inermis* against *Staphylococcus aureus, Streptococcus mutans,* and *Pseudomonas aeruginosa (Kannahi et al., 2013).*

Catharanthus roseus (Sadabhar)

Catharanthus roseus, commonly known as the Madagascar periwinkle or rosy periwinkle belonges to the family apocynaceae.

Description

In the wild, it is an endangered plant; the main cause of decline is habitat destruction by slash and burn agriculture. It is also however widely cultivated and is naturalised in subtropical and tropical areas of the world. It is so well adapted to growth in Australia, that it is listed as a noxious weed in Western Australia and the Australian Capital Territory, and also in parts of eastern Queensland.

Antimicrobial Activity

The ethanol, methanol, chloroform and aqueous extracts of leaves, flowers and stems of *Catharanthus roseus* were tested by Agar Well Diffusion Method *(Chaman et al., 2013).* Ethanolic leaf extract of *Catharanthus roseus* had shown antimicrobial activity against *Candida albicans, Pseudomonas aeruginosa,* and *Aspergillus niger* (with zone of inhibition 14, 13 & 8mm respectively). Ethanolic stem and flower extract had shown antimicrobial activity against gram positive bacteria *Staphylococcus aureus* and fungal strain *Aspergillus niger* (with zone of inhibition 19, 6 mm respectively by stem extract and 8, 10 mm respectively by flower extract).The antimicrobial activity may be due to the presence of alkaloids. (Ramya *et al.*, 2008) had also reported variable positive result of ethanolic leaf extract of Sadabahar for different bacterial strains including both gram positive and gram negative bacteria i.e. *Escherichia coli, Pseudomonas aeruginosa, Serratia marcescens, Salmonella typhii, Staphylococcus aureus, Streptococcus pyrogens, Bacillus cereus* and *Bacillus subtilis.*

Methanolic leaf, stem and flower extract of *Catharanthus roseus* had not shown antibacterial activity against gram positive and gram negative bacterial strains but it was effective against *Candida albicans*. Maximum antifungal activity was exhibited by methanolic flower extract of *Catharanthus roseus* (18mm zone of inhibition) followed by methanolic leaf extract (13 mm zone of inhibition) and minimum by methanolic stem extract (11 mm zone of inhibition). All plant parts in methanolic solvent had shown inhibition of *Candida albicans.* (Goyal *et al.*, 2008) reported that flower extract of *Catharanthus roseus* were inactive in inhibition of microbial strains (*Escherichia coli, Salmonella paratyphi, Kleibsella pneumonia, Bacillus aureus, Bacillus subtilis* and *Staphylococcus aureus*).

Hemidesmus indicus (Indian sarsaparilla)

Hemidesmus indicus is a species of plants that is found in the south Asia. It belongs to the family apocynaceae. It occurs over the greater part of India, from the upper Gangetic plains eastward to Assam and and in some places in central, western and South India. In Ayurveda it goes by the name of Ananthamoola, also known locally as Naruneendi or Nannari.

Description

It is a slender, laticiferous, twining, sometimes Prostrate or semi-erect Shrub. Roots are woody and aromatic. The stem is numerous, slender, terete, thickened at the nodes. The leaves are opposite, short-petioled, very variable, elliptic-oblong to linear-lanceolate. The flowers are greenish outside, purplish inside, crowded in sub-sessile axillary cymes.

Antimicrobial Activity

Hemidesmus indicus root extracts have been great potential as antimicrobial compounds against microorganisms. The antibacterial activity of the ethanol and aqueous extracts of *Hemidesmus indicus* roots were determined by Agar well diffusion assay *(Purohit et al., 2014)*. It has been observed that the ethanol and aqueous extracts of the root of *Hemidesmus indicus* exhibited moderate to significant antibacterial *activity against four tested bacterial* organisms as compared to the standard ciprofloxacin. The highest zones of growth inhibition were exhibited by ethanol extract against all the microorganisms compared to be aqueous extract. The ethanol extract produced a highest mean zone diameter of 19.35±3.28 mm at a dose of 200 mg/ml on *Staphylococcus aureus*, and lowest zone of growth inhibition was observed on *Pseudomonos aeruginosa*, which gave a zone of inhibition measuring 5.34±2.38 mm at a dose of 100 mg/ml.

Azadirachta indica (Neem)

Azadirachta indica, also known as Neem, Nimtree, and Indian Lilac. It is a tree in the mahogany family Meliaceae. It is one of two species in the genus *Azadirachta*, and is native to India and the Indian subcontinent including Nepal, Pakistan, Bangladesh and Sri Lanka. It is typically grown in tropical and semi-tropical regions. Neem trees now also grow in islands located in the southern part of Iran.

Description

Neem is a fast-growing tree that can reach a height of 15–20 metres and rarely 35–40 metres. It is evergreen, but in severe drought it may shed most or nearly all of its leaves. The branches are wide and spreading. The opposite, pinnate leaves are 20–40 centimetres long, with 20 to 31 medium to dark green leaflets about 3–8 centimetres long. The terminal leaflet is often missing. The petioles are short.

The flowers are arranged in more-or-less drooping axillary panicles which are up to 25 centimetres long. The inflorescences, which branch up to the third degree, bear from 150 to 250 flowers. An individual flower is 5–6 millimetres long and 8–11 millimetres wide, the fruit is a smooth (glabrous) olive-like drupe which varies in shape from elongate oval to nearly roundish, and when ripe is 1.4–2.8 centimetres by 1.0–1.5 centimetres.

Antimicrobial Activity

Ethanol extract from both dry and fresh bark extracts were more effective against *Staphylococcus aureus*compared to water extracts *(Francine, 2015)*. These results are the same as the ones obtained in study carried out by (Gajendrasinh *et al.*, 2012). In all cases, ethanol extracts were the best in terms of effectiveness against *Staphylococcus aureus.* According to the report done by (Kirtikar *et al.*, 1975), whose results are similar to the ones we obtained, they said that the active ingredients are slightly soluble in water and freely soluble in organic solvents such as alcohols, these ingredients include: azardirachtin, 1-maliantriol,salannin, nimbin, nimbdin and others.

Extract from fresh leaves were more effective than that from dry leaves. This inefficiency of dry leaves might be due to the fact that they were exposed to high temperature during the drying period thus there might beloss of some important components which could help in *Staphylococcus aureus* growth inhibition according to other studies, this may be caused by the slow response of *Staphylococcus aureus*to extract of dry neem leaf compared to the fresh leaf. This slower response isdue to the slower diffusion of active ingredients into thesolution from the dry neem leaves relative to the fresh leaves.

This was not the case for barks because for both dry and fresh bark extract the effect was the same as shown by p value calculated which was greater than the significance level this implies that there is no difference between their means. For comparing the effectiveness of barks to that of leaves, ethanol extracts from fresh barks were compared to ethanol extracts from fresh leaves; and there was no difference because the *p* value was greater than the significance level, this was also the case for ethanol extracts from dry barks when compared to ethanol extracts from dry leaves. This different from the study done by *(Mamman et al., 2001),* whereby the stem-bark extracts were the stem bark was found to be more effective than the leaf extract in terms of antibacterial activity. For all extracts used during this study, the bactericidal activity increased with the increase of the extract concentration, this means that the inhibition zone was higher on plates that contain extract with low dilution factor, this is also observed in the report done by *(Esimone et al. 1998)* which says that extract of plants inhibit the growth of various microorganisms at different concentrations. Active compound(s) may be present in insufficient quantities in the extracts to show activity with the concentration employed. Neem extracts with low concentrations didn't show effect on *Staphylococcus aureus* but by increasing the concentration of extract, effect was obtained as the dilution level decreases.

Puniuca granatum (pomegranate)

Pomegranate is a fruit-bearing deciduous shrub or small tree in the family Lythraceae that grows between 5 and 8 m tall. The pomegranate originated in the region of modern-day Iran and has been cultivated since ancient times throughout the Mediterranean region and northern India. It was introduced into America (Spanish America) in the late 16th century and California by Spanish settlers in 1769.

Today, it is widely cultivated throughout the Middle East and Caucasus region, north Africa and tropical Africa, the subcontinent, Central, the drier parts of southeast Asia, and parts of the Mediterranean Basin. It is also cultivated in parts of California and Arizona.

Description

It is a shrub or small tree growing 6 to 10 m high; the pomegranate has multiple spiny branches, and is extremely long-lived, with some specimens in France surviving for 200 years. *P. granatum* leaves are opposite or subopposite, glossy, narrow oblong, entire, 3–7 cm long and 2 cm broad. The flowers are bright red and 3 cm in diameter, with three to seven petals. Some fruitless varieties are grown for the flowers alone.

The edible fruit is a berry, intermediate in size between a lemon and a grapefruit, 5–12 cm in diameter with a rounded shape and thick, reddish skin. The number of seeds in a pomegranate can vary from 200 to about 1400.

Antimicrobial Activity

The peel of *Punica granatum* shows various therapeutic applications as Antibacterial, antifungal, antioxidant, antitumor, antiviral, antimalarial and antimutagenic effects as reported by different authors [3- 6]. During screening for antimicrobials, *Punica granatum* aqueous and methanolic extract was shown to be effective against *B. subtilis, B. megaterium, B. cereus, S. typhi, S. paratyphi A, P. vulgaris* and *S. aureus*. However, unlike aqueous and methanolic extract, ethanolic extract also show significant antimicrobial activity against *P. aeruginosa.* Acetic acid extract show antimicrobial activity against *B. megaterium* and *P. vulgaris,* whereas petroleum ether shows antimicrobial activity against *E. coli, B. megaterium, B. cereus, S. typhi, S. paratyphi A, P. vulgaris* and *P. aeruginosa.*

The dose dependent study using aqueous extract show significant antimicrobial activity against *S. typhi and P. vulgaris* at the concentration of 10 mg/ml. The dose dependent study using methanolic extract show antimicrobial activity against *S. typhi, P. vulgaris, B. cereus, B. megaterium, S. paratyphi A* at extract concentration of 10 mg/ml. The ethanolic extract shown to be effective against *B. cereus, P. vulgaris, S. typhi, E. coli and P. aeruginosa* at extract concentration of 10 mg/ml. *Punica granatum* peel Acetic acid extract shows that zone of inhibition with *P. vulgaris, B. megaterium,* but dose dependent study show significant antimicrobial activity against only *P. vulgaris* at 10 mg/ml extract concentration. *Punica granatum* peel Petroleum ether extract shows that zone of inhibition with *E. coli, B. megaterium, B. cereus, S. typhi, S. paratyphi A, P. vulgaris and P. aeruginosa* but dose dependent study show significant antimicrobial activity against *S. tyhphi* and *P. vulgaris* only at 10 mg/ml extract concentration. Tetracycline was used as positive control and DMSO as negative control for each tested extract.

Crude extract from pomegranate showed a considerable inhibitory effect against both genera *Trichophyton* and*Microsporum* with MIC of 125 and 250 μg/ml, respectively. The isolated compound punicalagin showed about the same MIC value as the crude extract, probably because punicalagin is the majority substance (Hajoori *et al.,* 2014).

Curcuma longa (Haldi)

Turmeric is a rhizomatous perennial pplants of the ginger family, Zingiberaceae. It is native to southwest India.

Description

Turmeric is a perennial herbaceous plant that reaches up to 1 m tall. Highly branched, yellow to orange, cylindrical, aromatic rhizomes are found. The leaves are alternate and arranged in two rows. They are divided into leaf sheath, petiole, and leaf blade. From the leaf sheaths, a false stem is formed.

The petiole is 50 to 115 cm long. The simple leaf blades are usually 76 to 115 cm long and rarely up to 230 cm. They have a width of 38 to 45 cm and are oblong to elliptic, narrowing at the tip.

Antimicrobial Activity

Antimicrobial susceptibility tests of different fractions of Curcuma. longa rhizome extract against S. aureus ATCC 6571 and clinical isolates show that all fractions of C. longa rhizome are highly active against standard and clinical isolates of S. aureus showing zone of inhibition ranges between 9 mm and 21 mm which was similar to the study of (Negi *et al.*, 1999) who reported the inhibitory effects of ethanol and hexane extract of turmeric against S. aureus. Further observations revealed that benzene extract was least active showing zone of inhibition of about 9 mm at the concentration of 50 mg/ml while methanolic extract was most active showing zone of inhibition of about 19 mm at the concentration of 50 mg/ ml. while inhibitory activity of all other fractions ranges between the two. The minimum inhibitory concentration (MIC) was studied for different fractions (100 mg/ml i.e., 2500 mg/disc) at 1/10 (250 mg/ disc) and 1/100 (25 mg/disc) dilutions respectively and results are compared with standard antibiotics as percentage. It was observed that dilution altered the activity gradually. In case of S. aureus ATCC 6571 percentage inhibition observed in first fraction of petroleum ether ranges from 73 to 63%, in case of fraction second of benzene it ranges from 84 to 68%, in case of fraction third of chloroform it ranges from 42 to 31%, in case of fraction fourth of methanol it ranges from 100 to 84% and in case of fraction five of aqueous it ranges from 73 to 57% and comparing it with clinical isolate of S. aureus in fraction first of petroleum ether ranges from 85 to 92%, in case of fraction second of benzene it ranges from 71 to 107%, in case of fraction third of chloroform it ranges from 57 to 71%, in case of fraction fourth of methanol it ranges from 21 to 42% and in case of fraction five of aqueous it ranges from 64 to 85%.

Senna alata

Senna alata is an important medicinal tree, as well as an ornamental flowering plant in the subfamily Caesalpinioideae. It also known asemperor's candlesticks candle bush. *S. alata* is native to Mexico, and can be found in diverse habitats. It is an invasive species in Austronesia.

Description

The shrub stands 3–4 m tall, with leaves 50–80 cm long.The leaves close in the dark. The inflorescence looks like a yellow candle. The fruit, shaped like a straight pod, is up to 25 cm long. Its seeds are distributed by water or animals. The seed pods are nearly straight, dark brown or nearly black, about 15 cm long and 15 mm wide. On both sides of the pods is a wing that runs the length of the pod. Pods contain 50 to 60 flattened, triangular seeds.

Antimicrobial Activity

Ethanol leaf extract of *Cassia alata* at the tested doses of 25 mg to 200 mg on five selected clinical isolates of pathogenic fungi, showed a dose dependent effect *(References)*. At 100 mg and 200 mg of the extract there was a higher statistical significant difference in activity than the positive control (Ketoconazole) on *Candidaalbican, Microsporum canis* and *Trichophyton mentagrophyte* than the ketoconazole 200 mg used as a positive control ($p<0.05$). The effect of ethanol extract of *Cassis alata* on *Penicillium notatum* at 100 mg did not show a statistical significant difference with the ketoconazole ($p>0.05$). However, at 200 mg the ethanol leaf extract had a higher antifungal activity on *Penicillium notatum* than ketoconazole ($p<0.05$). Ketoconazole was able to inhibit the growth of *Aspergillus niger* significantly higher than ethanol leaf extract at all the doses tested ($p<0.05$).

The minimum inhibitory concentration of the water leaf extract of *Cassia alata* for *Candida albicans, Aspergillus niger, Penicillium notatum, Microsporium canis* and *Trichophytonmentagrophytes* were 26.90 mg, 32.40 mg, 29.50 mg, 30.30 mg and 27.80 mg respectively obtained, while that of ethanol leaf extract of *Cassia alata* for *Candida albicans, Aspergillus niger, Penicillium notatum, Microsporium canis* and *Trichophyton mentagrophytes* were 5.60mg, 3.50 mg, 4.90 mg, 12.60 mg and 9.80 mg respectively

Centella asiatica (gotu kola)

Centella asiatica, commonly known as centella and gotu kola, is a small, herbaceous, plant of the family Mackinlayaceae or subfamily Mackinlayoideae of family Apiaceae, and is native to wetlands in Asia. Centella grows in tropical swampy areas. *Centella asiatica* is indigenous to the Indian subcontinent, Southeast Asia, and wetland regions of the Southeastern US.

Description

The flowers are white or pinkish to red in color, born in small, rounded bunches (umbels) near the surface of the soil. Each flower is partly enclosed in two green bracts. The hermaphrodite flowers are minute in size (less than 3 mm), with 5–6 corolla lobes per flower. Each flower bears five stamens and two styles. The fruit are densely reticulate, distinguishing it from species of Hydrocotyle which have smooth, ribbed or warty fruit.

Antimicrobial Activity

Methanolic extract exhibited different degree of growth inhibition against *Asperigellus niger* (MTCC 2723), *Pencillium expansum* (MTCC 2006), *Fusarium oxysporum* (MTCC 1755), *Xanthomonas compestries* (MTCC 2286), Lactobacillus acidophilus (MTCC 447), *Pseudomonas marginalis* (MTCC), Pseudomonas syringae (MTCC 1604), *Pseudomonas aeruginosa* (MTCC 1688), *Streptococcus mutans* (MTCC 890), *Steptococcus salivarious* (MTCC 1938) and *Staphylococcus aureus* (MTCC). methanolic extracts of *Centella. asatica* exhibited considerable antimicrobial activity against tested microbial strains. C. asatica is significant against *P. syringae* and moderate against other pathogens *F. oxysporum, L. acidophilus, S. salivarious* and *S. aureus* with 100 mg/ml DMSO. The results of MICs values are lowest at 0 and highest at 155 mg/ml for C. asatica. No inhibitions was observed with C. asatica on *P. aeruginosa* and *S. mutans*

Ocimum sanctum (Holy basil)

Ocimum sanctum is also known as *ocimum tenuiflorum.* It is an aromatic plant in the family of Lamiaceae which is native to the Indian subcontinent and widespread as a cultivated plant throughout the Southeast Asian tropics.

Description

It is an erect, many-branched subshrub, 30–60 cm tall with hairy stems and simple phyllotaxic green or purple leaves that are strongly scented.

Leaves have petioles and are ovate, up to 5 cm long, usually slightly toothed. The flowers are purplish in elongate racemes in close whorls.

Antimicrobial Activity

Antimicrobial activity of methanol extract of *Ocimum sanctum* was analyzed *(Bharathi et al., 2014,)* Among the three concentrations (100 mg/ml, 200, 300 mg/ml) used, maximum inhibitory zone was observed at 300 mg/ml followed by 200 mg/ml and 100 mg/ml. Maximum antibacterial activity was observed in the bacteria *Bacillus subtilis* (24 mm, 28 mm and 34 mm) followed by *Pseudomonas aeruginosa* (25 mm, 30 mm and 31 mm), *Staphylococcus aureus* (21 mm, 23 mm and 25 mm) and *Streptococcus pyogenes* (8 mm, 13 mm and 15 mm). The fungi *Penicillium* sp. (13 mm, 15 mm and 16 mm) showed more inhibitory activity when compared to *Aspergillus niger* (No zone, 10 mm and 12 mm). No zone of inhibition was observed in the negative DMSO control. The antimicrobial activity of chloroform extract of *Ocimum sanctum* was determined in the investigation and among the three concentrations (100 mg/ml, 200, 300mg/ml) used, maximum inhibitory zone was noticed at 300 mg/ml followed by 200 mg/ml and 100 mg/ml. Maximum antibacterial activity was observed in the bacteria *Bacillus subtilis* (19 mm, 23 mm and 29 mm) followed by *Pseudomonas aeruginosa* (20 mm, 25 mm and 26 mm), *Staphylococcus aureus* (16 mm, 18 mm and 20 mm) and *Streptococcus pyogenes* (No zone, 8 mm and 10 mm). The fungi *Penicillium* sp. (8 mm, 10 mm and 11 mm) showed more inhibitory activity than *Aspergillus niger*. No zone of inhibition was observed against *Aspergillus niger* and negative DMSO control. The antimicrobial activity of ethyl acetate extract of *Ocimum sanctum* was evaluated and among the three concentrations (100 mg/ml, 200, 300 mg/ml) used, maximum inhibitory zone was recorded at 300 mg/ml followed by 200 mg/ml and 100 mg/ml. Maximum antibacterial activity was observed in the bacteria *Bacillus subtilis* (16 mm, 20 mm and 26 mm) followed by *Pseudomonas aeruginosa* (17 mm, 22 mm and 23 mm), *Staphylococcus aureus* (13 mm, 15 mm and 17 mm) and *Streptococcus pyogenes* (No zone, No zone and 8 mm). The ethyl acetate extract of *Ocimum sanctum* showed resistance against *Penicillium* sp. and *Aspergillus niger*. No zone of inhibition was observed against *Penicillium* sp., *Aspergillus niger* and negative DMSO control.

Chromolaena odorata

Chromolaena odorata is a tropical and subtropical species of flowering shrub in the sunflower family. It is native to North America, from Florida and Texas to Mexico and the Caribbean, and has been introduced to South America, tropical Asia, west Africa, and parts ofAustralia.

Description

Chromolaena odorata is a rapidly growing perennial herb. It is a multi-stemmed shrub to 2.5 m tall in open areas. It has soft stems but the base of the shrub is woody. The plant is hairy and glandular and the leaves give off a pungent, aromatic odour when crushed. The leaves are opposite, triangular to elliptical with serrated edges. Leaves are 4–10 cm long by 1–5 cm wide (up to 4 × 2 inches). Leaf petioles are 1–4 cm long. The white to pale pink tubular flowers are in panicles of 10 to 35 flowers that form at the ends of branches. The seeds are achenes and are somewhat hairy.

Antimicrobial Activity

Our results were similar to previous findings on the effect of *C. odorata* extracts against pathogens. Leaf extracts demonstrated the best antimicrobial activity, followed by stem and root extracts. The best extraction solvent for antibacterial activity was methanol, followed by ethanol and hexane. Most of the antibacterial activities found in the aqueous, ethanol and methanol leaf extracts were against gram-positive bacteria (*B. subtilis, B. cereus, Staph. aureus* and *Staph. epidermidis*) and gram-negative bacteria (*E. coli, Kleb. pneumoniae, Neisseria gonorrhoeae, Ps. aeruginosa, Salmonella* Typhimurium and *Vibrio cholerae*) (Vital & Rivera, 2009; Maji *et al.*, 2010; Naidoo *et al.*, 2011; Mondal *et al.*, 2012; Eze *et al.*, 2013; Stanley *et al.*, 2014). Furthermore, it was found that the gram-negative bacteria *Entc. aerogenes* was not inhibited by water, ethanol, methanol or hexane leaf extracts, results which are in accordance with the leaf extract from *C. odorata* in Durban, South Africa (Naidoo *et al.*, 2011). *E. coli* and *Klebsiella pneumoniae* were inhibited by leaf extracts with acetone and benzene from *C. odorata* in India but not by water leaf extract (Maji *et al.*, 2010). The previous report found that the hexane leafextacts of *Callistemon viminalis* leave showed more potent inhibition against skin pathogen (*Staph. aureus, Strep. pyogenes* and the enteric *B. cereus*) than intestinal pathogen (*Shigella sonnei, Salmonella enteritidis* and *E. coli*) (Delahaye *et al.*, 2009). The factors affecting the quality of plant extracts are the nature of the plant material (season, topography and climate) and its origin (locations) (Tiwari *et al.,* 2011). The type of solvent used in the extraction procedure plays an important role in the diversity of compounds in the plant extracts (Tiwari *et al.,* 2011). *C. odorata* stem and root extracts in hexane showed better antibacterial activity compared with other solvents. Venkata *et al.,* (2012) reported that extracts from the root of *C. odorata,* using ethyl alcohol, methanol,

Chloroform, and methanol: chloroform: water in a ratio of 12:5:3 as solvents, exhibited activity against the same pathogen strains as in our results.

Phyllanthus amarus

Phyllanthus is the largest genus in the flowering plant family Phyllanthaceae. It originates from tropical America and has spread as a weed throughout the tropics and subtropics. In tropical Africa it occurs in most countries. It also occurs throughout the Indian Ocean islands.

Description

It is Monoecious, annual, erect, glabrous herb up to 60 cm tall, reddish; branchlets flattened, often slightly winged and sparsely hairy. Leaves alternate, distichous and crowded along lateral branchlets, simple and entire, sessile; stipules ovate-lanceolate to lanceolate. Flowers 1–2 in the axils of leaves, unisexual, pale green, often flushed red; male flowers at the base of branches, other leaf axils with 1 female flower and 1 male flower. Fruit an obtusely 3-lobed capsule 2–2.5 mm in diameter, smooth, hanging, 6-seeded. Seeds c. 1 mm long, with transverse ridges.

Antimicrobial Activity

Hexane, petroleum ether, chloroform, acetone and methanol extract of Phyllanthus leaves were tested for antibacterial activity against *Pseudomonas aeruginosa, Klebsiella pneumonia, Proteus mirabilis, Streptococcus faecalis, Enterobacter species, Serratia marcescens, Staphylococcus aureus* and *Escherichia coli* by agar well diffusion method. The results demonstrated methanol extract of *Phyllanthusamarus* for highest inhibitory activity against above bacterialspecies (Saranraj *et al.,* 2012). Similarly, in another study antimicrobial potential of *Phyllanthus amarus* were investigated using agar well diffusion method for activity against several drug resistant pathogens such as *Escherichia coli, Pseudomonas aeruginosa, Staphylococcus aureus* and *Klebsiella Species*. The results revealed minimum inhibitory concentration (MIC) of the ethanolic plant extracts on *Escherichia coli, Staphylococcus aureus, Pseudomona aeruginosa* and *Klebsiella Species* were at 10 mg/ml, 50 mg/ml, 150 mg/ml and 100 mg/ml while the minimum bactericidal concentration were at 50 mg/ml, 100 mg/ml, 150 mg/ml and 150 mg/ml respectively (Adegoke *et al.,* 2010). Further studies on hexane, chloroform, ethyl acetate, acetone andmethanol extract of stem bark extracts of *Phyllanthus amarus* demonstrated the antimicrobial activity for all these extracts with adiameter that ranges between 11 mm 24 mm against

Streptococcus pyogenes, Staphylococcus aureus, Salmonella typhi, Escherichia coli, Candidas albican, Aspergillus flavus (Ushie *et al.*, 2013). The antimicrobialactivity of the methanolic extract of *Phyllanthus amarus* as studiedby agar dilution method and disc diffusion showed significantconcentration-dependent antibacterial activity specifically forgram-negative microbes.

Callistemon viminalis

Callistemon viminalis, commonly known as weeping bottlebrush, or creek bottlebrush is a plant in the myrtle family, Myrtaceae. It is endemic to New South Wales, Queensland and Western Australia.

Description

Callistemonviminalis is a large shrub or small tree growing to 35 metres tall with hard, fibrous, furrowed bark, a number of trunks and usually pendulous branches. Its leaves are arranged alternately and are 25–138 millimetres long, 3–27 millimetres wide, more or less flat, very narrow elliptical to narrow egg-shaped with the narrower end towards the base and the other end tapering to a sharp point. The leaves have a mid-vein, 9-27 lateral veins and large number of conspicuous oil glands.

The flowers are bright red and are arranged in spikes on and around the ends of branches which continue to grow after flowering. The spikes are 35–50 millimeters in diameter and 40–100 millimeters long with 15 to 50 individual flowers. The petals are 3.4–5.9 millimetres long and fall off as the flower ages and the stamens are arranged in five bundles around the flower. Flowering occurs from September to December and often sporadically throughout the year. Flowering is followed by fruits which are woody capsules, 3.8–4.8 millimeters long and 5–6 millimeters in diameter.

Antimicrobial Activity

The crude extracts from the leaves of *Callistemon viminalis* showed antibacterial and antifungal activity against both the Gram-positive (*Bacillus cereus, Staphylococcus aureus*, MRSA, and *Streptococcus pyogenes*), Gram-negative bacteria (*Escherichia coli, Pseudomonas aeruginosa, Salmonella enteritidis*, and *Shigella sonnei*) and the fungus *Candida albicans*. However, the three crude extracts of *C. viminalis* were more potent antibacterial agents against the Gram-positive bacteria and fungus (MBCs of 0.8 – 6.3 mg/ml) than the Gram-negative bacteria (MBCs of 6.3 – 50 mg/ml). For each test microbe, the aqueous ormethanol extract produced a lower MIC and MBC than the corresponding hexane extract. The methanol extract's average zone of inhibition for MRSA [25.61 ± 2.11 mm] was larger than that of non-methicillin resistant *S. aureus* [17.41 ±1.10 mm] (Fig. *i* & *ii*). The growth of *P. aeruginosa* was also Inhibited but to a lesser extent by the methanol extract, with MIC of 12.5 mg/ml and inhibition zones as high as 14 mm. For the Gram-negative bacteria, (*Bacillus cereus,*

Staphylococcus aureus, MRSA, and *Streptococcus pyogenes*) zones of inhibition were all above 15 mm for all three extracts indicating their high antibacterial potency. For the Gram-positive bacteria *Escherichia coli, Salmonella enteritidis,* and *Shigella sonnei,* the aqueous extracts produced the strongest anitbacterial activity with lower MBC (6.3 – 12.5 mg/ml) and larger zones of inhibition (>15 mm) than those produced by the other two extracts while for *Pseudomonas aeruginosa* the methanol extract was the strongest (MBC 12.5 mg/ml, 11-15 mm zone of inhibition). The aqueous extract was more effective against the gastro-intestinal pathogens (*S. enteritidis, S. sonnei*) than the methanol extracts.

All three crude extracts were effective at inhibiting growth of the fungus *C. albicans* producing zones of inhibition of >15 mm for the methanol and hexane extracts and the lowest MIC and MBC's of 1.6 and 3.2 mg/ml respectively for the methanol crude extract.

Shorea robusta

Shorea robusta, also known as sal tree, is a species of tbelonging to the Dipterocarpaceae family. This tree is native to the Indian subcontinent, ranging south of the Himalaya, from Myanmar in the east to Nepal, India and Bangladesh. In India, it extends from Assam, Bengal, Odisha and Jharkhand west to the Shivalik Hills in Haryana, east of the Yamuna.

Description

Sal is moderate to slow growing, and can attain heights of 30 to 35 m and a trunk diameter of up to 2-2.5 m. The leaves are 10–25 cm long and 5–15 cm broad. In wetter areas, it is evergreen; in drier areas, it is dry-season deciduous, shedding most of the leaves in between February to April.

Antimicrobial Activity

The aqueous, methanol, petroleum and benzene extract of oleoresin of *Shorea robusta* were tested. *(Adlakha et al., 2104).* Different extracts inhibited the growth of used microorganisms. Aqueous extracts of Shorea robusta exhibits significant activity against Bacillus coagulans, Escherichia coli, Bacillus cereus and moderate inhibition on *Salmonella typhi* and *Bacillus subtilis* and less activity against *Proteus vulgaris* and *Pseudomonas fluorescence.* However, ethanolic extracts also exhibited significant activity against *Staphylococcus aureus, S. epidermidis* and *Escherichia coli, moderate inhibition* on *Candida albicans* and *Bacillus coagulans.* The results revealed methanol extract showed more significant activity. The petroleum ether and benzene extracts showed less inhibitory activity when compared with the above two extracts. The Petroleum ether showed activity against *Escherichia coli, Aspergillus flavus* and *Candida albicans* and whereas benzene extracts worked against *Bacillus licheniformis, Bacillus cereus* and *Aspergillus flavus.* It may be concluded that *Shorea robusta* resin have a stronger and broader spectrum of antimicrobial activity against a number of pathogenic microorganisms (Murthy *et al.,* 2011).

Mentha arvensis

*Mentha arvensis Pudina*wild mint, or corn mint belonges to the family Lamiaceae. It is native to the temperate regions of Europe and western and central Asia, east to the Himalaya and easternSiberia, and North America.

Description

Wild mint is a herbaceous perennial plant generally growing to 10–60 cm and rarely up to 100 cm tall. It has a creeping rootstock from which grow erect or semi-sprawling squarish stems. The leaves are in opposite pairs, simple, 2–6.5 cm long and 1–2 cm broad, hairy, and with a coarsely serrated margin. The flowers are pale purple (occasionally white or pink), in whorls on the stem at the bases of the leaves. Each flower is 3 to 4 mm long and has a five-lobed hairy calyx, a four-lobed corolla with the uppermost lobe larger than the others and four stamens. The fruit is a two-chambered carpel.

Antimicrobial Activity

Antimicrobial activity of extract from *Mentha arvensis* was tested against *Escherichia coli* (ATCC 25922), *Pseudomonasaeruginosa* (ATCC 15442), *Shigella fl exineri* (ATCC 12022), *Klebsiella pneumoniae* (ATCC 10031) and *Sthaphylococcus aureus* (ATCC 12692) by using the agar diffusion method. (Romeiro, 2001). The ethanolic extract obtained from *M. arvensis* inhibited the growth of the bacterial strains; *Sthaphylococcus aureus* (Gram positive, inhibition zone diameter mean 21 mm) was the most susceptible of all the test microorganisms in a similar way to that of tetracycline. This result indicates that *M. arvensis* extract has an antibacterial potential similar to that of a commercial drug. No significant differences were detected between the *E. coli, P. aeruginosa, S. Flexineri* and *K. pneumoniae* inhibitionzone diameters.

Zingiber officinale

Ginger (*Zingiber officinale*) is a flowering plant whose rhizome, ginger root or simply ginger, is belonges to the family Zingiberaceae. Ginger originated in the tropical rainforest in Southern Asia. Although ginger no longer grows wild, it is thought to have originated on the Indian subcontinent.

Description

Ginger produces clusters of white and pink flower buds that bloom into yellow flowers. Because of its aesthetic appeal and the adaptation of the plant to warm climates, it is often used as landscaping around subtropical homes. It is a perennial reed-like plant with annual leafy stems, about a meter (3 to 4 feet) tall. Traditionally, the rhizome is gathered when the stalk withers; it is immediately scalded, or washed and scraped, to kill it and prevent sprouting. The fragrant perisperm of the Zingiberaceae is used as sweetmeats by Bantu, and also as a condiment and sialagogue.

Antimicrobial Activity

Water was used as a solvent to extract the *Zingiber officinale* juice. Imokawa (2008) indicated that the substances responsible for the spicy characteristics of *Z. officinale* are, for the most part, insoluble in water, whereas the desired proteases are extracted with water. Therefore, the aqueous extract is non-irritating and safe to use on human skin (Thompson, 1973). Propylene glycol was also used as an extraction solvent (Grégio, 2006); the goal was to maintain the antimicrobial activity and to compare the stability of the two extracts.The results for the *Z. officinale* rhizome extracts suggest their proteolytic activity is inferior to that of papain. The calculation was carried out using the mass of the rhizome used in the replicates, the dilution, and the volume used in the reaction. The results are expressed in PU/g or mL of the sample; thus, one gram of papain showed 443.30 PU, whereas the aqueous extract of the rhizome showed 338.14 PU/g of juice, and the glycolic extract showed 691.68 PU/g of juice. The activity was lower than that of papain under the same experimental conditions. The papain used was of high quality and highly purified, whereas the ginger extracts were of crude quality. The results corroborate Ha *et al.,* (2012); those authors assessed papain, bromelain, actinidin and zingibain. The activity of papain was approximately twenty times higher than that of zingibain, but the results indicated that the zingibain protease preparation was the most effective at hydrolyzing meat connective tissue proteins.

The results in the antimicrobial assay corroborate Jagetia *et al.,* (2003), who administered *Zingiber officinale* intraperitoneally and observed antimicrobial activity against *Pseudomonas aeruginosa, Salmonella typhimurium, Escherichia coli* and Candida albicans. Other studies show that hydroethanolic ginger extract exhibits potent antibacterial activity against both Gram-positive and Gram-negative bacteria, including *Staphylococcus aureus, Streptococcus pyogenes/ pneumonia* and *Haemophilus influenzae* (Akoachere *et al.,* 2002). Yet others have shown antibacterial activity against the Gram-negative bacteria *Pseudomonas aeruginosa, Salmonella typhimurium* and *Escherichia coli,* for which the minimum inhibitory concentration (MIC) of ginger extracts ranged from 0.0003 μg/mL to 0.7 μg/mL, while the minimum bactericidal concentration (MBC) ranged until 2.04 μg/mL for ginger (Jagetia *et al.,* 2003).

REFERENCES

Dev Sukh, (2012). Prime Ayurvedic Drugs-A Modern Scientific Appraisal, (Edn2), Ane Books Pvt. Ltd, New Delhi, India.

Sukanya, SL. Sudisha, J. Hariprasad, P. Niranjana, SR. Prakash, HS. Fathima, SK. Antimicrobial Activity of Leaf Extracts of Indian Medicinal Plants against Clinical and Phytopathogenic Bacteria. (2009). Afr J Bio.8(23): 6677-6682.

Marikani, K.Sharma, R. and Narayanan (2009). Phytochemistry and Immunopharmacological Investigation of Pharmacologyonline. 3: 653–662. Retrieved from http://www.unisa.it/download/1966_11225_1606014532_70.Kannan.pdf.

Kannan and Marikani (2010). An Immuno-Pharmacological Investigation of Indian Medicinal Plant *Nyctanthes arbor-tristis* Linn. World Applied Sciences Journal *11*(5):495–503. Retrieved from http://www.idosi.org/wasj/wasj11(5)/1.pdf.

Kannan, M. Singh, A. J. A. R., Kumar, T. T. A., Jegatheswari, P., & Subburayalu, S. (2007). Studies on Immuno-bioactivities of *Nyctanthes arbor-tristis*. African Journal of Microbiology Research 88–91.

Dheeba, B, Sampath Kumar P, R. R. S. P. and M. K. (2010). Phytochemical Studies and Evaluation of Antioxidant Potential of Various Extracts of *Aegle marmelos* Bark. Pharmacologyonline *3*: 831–839.

Kannan and Marikani (2010). An Immuno-Pharmacological Investigation of Indian Medicinal Plant *Nyctanthes arbor-tristis* Linn. World Applied Sciences Journal *11*(5): 495–503. Retrieved from http://www.idosi.org/wasj/wasj11(5)/1.pdf.

Aburjai, T. Darwish, R. M., Al-Khalil, S. Mahafzah, A. & Al-Abbadi, A. (2001). Screening of Antibiotic Resistant Inhibitors from Local Plant Materials Against Two Different Strains of *Pseudomonas aeruginosa*. Journal of Ethnopharmacology. *76*(1): 39–44. Retrieved from http://www.ncbi.nlm.nih.gov/pubmed/11378279.

Ahmad, I. & Beg, AZ. (2001). Antimicrobial and Phytochemical Studies on 45 Indian Medicinal Plants against Multi-drug Resistant Human Pathogens. Journal of Ethnopharmacology. *74*(2):113–23. Retrieved from http://www.ncbi.nlm.nih.gov/pubmed/11167029.

Ahmad, V. U., Ahmad, W. U., Aliya, R. Baqai, F. T. Iqbal, S. Khatoon, R., Siddiqui, S. (1994). New Natural Products from Terrestrial Medicinal Plants and Marine Algae. Pure and Applied Chemistry. *66*(10-11):2311–2314. doi:10.1351/pac199466102311.

Chomnawang, M. T., Surassmo, S., Nukoolkarn, V. S.& Gritsanapan, W. (2005). Antimicrobial Effects of Thai Medicinal Plants Against Acne-inducing Bacteria. Journal of Ethnopharmacology. *101*(1-3): 330–3. doi:10.1016/j.jep.2005.04.038.

Crops, S. Agriculture, S. & Republic, C. (n.d.). Screening for Antimicrobial Activity of Some Medicinal Plants Species of Traditional Chinese Medicine. Czech J. Food Sci. *Vol.*, *21*(3):107–110.

Ko, WT. Adal, KA. Tomecki, KJ. (1998). Infectious Diseases. Medical Clinic of North America. 82(5): 1001-1031.

Jawetz E, Janet S, Nicholas L, Edwards E (1978). Skin Microorganisms, In: Medical Microbiology. Lange International, New York. 25-27.

Mothana, RA. Lindequist, U. Antimicrobial Activity of Some Medicinal Plants of the Island Soqotra. Journel of Ethnopharmacol. 96(1-2): 177-181.

Okigbo RN, Anuagasi CL, Amadi JE. (2009). Advances in Selected Medicinal and Aromatic Plants Indigenous to Africa. J MedPlant Res.3(2): 86-95.

Rios, JL. Recio, MC. (2005). Medicinal Plants and Anti-microbialactivity. J Ethnopharmacol .100: 80-84.

Chanda, S. Rakholiya, K.(2011) Combination Therapy-Synergism between Natural Plant Extracts and Anti-biotics Against Infectious Diseases. Microbiology Book Series 520-529.

Harishchandra, MR. Rajan, PR. Singh, SRP.(2012). Study of Krimighna Effect of Nimba (Azadiracta indica) Patra as Rakshoghna Dhoopan by Culture and Sensitivity Method W.S.R. to Pyogenic Bacteria. International Journel of Pharmacy 3(6):142-146.

Nascimento, GF. Lacatelli, J. Freitas, PC.Silva, GL. (2000). Antibacterial Activity of Plant Extracts and Phytochemicalson Anti-biotic-resistant Bacteria. Brazilian Journel of Microbiology 31(4): 886-891.

Dahanukar, SA. Kulkarni, RA. Rege, NN.(2000). Pharmacology of Medicinal Plants and Natural Products. Indian Journel of Pharmacology 32: 81-118.

Silva, MSP. Brandao, DO. Chaves, TP. Filho, ALNF. Costa, EMDB. Santos, VL. (2012). Study Bioprospecting of Medicinal Plant Extracts of the Semiarid Northeast: Contribution to the Control of Oral Microorganisms. Eviourment-Based Comp Alt Med. 2012: 1-6.

Saranraj, P. Sivasakthivelan, P. (2012). Screening of Antibacterial Activity of the Medicinal Plant *Phyllanthus amarus* Against Urinary Tract Infection Causing Bacterial Pathogens. Applied Journal of Hygiene 1(3):19-24.

Adegoke, AA. Iberi, PA. Akinpelu, DA. Aiyegoro, P.(2010). Studieson Phytochemical Screening and Anti-microbial Potentials of *Phyllanthus amarus* against Multiple Anti-biotic Resistant Bacteria. International Journal of Applied Research in Natural Products 3:6.

Ushie, O. Neji, P. Etim, E.(2013). Phytochemical Screening and Anti-microbial Activities of *Phyllanthus amarus* Stem Barkextracts. International Journal of Modern Biology and Medicines 3:101-112.

Chandrasekaran, M., & Venkatesalu, V. (2004). Anti-bacterial and Anti-fungal Activity of *Syzygium jambolanum* Seeds. Journal of Ethnopharmacology, *91*(1), 105–8.doi:10.1016/j.jep.2003.12.012.

MacGaw, L. J., A.K. Jaguar and VanStaden. J. (2002). Isolation of Basarones, An Anti-bacterial and Anthermintic Compound, from Acores. South African J. Bot. 68:31-35.

Essawi, T., and M. Srour 2000. Screening of Some Palestinian Medicinal Plants for Anti-bacterial Activity. J. Ethnopharmacol 70: 343-349.

Ramya S, Govindaraji V, Kannan K N, Jayakumararaj R. (2008) *In Vitro* Evaluation of Anti-bacterial Activity Using Crude Extracts of *Catharanthus roseus L.* (G.) *Don,* Ethno Botanical Leaflets, 12:1067-72.

Goyal P, Khanna A, Chauhan A, Chauhan G, Kaushik P. (2008). In vitro Evaluation of Crude Extracts of *Catharanthusroseus* for Potential Anti-bacterial Activity, International Journal of Green Pharmacy, 2(3):176-181.

Gajendra Singh PR, Bhavika MK, Rohit S, Hetal A, Prajapati PK. (2012). *In vitro* Anti-bacterial Study of Two Commonly Used Medicinal Plants in Ayurveda: Neem (*Azadirachta indica L.*) and Tulsi (*Ocimum sanctum L.*). IJPBA; 3(3):582-586.

Murthy KSR, Lakshmi N, Ramulu DR. (2011). Biological Activity and Phytochemical Screening of the Oleoresin of *Shorea robusta* Gaertn. f. Trop Subtrop Agroeco. 14: 787-791.

Romeiro R.(2001). 2todos em Bacteriologia de Plantas. Viçosa, Editora UFC.

Imokawa G. (2008) Recent Advances in Characterizing Biological Mechanisms Underlying UV-induced Wrinkles: A Pivotal Role of Fibrobrast - Derived Elastase. Arch Dermatol Res. 300:S7-S20.

Grégio AMT, Fortes ESM, Rosa EAR, Simeoni RB, Rosa RT . (2006). Anti-microbial Activity from Zingiber Officinalle on Oral Cavity Pathogens. Estud Biol.28(62):61-6.

Ha M, Bekhit AEDA, Carne A, Hopkins DL.(2012) Characterisation of Commercial Papain, Bromelain, Actinidin and Zingibain Protease Preparations and their Activities Toward Meat Proteins. Food Chem. 134:95-105.

Jagetia GC, Baliga MS, Venkatesh P, Ulloor JN. (2003) Influence of Ginger Rhizome (*Zingiber officinale* Rosc.) on Survival, Glutathione and Lipid Peroxidation in Mice after Whole-body Exposure to Gamma Radiation. Radiat Res. 160:584-92.

Akoachere JF, Ndip RN, Chenwi EB, Ndip LM, Njock TE, Anong DN. (2002). Antibacterial Effect of *Zingiber officinale* and Garcinia Kola on Respiratory Tract Pathogens. East Afr. Med. J., 79:588-92.

Jagetia GC, Baliga MS, Venkatesh P, Ulloor JN. (2003). Influence of Ginger Rhizome (*Zingiber officinale* Rosc.) on Survival, Glutathione and Lipid Peroxidation in Mice After Whole-body Exposure to Gamma Radiation. Radiat Res. 160:584-92.

Medicinal and Nutritional Values of Plants
Edited by: Alka Chauhan and Pawan Kumar 'Bharti'
ISBN: 978-93-5056-883-5
Edition: 2017
Published by: Discovery Publishing House Pvt. Ltd., New Delhi (India)

6

PGPR Assisted Plant Growth Regulation
An Overview

[1]Prasann Kumar

ABSTRACT

The high tech agricultural methods have tried to offset the adverse effect of population pressure on the productivity has not only rendered the agricultural field less productive, but has severely damaged the population dynamics of soil-microflora. The soil microorganisms are essential for the supply of minerals to the plants and they help in mineralization of most the macronutrients including sulphur and phosphorus.[1]

Key words: Agriculture, Biotic, Colony, Diffuse, Efficient, Fungus, Glomus,

INTRODUCTION

The group of root colonizing beneficial soil microorganisms known to enhance plant growth and yield by suppressing diseases, fixing atmospheric nitrogen, solubilising/ translocating P, K, Fe and other nutrients, and producing bioactive substances that stimulate root prolifiration are called Plant growth promoting rhizobacteria (PGPR) or probiotic rhizobacteria (Kloepper *et al.*, 1980, Hass and Keel, 2003). We are interested to know the facts that how PGPR is responsible for the enhanced growth of plants, these are described as follow:

- Biological N-fixation.
- Nutrient solubiliztion/translocation.
- Suppression of plant diseases.
- Production of phytohormones.
- Inducing resistance against abiotic stresses.
- Problem as a consequence of increases in and environmental damage and worldwide population growth, global food production may soon be insufficient to feed all of the world's people.
- In this regard, the world's population, which is currently around 7 billion people, has been projected to increase to around 10 billion in the next 50 years.

[1] Department of Plant Physiology, Institute of Agricultural Sciences, Banaras Hindu University, Varanasi, 221005, U.P., India

- To feed all of these individuals it is absolutely essential that agricultural productivity be significantly increased within the next few decades.
- However, providing sufficient food for an ever-increasing world population is not an easy task; it will require a variety of different strategies and approaches.
- To produce more food, the world will require more agricultural land; greater use of chemicals including fertilizers, pesticides and herbicides; more farm mechanization; greater use of transgenic crops; and the expanded use of plant growth-promoting microorganisms.
- These points keep in mind to develop a strategies or mechanism for Plant growth promotion.
- Without affecting the soil health and environment.
- Maintain sustainability in food production.
- To minimize the cost of production by fixation of atmospheric Nitrogen, Solubilization of Phosphorus and Potassium, production or synthesis of growth regulators e.g. Auxin, GA3, cytokinin.
- To minimize the population of rhizospheric plant pathogen by production of antibiotic compounds e.g. HCN.

- These points keep in mind to develop a strategies or mechanism for Plant growth promotion.
- Without affecting the soil health and environment.
- Maintain sustainability in food production.
- To minimize the cost of production by fixation of atmospheric Nitrogen, Solubilization of Phosphorus and Potassium, production or synthesis of growth regulators e.g. Auxin, GA3, cytokinin.
- To minimize the population of rhizospheric plant pathogen by production of antibiotic compounds e.g. HCN.

PLANT GROWTH PROMOTING BACTERIA

I am giving about the some points about the plant growth promoting bacteria. These are as follow:

- Most soils contain an enormous diversity of microorganisms including bacteria, actinomycetes, fungi, algae and protozoa.
- It has been suggested that a typical gram of soil contains ~9×10^7 bacteria, 4×10^6 actinomycetes, 2×10^5 fungi, 3×10^4 algae, 5×10^3 protozoa and 3×10^1 nematodes (Alexander 1991).
- The numbers of these organisms in any one soil compared to another may vary greatly.
- Soil bacteria in particular have the ability to grow rapidly and to utilize a very wide range of different substances as nutrient sources.

- Many bacteria are dispersed within the soil, often attached to soil particles; many interact with the roots of plants.
- It is quite common for the concentration of bacteria that is found around the roots of plants, i.e. in the rhizosphere, to be much greater than the other place.

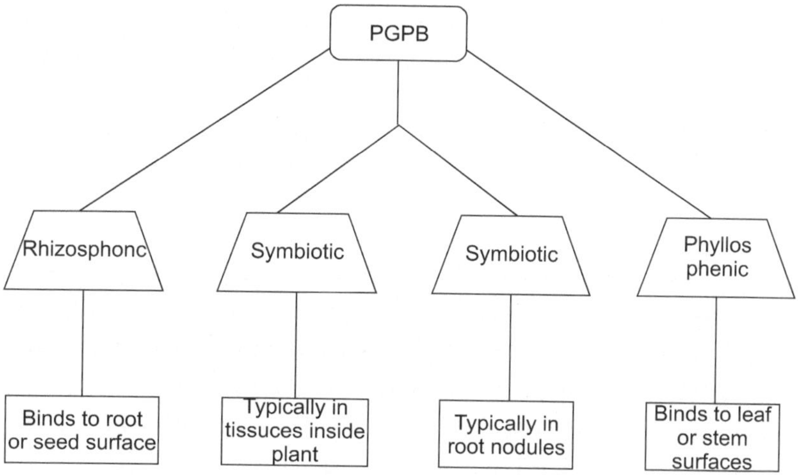

Fig. 6.1: PGPR interaction with plants in diverse ways

(**Source:** Review literature, 2016)

- **PGPR** are soil bacteria capable of colonizing the root systems of many cultures and impact positively the plant physiological process.
- These bacteria are involved in the plant resistance to biotic and/or abiotic stresses.
- Though their mechanisms of action, PGPR are currently classified into four groups:
  - (*i*) *Biofertilizers* for their ability to solubilize mineral phosphorus, potassium and to fix atmospheric nitrogen.
  - (*ii*) *Phytostimulators* for their ability to produce plant hormones.
  - (*iii*) *Rhizoremediators* for their capacity to degrade organic pollutants.
  - (*iv*) *Biopesticides"* for their ability to produce siderophores, to synthesize antibiotics, enzymes, and/or fungicidal compounds.
- These abilities are of great agriculture importance in terms of improving soil fertility and crop yield, thus reducing the negative impact of chemical fertilizers on the environment.
- Micro environment surrounding the root system is referred to as rhizosphere and bacteria colonizing in these zones called rhizobacteria.
- It providing the mechanical support and facilitating water and nutrient uptake, plant roots also synthesize, accumulate, and secrete chemical compounds into the soils are generally called as root exudates.

- These compounds act as chemical attractants for a vast number of heterogeneous, diverse and actively metabolizing soil microbial communities.
- These compounds modify the chemical and physical properties of the soil and regulate the structure of soil microbial community in the immediate vicinity of root surface.
- Some of the exudates act as repellants against microorganisms.
- The composition of these exudates is dependent upon the physiological status and species of plants and microorganisms.
- Microbial activity in the rhizosphere affects rooting patterns and the supply of available nutrients to plants, thereby modifying the quality and quantity of root exudates.

Nitrogen fixation is limited to prokaryotes. Some eubacteria and a few archebacteria can fix nitrogen-but no eukaryotic cells can do this. Some N-fixing bacteria are free-living whereas other form symbiotic associations with plants. I am giving the example of free living nitrogen fixing bacteria. These are:

(*a*) Obligate anaerobes, e.g. *Clostridium pasteurianum*

(*b*) Facultative anaerobes, e.g., *Klebsiella*, a close relative of *E. coli.*

(*c*) Photosynthetic bacteria, e.g., *Rhodobacter*

(*d*) Many *Cyanobacteria*

(*e*) Obligate aerobes such as *Azotobacter*

(*f*) Some *Methanogens*

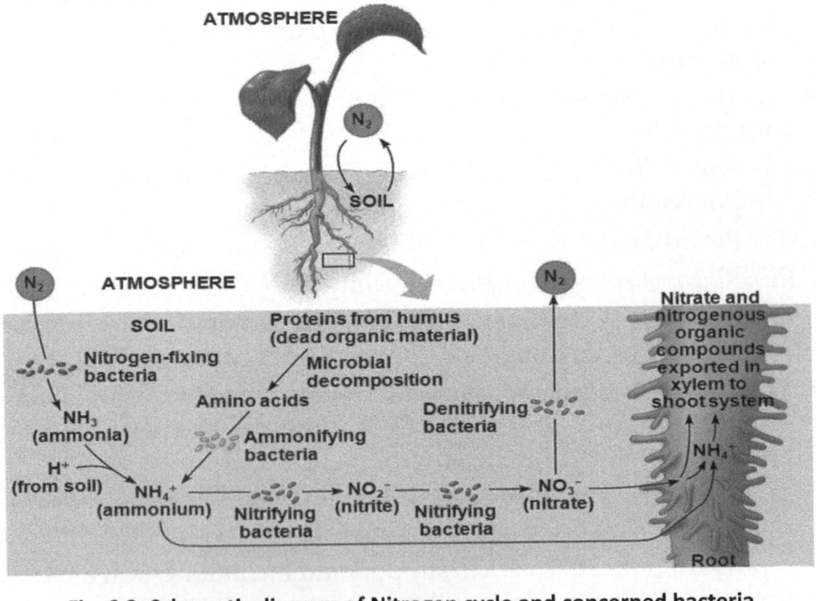

Fig. 6.2: Schematic diagram of Nitrogen cycle and concerned bacteria

(Source: Review Literature, 2016**)**

Since nitrogenase is inactivated by O_2, the fixation of N_2 must occur under conditions which are anaerobic at least locally. For anaerobes there is no problem. Facultative organism such as purple photosynthetic bacteria or *Klebsiella* fixes N_2 only when anaerobic. Other organisms have protective mechanisms. In azotobacter, an obligat aerobe, the O_2 concentration inside the cell is held down by partial uncoupling of a highly active respiratory chain. This wastes carbohydrates, but if growth is limited by absence of nitrogen compounds then this is justifiable. In Cyanobacteria O_2 is actually generated by photosynthesis. Fixation of N_2 occurs in special cells known as heterocysts which do not photosynthesize but are devoted solely to N_2 fixation (figure 6.2).

SYMBIOTIC NITROGEN FIXING BACTERIA

Symbiotic bacteria are protected from oxygen by inhabiting a plant host. Bacteria of the genus *Rhizobium* and *Bradyrhizobium* inhabit the root nodules of leguminous plants (e.g. peas, beans, clover, alphafa, soybeans). Other symbiotic associations occur but are less important. *Anabena azollae*, a nitrogen fixing cyanobacterium, lives in pores on the fronds of a water fern called *Azolla*. This symbiotic partnership is used to enrich paddies with organic nitrogen. Some of the known species of Azolla are *Azolla mexicana, Azolla pinnat, Azolla caroliniona, Azolla filiculoides* and *Azolla micropylla*. The method followed for mass cultivation of *Azolla* is as under the microplots (20 m^2) are filled with water upto a level of about 10 cm and are supplemented with 4-20 kg P_2O_5/ha. Water filled plots with approximate pH 8.0 are inoculated with *Azolla* (0.5 kg/m^2) and are left at a temperature ranging between 15-30°C . The insecticide (furadon) is also added to check the attack of insects. There weeks later *Azolla* mat is harvested and dried for further use as green manure. Two ways of its application in the rice fields have been recognized (Singh, 1979, 1980); (*a*) adding *Azolla* in the soil before rice plantation, (*b*) Rice transplantation is followed by introduction of *Azolla*. Using *Azolla* as a biofertilizers in rice fields, to a certain extent, can compensate the use of urea or ammonium phosphate. Rhizobium is also found free in the soil but only fixes N_2 when inside the root nodules of its host plant, in a strictly controlled microaerophilic environment. Oxygen is required to generate sufficient respiratory energy to drive N_2 fixation. But too much oxygen inactivates nitrogenase. In root nodules the O_2 level is regulated by a special hemoglobin-leghemoglobin. The globin protein is encoded by plant genes but the heme cofactor is made by the symbiotic bacteria. This is produced only when the plant is infected with *Rhizobium*. The plant root cells convert sugar to organic acids which they supply to the bacteroids. In exchange, the plant receives amino-acids (rather than free ammonia). Specific strains of bacteria are found inhabiting specific plant species. For example, a carbohydrate binding protein (lectin) on the surface of root cells of clover (*trifolium*) specifically binds to lipopolysaccharides of *Rhizobium trifolii* which contains 2-deoxyglucose. The bacteria then enter and produce cytokinin (a type of plant hormone) which promote the division of plant cells to form nodules. The bacteria lose their outer membranes and become irregular in shape–bacteroids.

NITROGENASE AND ITS FUNCTIONAL ROLE

Nitrogenase contains the two proteins molybdoferredoxin and azoferredoxin. These must be supplied with reducing equivalents by other proteins that vary. Here we considered nitrogenase from *Klebsiella*, a close relative of *E.coli* where the accessory proteins are flavodoxin and pyruvate flavodoxin reductase. In most bacteria electrons are passed from NAD(P)H or pyruvate to ferredoxin, an FeS protein. If iron is in short supply ferredoxin is replaced by flavodoxin, a flavoprotein. In *Klebsiella* there is no ferredoxin and flavodoxin (*NifF* protein) is used all the time. Azoferredoxin transfers electrons from reduced flavodoxin (or ferredoxin) to molybdoferredoxin. Molybdoferredoxin is an alpha2/beta2 tetramer. The alpha and beta subunits are similar but distinct and are encoded by genes *nifK* and *nifD*. Each tetramer contains 2Mo and several FeS groups. The molybdenum is part of a low molecular weight cofactors containing Mo bound to a Fe_7S_8 cluster and to homocitrate. This MoFe cofactor is unique to nitrogen fixation and distinct from the Mo-pterin cofactor of other Mo protein (e.g. nitrate reductase, xanthine oxidase). Azoferrerodoxin is a dimer of identical subunits encoded by *nifH* and contains a single Fe_4S_4 groups per dimer. Azoferredoxin is modified by the *NifM* protein. Molybdoferredoxin from one genus can often interact with azoferredoxin from another genus to give active enzyme. These two proteins have several alternative names:

Molybdoferredoxin = component I, MoFe protein, or 'nitrogenase'

Azoferredoxin = component II, Fe protein, or nitrogenase reductase

Nitrogenase is not very fast (the turnover number is fifty moles/min per mole of Mo) and so about 2-5% of the total cell protein is nitrogenase. The reaction $N_2 + 3H_2 = 2NH_3$ actually released energy. However, the activation energy needed to break the N_2 triple bond is very high and in practice energy, as ATP, is consumed by NifH protein (azoferredoxin). If there is an excess of azoferredoxin then ATP tends to be wasted. In *Klebsiella* nifHDK form an operon that keeps the ratio of components constant (table 6.1, 6.2, 6.3 & 6.4).

Table 6.1: Data of Total Nitrogen Fixation

Sl. No.	Type of fixation	N_2 fixed (10^6 metric t. per year)
A. Non-biological		
	Industrial	about 50
	Combustion	about 20
	Lightning	about 10
	Total	about 80

B. Biological		
	Agricultural land	about 90
	Forest and non-agricultural land	about 50
	Sea	about 35
	Total	about 175

(**Source:** Review Literature, 2016)

Table 6.2: N_2 Fixed by Various Agents in Wetland Rice Fields

Indigenous	**kg N/ha per crop of rice**
N_2-fixation associated with rice rhizosphere	**1-7**
N_2-fixation associated with straw	**2-4**
Total heterotrophic N_2-fixation	**1-31**
Cyanobacteria (surface)	**0-80**
Introduced	**kg N/ha per crop of rice**
Azolla	10-50 (fields)
Aquatic legume (Sesbania, Croteralia, Aeschynomene, Indigofera etc.)	**20-260**

(**Source:** Review Literature, 2016)

Table 6.3: Rates of Nitrogen Fixation for Some Common Agricultural Crops and Agro Forestry Trees

Crops	**N_2 fixed, kg/ha/yr**
Soybean	14.7-263
Alfalfa (*Medicago sativa*)	229-290
Red clover (*Trifolium pratense*)	154
Bean (*Phaseolus vulgaris*)	10
Pea (*Pisum sativum)*	17-69
Chick Pea	67-141
Acacia mearnsii	200
Gliricidia	13
Leucaena	100-500
Erythrina	60
High potential: Acacia mangium, Casuarina equisetifolia,	100-300
Low potential: Faiderbia albidia, A. Senegal	20
Azolla/anabaena	70
Casuarina	58, 113, 218 **(various estimates)**

(**Source:** Ladha *et al.*, 1993)

Table 6.4: PGPR (Free living) with Ability to FIX-N_2

PGPR	Relationship to host	Host crops	References
Azospirillum sp.	Rhizospheric	Maize Rice Wheat	Malik *et al.*, 1997 Boddey *et al.*, 1986
Azoarcus sp.	Endophytic	Kallar grass Sorghum	Hurek *et al.*, 2002 Stein *et al.*, 1997
Azotobacter sp	Rhizospheric	Maize Wheat	Pandey *et al.*, 1998 Mrkovacki and Milic, 2001
Bacillus polymyxa	Rhizospheric	Wheat	Omar *et al.*, 1996
Burkholderia sp	Endophytic	Rice	Baldani *et al.*, 2001
Cyanobacteria	Rhizospheric	RiceWheat	Hashem, 2001 Obreht *et al.*, 1993
Gluconacetobacter	Endophytic	Sorghum	Isopi *et al.*, 1995
Herbaspirillum sp.	Endophytic		James *et al.*, 2002 James *et al.*, 1997 Pimentel *et al.*, 1991

PROPOSING MODEL OF PGPR USED IN FIELD

- *Pseudomonas* rhizobacteria, primarily of the *P.fluorescens, P. putida, P. cepacia, and P. aureofaciens* applied to seeds, roots of plant have resulted in the less diseases in several crops, such as damping-off, soft rot, and consistent increase in growth and yield of plants.
- *Bacillus spp.* especially *B. cereus* provides effective biocontrol of damping-off disease of legume.
- Some of them are sold commercially, *B. subtilis* is sold as Kodiak and *P. fluoresecens* is sold as Dagger G.
- All have given good results in experimental trials.

APPROACH TO COMMERCIALIZING PGPR

- Further study on the factors that influence on the inconsistent performance of PGPR applied to the field.
- Improvement the survival and proliferation of PGPR by determination the optimal concentration, timing and placement of inoculants.
- Enhancement PGPR functions by manipulation of the host plant, substrates for PGPR, or through agronomic practices.
- Develop better formulation: shelf life, compatibility with current application practices, cost, and ease of application.

P-SOLUBLIZATION THROUGH PSB

- After nitrogen, phosphorus (P) is the second essential macronutrient for plant growth and development.

- Generally, Substantial amount of phosphorus (P) occurs in soil ranging from 400 to 1200 mg/kg of soil, in mineral forms e.g., apatite, hydroxy-apatite and oxy-apatite, or organic forms such as, inositol-phosphate(soil-phytate) phosphomono-esters, phosphodi-esters and phospho-triesters.
- However, the concentration of soluble forms of P in soil is usually ~1mg/kg or less.
- The ability of some microorganisms to convert insoluble phosphorus (P) to an accessible form, like orthophosphate, is an important trait in a PGPR for increasing plant yields (figure 6.3).

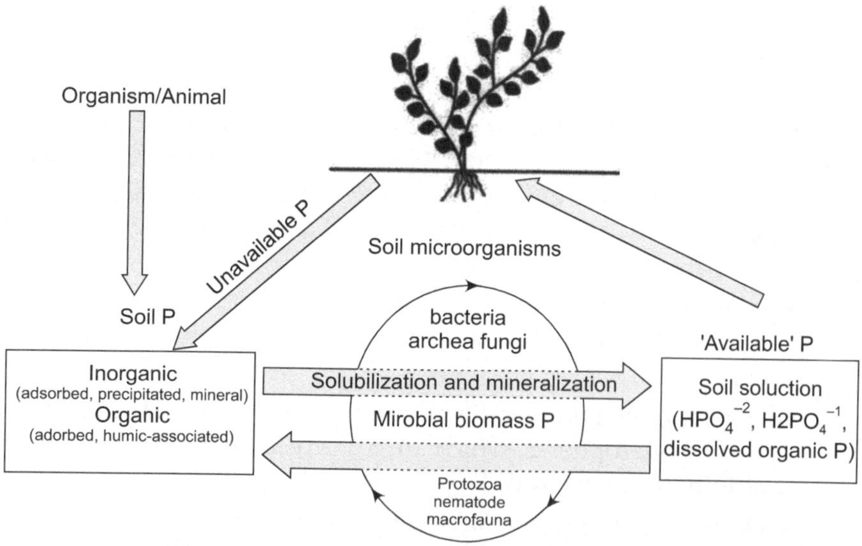

Fig. 6.3: Schematic diagram of P-solublization

(Source: Review Literature, 2016**)**

PHYTOHORMONES PRODUCTION THROUGH PGPR

- A wide range of microorganisms found in the rhizosphere are able to produce substances that regulate plant growth and development.
- Plant growth promoting rhizobacteria produce phytohormones such as auxins, cytokinins, gibberellins.
- Indole Acetic Acid (IAA): Among plant growth regulators, IAA is the most common natural auxin found in plants and its positive effect on root growth.
- Up to 80% of rhizobacteria can synthesize indole acetic acid (IAA) colonized the seed or root surfaces to stimulate cell proliferation and enhance the host's uptake of minerals and nutrients from the soil.

- Tryptophan is an amino acid commonly found in root exudates, has been identified as main precursor molecule for biosynthesis of IAA in bacteria.
- Several plant growth promoting rhizobacteria like *Azotobacter sp., Rhizobium sp., Pseudomonas fluorescens, Bacillus subtilis, Pantoea sp, and Rhodospirillum sp.,* can produce cytokinins or gibberellins or both that promote plant growth.

SIDEROPHORE PRODUCTION THROUGH PGPR

- Iron is an essential nutrient for life. However, in most aerobic microbial habitats, Fe^{2+} is oxidized to Fe^{3+}, forming insoluble compounds that are unavailable to microorganisms.
- In those circumstances, some bacteria produce low-molecular mass iron chelators with high affinity for iron termed siderophores.
- Siderophores are low molecular weight, extracellular compounds with a high affinity for ferric iron, that are secreted by microorganisms to take up iron from the environment and their mode of action in suppression of disease were thought to be solely based on competition for iron with the pathogen.
- Iron occurs mainly as Fe^{3+} forms insoluble hydroxides and oxy-hydroxides, and it is not easily available to both plants and micro-organisms.
- Under iron-limiting conditions to acquire iron, bacteria secret low molecular weight siderophores, which are iron chelators with exceptionally strong affinity for ferric iron (Fe^{3+}).
- Despite their preferential affinity for (Fe^{3+}), they can also chelate several other metals such as, magnesium, manganese, chromium (III), gallium (III), cadmium, zinc, copper, nickel, arsenic and lead, with variable affinities.
- Supply of iron to growing plants under heavy metal pollution becomes more important as bacterial siderophores help to minimize the stress imposed by metal contaminants.
- The hormone ethylene, which is found in all higher plants, is an important modulator of normal plant growth and development.
- Many aspects of the growth of plant tissues such as roots, stems, leaves, flowers and fruits, as well as all stages of plant development are affected by ethylene.
- Within any particular plant, ethylene synthesis is affected by a number of different factors including temperature, light, gravity, nutrition and the presence of various types of biological stress to which the plant maybe subjected.

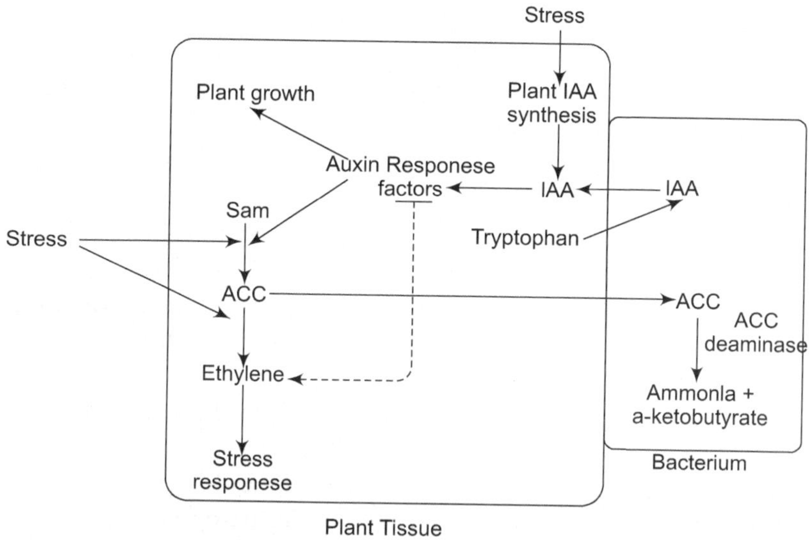

Fig. 6.3: How plant growth-promoting rhizobacteria that produce both ACC deaminase and synthesize IAA may facilitate plant growth

(Source: Review Literature, 2016**)**

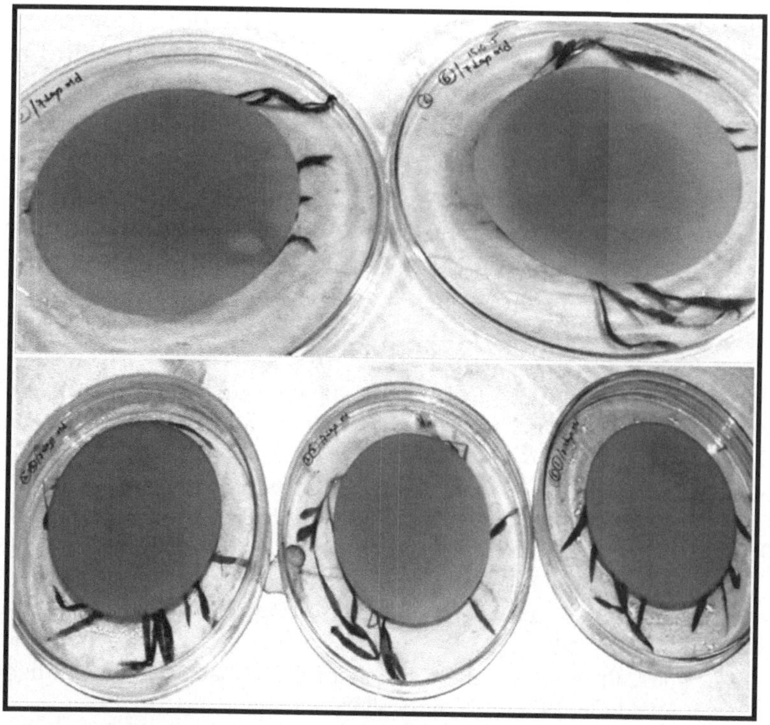

Fig. 6.4: HCN production through sorghum plant inoculated with mycorrhiza

(Source: Based on the experiment of author**)**

HCN PRODUCTION THROUGH PGPR

- Hydrogen cyanide is a broad spectrum antimicrobial compound involved in biological control of root disease by many plant associated fluorescent pseudomonads.
- Pseudomonas fluorescens HCN inhibited the mycelial growth of Pythium in vitro.
- HCN first inhibits the electron transport, and the energy supply to the cell is disrupted leading to the death of the organisms.
- It inhibits proper functioning of enzymes, natural receptors mechanism of inhibition and is also known to inhibit the action of cytochrome oxidase.
- Further, they noted that the enzyme HCN synthase is encoded by three biosynthetic genes (henA, henB and henC).
- HCN is produced by many rhizobacteria and is postulated to play a role in biological control of pathogens (figure 6.4)

CONCLUSION

Plant growth promoting rhizobacteria (PGPR) are a heterogeneous group of bacteria that can be found in the rhizosphere, at root surfaces and in association with roots, which can improve the extent or quality of plant growth directly and/or indirectly. In last few decades a large array of bacteria including species of *Pseudomonas, Azospirillum, Azotobacter, Enterobacter,, Arthrobacter, Bacillus, and Rhizobium* have reported to enhance plant growth. The direct promotion by PGPR entails either providing the plant with plant growth promoting substances that are synthesized by the bacterium or facilitating the uptake of certain plant nutrients from the environment. The indirect promotion of plant growth occurs when PGPR prevent deleterious effects of one or more Phytopathogenic micro-organisms.

REFERENCES

Baldani, V.L.D., J.I. Baldani and J. Dobereiner. 2000. Inoculation of Rice Plants with the Endophytic Diazotrophs *Herbaspirillum seropedicae* and *Burkholderia* spp. Biology and Fertility of Soils 30:485–491.

Boddey, R.M., Baldani, V.L.D., Baldani, J.L. and J. Dobereiner. 1986. Effect of Inoculation of *Azospirillium* spp. On Nitrogen Accumulation by Field Grown Wheat. Plant and Soil 95:109-121.

Haas, D. and C. Keel. 2003. Regulation of Anti-biotic Production in Root Colonizing *Pseudomonas* spp. and Relevance for Biological Control of Plant Disease. Annu. Rev. Phytopathol. 79:117-153.

Hashem, M.A. 2001. Problems and Prospects of Cyanobacterial Biofertilizer for Rice Cultivation. Aust J Plant Physiol. 28:881–888.

Hurek, T., L.L. Handley, B. Reinhold-Hurek, Y. Piche. 2002. *Azoarcus* Grass Endophytes Contribute Fixed Nitrogen to the Plant in an Unculturable State. Mol. Plant-Microbe Interact., 15: 233-242.

Isopi, R., P. Fabbri, M. del Gallo, and G. Puppi.1995. Dual Inoculation of *Sorghum bicolor* (L.) Moench ssp. *bicolor* with Vesicular Arbuscular Mycorrhizas and *Acetobacter diazotrophicus*. Symbiosis 18:43-55.

James, E. K., F. L. Olivares, J. I. Baldani, and J. Dobereiner. 1997. Herbaspirillum, An Endophytic Diazotroph Colonizing Vascular Tissue in Leaves of Sorghum Bicolor L. Moench. J. Exp. Bot. 48:785–797.

James, E. K., P. Gyaneshwar, P. N. Mathan, W. L. Barraquio, P. M. Reddy, P. P. Iannetta, F. L. Olivares, and J. K. Ladha. 2002. Infection and Colonization of Rice Seedlings by the Plant Growth-promoting Bacterium *Herbaspirillum seropedicae* Z67. Molec. Plant-Microbe Interact 15:894–906.

Kloepper, J.W., Leong, J., Teintze, M. and Schroth, M.N. 1980. Enhanced Plant Growth by Siderophores Produced by Plant Growth-promoting Rhizobacteria. Nature 286: 885–886.

Ladha, J.K. and P.M. Reddy 1995. Extension of Nitrogen Fixation to Rice: Necessity and Possibilities. Geo. J. 35: 363–372.

Malik, K.A., B. Rakhshanda, S. Mehnaz, G. Rasul, M.S. Mirza, S. Ali. 1997. Association of Nitrogen-fixing Plant-growth Promoting Rhizobacteria (PGPR) with Kallar Grass and Rice. Plant Soil 194:37-44.

Mrkovacki, N., S. Mezei, N. Cacic. 2003. Population Dynamics of Azotobacter Chroococcum in Sugarbeet Rhizosphere Depending on Mineral Nutrition. Zbornik Matice Srpske Za Prirodne Nauke 104: 91 – 97.

Obreht, Z.N., W. Kerby, M. Gantar, P. Rowell (1993). Effect of Root Associated N2-fixing Cyanobacteria on the Growth and Nitrogen Content of Wheat (*Triticum vulgare*) Seedlings. Biol. Fert. Soils. 15: 68-72.

Omar, M.N.A., N.M. Mahrous and A.M. Hamouda. 1996. Evaluating the Efficiency of Inoculating Some Diazatrophs on Yield and Protein Content of 3 Wheat Cultivars Under Graded Levels of Nitrogen Fertilization. Ann. Agric. Sci. 41:579-590.

Pandey A, L.M.S. Palni. 1998. Isolation of *Pseudomonas corrugate* from Sikkim, Himalaya. World J of Microbiol. and Biotec. 14 (3): 411–413.

Pimentel, J.P., F. Olivares, R.M. Pitard, S. Urquiaga, F.D. Akiba, J. bereiner. 1991. Dinitrogen Fixation and Infection of Grass Leaves by *Pseudomonas rubrisubalbicans* and *Herbaspirillum seropedicae*. Plant Soil 137:61–65.

Singh, P.K. 1979. In: Nitrogen and Rice, IRRI, Philippines, p. 407.

Singh, P.K. 1980. Curr.Sci. 49:155

Stein, T., N. Hayen-Schneg and I. Fendrik. 1997. Contribution of BNF by *Azoarcus* sp. BH72 in *Sorghum vulgare*. Soil. Biol. Biochem. 29: 969-971.

Medicinal and Nutritional Values of Plants
Edited by: Alka Chauhan and Pawan Kumar 'Bharti'
ISBN: 978-93-5056-883-5
Edition: 2017
Published by: Discovery Publishing House Pvt. Ltd., New Delhi (India)

7 Medicinal Uses of Some Potential Ethno-medicinal Threatened Plants of Tarai Region of Udam Singh Nagar, Uttrakhand

An Overview

[1]Jagdish C. Arya, [1]G. C. Joshi, [3]Geeta Tewari, [2]Lalit M. Tewari, [1]Naveen Pandey, [2]Brij M. Upreti and [2]Kamal Kishor

ABSTRACT

Survey was conducted for the documentation of ethno-medicinal uses of some threatened plants from Udham Singh Nagar district. The tarai region of Uttarakhand plays a vital role from biodiversity point of view. Due to overexploitation and industrialization 13 valuable medicinal plants of tarai region are classified under threat categories by the IUCN. Group discussion, personal interview were conducted to explore the ethno-medicinal knowledge of the local people. A list of 14 medicinal plants were prepared, identified and preserved for future reference. Total 12 plant belonging to different families were identified of which 2 plants belong to the same family apocynaceae (Holarrhena, rauwolfia). Documented plant species were categorized as critical endangered (CR) 01, vulnerable (VU) 10, near threatened (NT) 03. Than different plant species further divided into herbs (10), shrubs (01), tree (01) and climber (02). If the rate of exploitation full fill the demand of these species in both paharmaceutical industries and traditional system continues, there is a probability of extinction of there species from their natural habitat in near future and the loss of natural resoruces directly affect to biodiversity of the state.

Key words: Tarai, Medicinal plant, IUCN, Endengerd plants.

INTRODUCTION

The Indian Himalayan Region (27 50′-37 06′N and 72°30′-97°25′E) covered approximately 8 million km^2 in surface area and occupying a length of approximately 3000 km. It is one of the most fragile mountain regions in the world and holds an enormous repository of biological, ethnic diversity; traditional culture, and much tribal wisdom, approximately 500 tribal and aboriginal communities in India live in close proximity to forests since time immemorial (Prakash, 2011). More than 80 percent of South Asia's 1.4 billion

[1] Regional Research Institute of Himalayan Flora, CCRAS, Thapla, Ranikhet, India
[2] Department of Botany, Kumaun University, Nainital, India
[3] Department of Chemistry, D. S. B. Campus, Kumaun University, Nainital, India

people have no access to modern health care; they rely on traditional medicine using native species (Bisht *et al.*, 2006). The Indian Himalayan Region is also a favourable habitat for major tribal communities like *Bhotias, Boaxas, Tharus, Rajis, Jaunsaries, Shaukas, Kharvar* and *Mahigiri.* From ancient period these communities mainly rely heavily and *directly* on the endemic vegetation for their daily needs such as food, fodder and medicines (Swe and Win, 2005). This Region supports about 18,400 species of plants, out of 1748 species which have been reported as medicinal plants; 701 species occur in Uttarakhand state (Samant *et al.*, 1998).

Uttarakhand is situated between the longitudes of 77°35′5″-81°2′25″ E and the latitudes of 28°43′.45″-31°8′10″N at the transjunction of Nepal, Tibet and India. In the north, natural water separates it from the Tibet, Kali reveres defines it's eastern border with the kingdom of Nepal, Yamuna-Tons rivers separates it from the state of Himachal Pradesh in the west and southern limit of Tarai belt almost demarcates it's southern boundary with the state of Uttar Pradesh. Uttarakhand includes 13 districts extends over an area of 53,485 km^2 with a total forest area of about 65% represent 1.68% of the land area of the country (Shrivastava & Singh, 2005).

Materials and Methods

Field survey was conducted during 2009-2013 to document the ethnomedicinal information about the plants. A semi structured questionnaire was used to collect the ethnomedicinal information and traditional healer's attitude about preservation of ethnomedicinal knowledge and the medicinal plant resources. Field survey was conducted taking traditional healers as a guide and voucher specimens of important medicinal plants used in traditional medicine were collected. The local names and traditional medicinal uses of plants were determined with the help of traditional healers. The voucher specimens were identified with the help of relevant taxonomic literature and CCRAS were also consulted for identification of the medicinal plants. Udham Singh Nagar is basically an industrial district, and many industry-related professions are prevalent here; it is a perfect example of "Unity in Diversity" for which India is so widely known—different cultures, religions, and life styles are blended in absolute harmony. The respondents were interviewed in their own houses and in nearby places falling within the study area where they would normally go to collect medicinal plants. The vernacular names were selected as mentioned by two or more of the people. The information, thus collected, was used to express species diversity for each plant community type. The species so collected were preserved for taxonomic identification following Jain and Rao (1977) and identified following Gupta (1968) and research publications. The identified specimens were further confirmed by comparing them with reference specimens preserved in the herbaria of Kumaun University, Nainital; and

CCRAS Ranikhet. Voucher specimens were submitted in the CCRAS Ranikhet. The identified species were further classified according to local names, habits different parts used traditionally and the disease treatment.

Results and Discussion

It has been estimated that there are approximately 35,000 to 70,000 plant species that have been used at one time or the other in one culture or another for medicinal purposes in the world (Pala & Todaria, 2010). In India, nearly 9,500 registered herbal industries and a multitude of unregistered cottage-level herbal units depend upon the continuous supply of medicinal plants for manufacture of herbal medical formulations based on Indian Systems of Medicine (Ved & Goraya, 2008). About 75% of these medicinal plants are taken from tropical forests while 25% from temperate forests (Kumar *et al.*, 2011). The sudden rise in the demand of herbal products and plant based drugs across the world resulting in the heavy exploitation of medicinal plants. Habitat degradation, unsustainable harvesting and over-exploitation have already led to the extinction of more than 150 plant species in the wild and most of medicinal plant species are becoming threat. It is estimated that 10% of all plant species are currently endangered in India (Pandey *et al.*, 2005; Singh & Rawat, 2011) and about 25,000 plant species are on the verge of extinction throughout the world (Jain and Sastry, 1980). In order to classify and update the list of threatened species, the International Union for Conservation of Nature and Natural Resources (IUCN) has recognized the categories on the basis of geographical range, populations and fragmentations of populations. The earlier categories, Extinct, Endangered, Vulnerable and Rare, have been now categories as Extinct (EX.), Extinct in the Wild (EW), Critically Endangered (CR), Endangered (EN), Vulnerable (VU), Conservation Dependent (CD), Data Deficient (DD), Low Risk (LR), Not Evaluated (NE) (Nayar, 1996; Prakash, 2011).

Tarai region of district Udham Singh Nagar are highly rich medicinal plants diversity. During the field study and scrutiny of available literature, the 14 medicinal plants are recorded threatened in Red Data Book of Indian plants (Nayar & Sastry, 1987, 1988, 1990). These threatened medicinal plants, which are facing the threat of habitat degradation and over exploitation, industrialization are categorized under various threat categories such as 10 species are Vulnerable (*Holarrhena pubescens* (Buch.-Ham) Wall ex G. Don., *Tinospora cordifolia* L., *Hemidesmus indicus* (L.) R. Brown., *Baccopa monnieri* (L.) Pennl., *Tribulus terrestris* L., *Clerodendrum serratum* (L.) Moon, *Curculigo orchioides* Gaertn., *Gloriosa superba* L., *Rauwolfia serpentina* (L.) Benth. ex. Kurz., *Curcuma angustifolia* Roxb). One species is Critically Endangered (*Acorus calamus* L.) and 3 species are Low Risk Near Threatened, *Costus speciosus* (Koen. ex Retz.) Sm. *Celastrus paniculatus* Willd., *Baliospermum montanum* Muell. (table 7.1, figure 7.1 & figure 7.2).

Botanical Descriptions

Acorus calamus Linn.

Fam. Araceae

Ver. Name: Vach.

Herb. Leaves uniform, with wavy margin. Spadix long, sessile, cylindrical. Flowers bisexual, the strongly aromatic fibrous root stock.

Fls. & Fr.: June- September

Distribution: Marshy places

Nativity: Reg Bor Temp (Bor Temperate Region)

RKT: 23539

Baccopa monnieri (L.) Wettst.

Fam. Scrophulariaceae

Ver. Name: Jalneem

Prostrate much branched herbs. Leaves sessile, opposite, oblong, entire, crenulate, and obtuse. Flowers bluish- purple or white, solitary, axillary. Capsules ovoid, glabrous.

Fls. & Fr.: Aug-Nov.

Distribution: Occasional in wet and marshy places in Tarai region.

Nativity: Cosmop (Cosmopolitation)

RKT – 30840

Baliospermum montanum Muell.- Arg.

Fam: Euphorbiaceae

Vern. Name: Danti

A stout under shrubs. Leaves alternate, variable in shape and size, upper lanceolate, palmately 3-5 lobed, coriaceous, acute or acuminate, sinuate-toothed. Flower greenish small. Capsule 3-lobbed and pubescent.

Fls. & Fr. September-December.

Distribution: Frequent on the edge of the Sal forest in Tarai region.

Nativity: Indo Malaya (Indian Orientation of Malaya)

RKT : 39465

Celastrus paniculatus Willd.,

Fam: Celastraceae

Ver.Name : Malkangani

A large woody climber. Leaves obavate orbicular elliptic or oblong–lanceolate, short-acuminate, crenate. Flower pale green. Capsule globose, bright yellow when ripe. Seeds black, enclosed in a red arillus.

Fls. & Fr.: April-October

Distribution: Climbing on the shrubs and trees.

Nativity: As Trop Malaya (Asian Tropical of Malaya)

RKT: 36340

Clerodendrum serratum (L.) Moon,

Fam: Verbanaceae

Ver. Name: Bharangi.

Shrub. Leaves opposite, oblong elliptic-oblong or oblanceolate, serrate, smooth, base cuneate. Flowers bluish-white, in terminal. Drupes black.

Fls. & Fr.: August-April

Distribution: Occasional in the forest or waste places.

Nativity: Ind Or Burma (Indian Orientation of Burma)

RKT : 37163

Costus speciosus (Koen. ex Retz.) Sm.

Fam.: Zingiberaceae

Ver. Name: Kemuk/Kebuk

Herb. Leaves large, alternate. Flower large white in dense terminal oblong spikes. Capsules bright red.

Fls. & Frt.: July-September.

Distribution: Commonly on forest edges in Tarai and bhabar region

Nativity: Ind Or Malaya (Indian Orientation of Malaya)

RKT: 39079

Curculigo orchioides Gaertn.,

Fam.: Hypoxidaceae

Ver. Name: Kali Musali

Perennial herb, with a short or root stock. Leaves linear lanceolate, sessile. Flowers in racemes, bright yellow. Fruits capsules. Seeds black

Fls. & Frt.: July-November

Distribution: Open forest localities.

Nativity: As Trop (Asian Tropical)

RKT: 39468

Curcuma aungustifolia **Roxb.**

Fam.: Zingiberaceae

Ver. Name: tikhur

Annual –perennial herb, with globose root stock, Leaves erect, lanceolate, acute or acuminate. Flowers white or yellow. Capsule ovoid, reddish brown and small.

Fls. &Frt.: June- August

Distribution: Frequently: Commonly cultivated in gardens widely, distributed in Tarai region

Nativity: Amphig Trop (Amphegion Tropical)

RKT: 30841

Gloriosa superba Linn.

Fam.: Colchicaceae

Ver. Nam. : Kalihari

Glabrous scrambling herb. Leaves sub-sessile, oblong-lanceolate, acuminate, tip linear spirally twisted. Flowers solitary, yellow with a blotch of bright red. Capsules oblong.

Fls. & Frt.: August-Novemeber

Distribution: Cultivated or wildly distributed near cultivated land areas.

Nativity: As Tropical (Asian Tropical)

RKT: 36864

Hemidesmus indicus (L.) R. Brown.

Fam.: Asclepiadaceae

Ver. Name: Dudhibel

Twining shrubs. Leaves linear-lanceolate or elliptic-oblong, acuminate. Flower in axillary, cymes. Follicles in pairs and slender.

Fls. & Frt.: August-September

Distribution: Frequently in the forest edges.

Nativity : Zeylan

RKT: 22373

Holarrhena pubescens **(**Buch.-Ham) Wall ex G.Don.

Fam.: Apocynaceae

Ver. Name : Kutaj

Small deciduous tree. Leaves opposite, elliptic-oblong, acute or acuminate, sub-coriaceous. Flower white or creamy colour. Seed numerous, linear, brown grey.

Fls. & Frt.: May-December

Distribution: Common on forest edges.

Nativity: As Trop (Asian Tropical)

RKT: 39202

Rauwolfia serpentina **(L.)** Benth. ex. Kurz.

Fam.: Apocynaceae

Ver. Name: Sarpgandha

Small glabrous shrub. Leaves whorled, long, lanceolate or elliptic-lanceolate acute or acuminate. Flowers pink in terminal or axillary, many flowered. Drupe single, purplish-black when ripe.

Fls. & Frt.: March–June.

Distribution: Occasional in the forest surface.

Nativity : Ind Or Java (Indian Orientation of Java)

RKT : 24919

Tinospora cordifolia Miers.

Fam.: Menispermaceae

Ver. Name : Gurj

A climber; stem smooth, with light papery bark. Leaves broadly ovate or orbicular, deeply cordate, acuminate. Flowers greenish yellow. Drupes ovoid, smooth.

Fls. &Frt.: February-April

Distribution: Commonly climbing on trees.

Nativity: Ind Or (Indian Orientation)

RKT : 31153

Tribulus terrestris L.,

Fam.: Zygophyllaceae

Ver. Name: Gokharu

Prostrate branched herb, Leaves paripinnate, leaflet hairy, mucronate. Flowers yellow. Fruits 5 angled globose.

Fls. &Frt.: August–December

Distribution: Frequently distributed on waste lands or sandy places.

Nativity: Amphig Trop (Amphegion Tropical)

RKT: 22561

Table 7.1: Threatened Categories of Medicinal Plants of Tarai Region of Uttarakhand

S. No.	Medicinal plants	Habit	Useful part	Medicinal uses
1	*Acorus calamus* L. (CR)	Herb	Rhizome/ Roots	Root powder is used to cure fever and worm infestation among children. Leaves and flowers decoction juice is given to cure cough. Branched, aromatic rhizomes are used medicinally as a carminative, a stimulant to the central nervous system, and as a tonic. Leaves and root stock are used in the preparation of perfumes, hair powders. Fresh root stock is used in confectionery and as a substitute for ginger.
2	*Baccopa monnieri* (L.) Pennl. (VU)	Herb	Whole plant	Plant is a nerve tonic. Stems and leaves are used for snake bite. Paste of whole plant used in treatment of cough, cold, fever and also used as blood purifier.

3	*Baliospermum montanum* Muell. Arg. (NT)	Shrub	Leaf, Root and Seed	Seeds purgative, leaf decoction is given in asthma, latex used for body ache and pain of joints.
4	*Celastrus paniculatus* Willd. (NT)	Climber	Bark. Root & Seed	Bark abortifacient. Seeds bitter, laxative, emetic, stimulant, aphrodisiac, oil from seeds in beriberi, powerful stimulant. Leaf juice is given as an antidote to overdose of opium, seeds made into a paste with cow's urine to cure scabies.
5	*Clerodendrum serratum* (L.) Moon, (VU)	Herb	Root	Young shoots and roots are ground in equal quantity and little gur is added to the taste. This preparation is given in the dose to cure thyroid.
6	*Costus speciosus* (Koen. ex Retz.) Sm. (NT)	Herb	Rhizome	Juice of stem used for dysentery, rhizome has been used for diabetes, fever, asthma, intestinal worms,
7	*Curculigo orchioides* Gaertn. (VU)	Herb	Root	Root is made into paste and applied externally as an antidote against Snake bite. Root powder/paste are administrated orally for Worm infestation. Root is boiled with milk and given in general debility.
8	*Gloriosa superba* L. (VU)	Herb	Rhizome	Tubers are used for elimination of intestinal worms. Rhizome paste is applied externally on ringworm and other skin diseases. Leaf juice is used to kill head lice.
9	*Hemidesmus indicus* (L.) R. Brown. (VU)	Herb	Root	Root of plant and Cumin seeds are grounded in equal quantities, some sugar is mixed and given internally to reduce Body Heat. Leaf juice mixed with some water is given in Fever.
10	*Holarrhena pubescens* (Buch.-Ham) Wall ex G.Don. (VU)	Tree	Bark	Roots are finely ground and powdered. This is boiled in water add given in filarial. Roots and stem powdered when dried and kept as home remedy. It is given in diarrhoea and dysentery.
11	*Rauwolfia serpentina* (L.) Benth. ex. Kurz. (VU)	Herb	Root	Powder of dry root is given internally for three days to cure Ulcers. Dried root powder is given orally to reduce high blood pressure. Leaf juice is used as remedy for the removal of opacities of cornea. Root paste is applied on cuts, wounds, or boils.

12	*Tinospora cordifolia* L. (VU)	Climber	Stem	Stem is used to increase the appetite, prevent the periodic return of diseases, and reduce fever. Infusion of powdered stem is used to restore health and stimulates sexual excitement. Starch from roots and stems are nutrients and are used against chronic diarrhea and dysentery. Juice of a fresh plant increases the flow of urine and is used for gonorrhoea.
13	*Tribulus terrestris* L. (VU)	Herb	Fruit	The fruits and seeds are powdered and used in backache. Fruits cooling, diuretic tonic, used in kidney disease and gravel.
14	*Curcuma angustifolia Roxb.* (VU)	Herb	Root/ rhizome	Green rhizome is crushed to make a fine paste. It is applied externally over the affected skin.

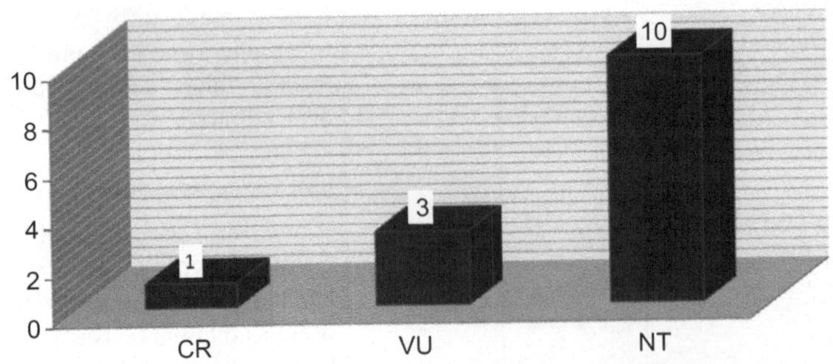

Fig. 7.1: Plant species catogoriserd within Critically Endengered (CR), Vulnerable (VU) and Near Threatend (NT).

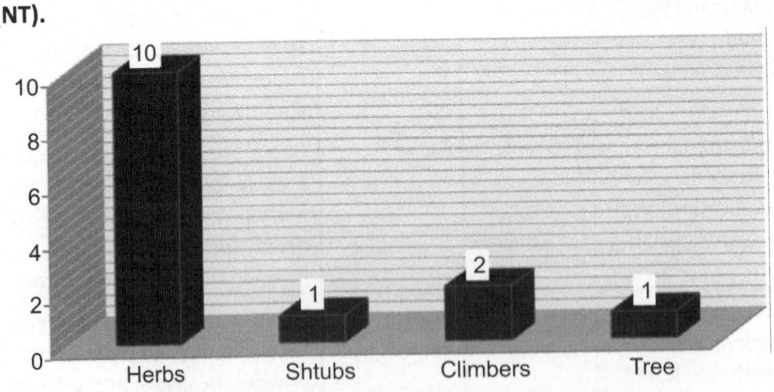

Fig. 7.2: Habit viz. Distribution of plant species.

Interest in green medicine is due to many reasons that the number of diseases are increasing day by day and prices spent on medicines are also increasing. Even some diseases like asthma, cancer, diabetes, jaundice, rheumatism, and arthritis are still incurable in allopathic systems of medicine.

Due to excesive use of this medicinal plant biodiversity resulting in extinction of many useful species has also posed a serious concern to the medical scientists and researchers.

Medicinal plants have become one of the main concerns of the world conservation organizations. Systematically more attempts to study and document the such medicinal plants of the Indian sub continent are seriously needed. There is also a need to establish herbal drug centers for collecting, processing and preparation of ethno-medicine and to develop cultivation, farming and documentation of potential and promising ethnomedicinal plants in social forestry operation for improving the life and economy of the local tribal and rural peoples. Hot spots are also required for the protection and conservation of valuable biodiversity. Therefore, there is urgent need to document complete biodiversity, prioritize useful threatened plants, and conserve them in-situ and ex-situ for sustainable utilization in health care and human welfare.

REFERENCES

Bisht, A. K., Bhatt, A., Rawal, R. S. and Dhar, U. 2006. Prioritization and Conservation of Himalayan Medicinal Plants: *Angelica glauca* Edgew. As a Case Study. *Ethnobotany Research & Applications* 4: 011-023.

Jain, S. K. and Sastry, A. R. K. 1980. Threatened Plants of India State-of-art Report. Botanical Survey of India, Howrah, 1-48.

Kumar, M. M., Sheikh, A. and Bussmann, R.W. 2011. Ethno Medicinal and Ecological Status of Plants in Garhwal Himalaya, India. *Journal of Ethnobiology and Ethnomedicine* 7: 32.

Nayar, M. P. 1996. Hot Spots of Endemic Plants of India, Nepal and Bhutan, Tropical Botanic Garden and Research Institute. Palode, Thiruvananthpuram-695562: 1-252.

Nayar, M. P. and Sastry, A. R. K (Eds.) 1990. Red Data Book of Indian Plants Vol. 3. Botanical Survey of India, Calcutta.

Nayar, M. P. and Sastry, A. R. K. (Eds) 1988. Red Data Book of Indian Plants Vol. 2. Botanical Survey of India, Calcutta.

Nayar, M. P. and Sastry, A. R. K. (Eds.) 1987. Red Data Book of Indian Plants Vol. 1. Botanical Survey of India, Calcutta.

Pala, N. A., Negi, A. K. and Todaria, N. P. 2010. Traditional Uses of Medicinal Plants of Pauri Garhwal, Uttrakhand, *Nature and Science* 8(6): 57-61.

Pandey, A. K., Patra, A. K. and Shukla, P. H. 2005. Medicinal Plants in Satpura Plateau of Madhya Pradesh: Current Status and Future Prospects *Indian Forester* 131(7): 857-883.

Prakash, A. 2011. Uses of Some Threatened and Potential Ethnomedicinal Plants Among the Tribals of Uttar Pradesh and Uttrakhand in India, Forest Biodiversity *Earth's Living Treasure* 93-99.

Samant, S. S., Dhar, U. and Palni, L. M. S. 1998. Medicinal Plants of Indian Himalaya: Diversity Distribution Potential Value. Almora: G.B. Pant Institute of Himalayan Environment and Development.

Singh, G. and Rawat, G. S. 2011. Ethnomedicinal Survey of Kedarnath Wildlife Sanctuary in Western Himalaya, India. *Indian Journal of Fundamental Applied Life Science* 1: 35-36.

Srivastava, S. K. and Singh, D. K. 2005. Glimpses of the Plan Wealth of Uttaranchal. Bishan Singh Mahendra Pal Singh, Deharadun.

Swe, T. and Win, S. 2005. Herbal Gardens and Cultivation of Medicinal Plants in Myanmar Regional Consultation on Development of Traditional Medicine in the South East Asia Region, Department of Traditional Medicine, Ministry of Health, Myanmar, Pyongyang, DPR Korea, World Health Organization (Regional office for South-East Asia): 22-24.

Ved, D. K. and Goriya, G. S. 2008. Demand and Supply of Medicinal Plants in India. Bishan Singh Mahendra Pal Singh, Deharadun & FRLHT, Banglore, India.

Bacopa monnieri (Linn.) Pennel

Acorus calamus Linn.

Rauvolfia serpentina Benth

Baliospermum montanum Muell. Arg.

Costum speciosus (Koenig)Sm

Clerodendrum serratum Linn.

Celastrus paniculatus Willd.

Curculigo orchioides gaerthn

Ilolarrhena antidysenterica Wall

Hemidesmus indicus (Linn.) R.Br.

Gloriosa superba Linn.

Tinospora cordifolia (Willd). Miers.

Medicinal and Nutritional Values of Plants
Edited by: Alka Chauhan and Pawan Kumar 'Bharti'
ISBN: 978-93-5056-883-5
Edition: 2017
Published by: Discovery Publishing House Pvt. Ltd., New Delhi (India)

8 Lentil (*Lens Culinaris* Medikus) Cultivation in India

An Ancient Crop of Modern Times

[1]Sandeep Sharma and [2]Arti Katiyar

ABSTRACT

Lentil (*Lens culinaris* Medikus sub sp. culinaris) commonly known as Masoor, plants are slender, semi-erect annuals legumes with purse like pods containing 1 or 2 lens shaped seeds. The word lentil comes from the Latin lens, and indeed, shaped like the double convex optic lens which took its name from the lentil. Lentils were among the earliest of human kinds plant domesticate and associated with the start of the 'agricultural revolution about 10,000 year ago in the near East. It is among the oldest domesticated crop in the world. It is a cool season food legume playing a significant role in human and animal nutrition as well as soil fertility maintenance. It can be grown in rotation to cereal crops which promote sustainable cereal-based production systems with a potential of fixing free nitrogen reached up to 107 kg ha-1. It is the most important crop because of its high protein content and fast cooking characteristic. The present study tries to analysis the current scenario of lentil, its uses, and constraints to increasing production of lentil in India.

INTRODUCTION

Lentil (*Lens culinaris*) from the family *Leguminosae*, are an ancient Mediterranean crop grown more than 8500 years ago and said to have been found in Egyption tombs dating from 2400BC. Lentils are grown as an annual crop during cool seasons and in areas of limited rainfall. Lentil is a short stature, annual, self-pollinated, high value crop species. Lentil highly nutritious food legume primarily cultivated for seed and eaten as dhal presented in (table 8.1). Lentil is an important rabi crop. It is one of the oldest pulse crops with the potential to grow in dry land areas. In India it is mostly grown in northern plains, central and eastern parts of India. It is grown in about 1053 thousand hectares

---

[1] Senior Research Fellow, Division of Social Sciences, ICAR-Indian Institute of Pulses Research, Kanpur-208024, U.P., (India).
[2] Senior Research Fellow, Division of Crop Protection, ICAR-Indian Institute of Pulses Research, Kanpur-208024, U.P., (India).

of land with the production of about 653000 tons. Global lentil production in 2009 was 4.5 million metric tons, the top producers being Canada, India, Turkey and the United States. Canada is the leading lentil exporting nation. The major importing countries are Spain, Colombia, Egypt, Algeria and Sri Lanka. India, Turkey, Ethiopia, China, Syria, Iran and Bangladesh are among the top ten producers. On average about 70% of global production is consumed in the developing countries where it is produced. About a quarter of global production is from India most of which is consumed in India itself. In 2010 the area of lentil worldwide was 4.2 million hectares and the average worldwide yield was 1.1 metric tons a hectare. Lentil production in India has always been important as it is the one of the most important rabi crops in the country (figure 8.1). India has been producing lentil since 1st century AD and has always been an important producer of the crop. In fact, India was the largest producer of the lentil crop in the world until recently Canada took over the lead leaving India at the second place. Indian production of this crop hovers around 10 lakh metric tons per year that is cultivated on about 14 lakh hectares of land. Masur crop is grown in India in the winter season in the following states.

- Uttar Pradesh
- Madhya Pradesh
- Bihar
- West Bengal
- Rajasthan
- Haryana
- Punjab
- Assam
- Maharashtra

Fig. 8.1: Lentil plants in the field before flowering

Around 90% of the production comes from the top four states in the list pertaining to the eastern and the northern part of the country (Cokkizgin and Munqez 2013, FAOSTAT 2013). The southern part of the country hardly contributes to India's total production. Uttar Pradesh accounts for the maximum production in the country contributing to around 45% of the country's production as well as for the maximum area under masur cultivation (table 8.2). The crop is both cultivated as a primary crop and a secondary crop in the country. Sagar, Jabalpur, Bundelkhand and Bhopal in Madhya Pradesh, Kanpur in Uttar Pradesh and Kota in Rajasthan are the districts where masur is cultivated primarily.

Table 8.1: Nutritional Value of Lentil

S.No.	Nutrient	Amount (100 grms)
1	Ash	2.7 g
2	Carbohydrate	57.09 g
3	Energy	338 kcal
4	Energy (Calories)	1414 kj
5	Fat (Lipids)	0.96 g
6	Fiber, Total dietary	30.5 g
7	Protein	28.06 g
8	Water	11.19 g
9	Calcium (Ca)	51 mg
10	Copper (Cu)	0.852 mg
11	Iron (Fe)	9.02 mg
12	Magnesium (Mg)	107 mg
13	Manganese (Mn)	1.429 mg
14	Phosphorus (P)	454 mg
15	Potassium (K)	905 mg
16	Sodium (Na)	10 mg
17	Zinc (Zn)	3.61 mg
18	Folate food	433 mcg
19	Niacin	2.621 mg
20	Panthothenic acid	1.849 mg
21	Riboflavin	0.245 mg
22	Thiamin	0.475 mg
23	Vitamin A	39I U
24	Vitmin B_6	0.535 mg
25	Vitamin C	6.2 mg
26	Vitamin E	0.33 mg

27	Alanine	1.172g
28	Arginine	2.168g
29	Aspartic acid	3.102g
30	Cystine	0.368g
31	Glutamic acid	4.35g
32	Glycine	1.14g
33	Histidine	0.79g
34	Isoleucine	1.212g
35	Leucine	2.034g
36	Lysine	1.957g
37	Methionine	0.238g
38	Phenyalalanine	1.383g
39	Proline	1.172g
40	Serine	1.293g
41	Threonine	1.006g
42	Tryptophan	0.251g
43	Tyrosine	0.75g
44	Valine	1.392g
45	Fatty acid	0.135g

Source: USDA Nutrient Database

Table 8.2: All India Area, Production and Yield of Lentil

Years	Area (million hectares)	Production (million tons)	Yield (kg/ha)
2000-01	1.48	0.92	619
2001-02	1.47	0.97	664
2002-03	1.38	0.87	634
2003-04	1.39	1.04	743
2004-05	1.47	0.99	675
2005-06	1.51	0.95	629
2006-07	1.47	0.91	621
2007-08	1.31	0.81	622
2008-09	1.38	0.95	693
2009-10	1.48	1.03	697
2010-11	1.60	0.94	591
2011-12	1.56	1.06	678
2012-13	1.42	1.13	797

Source: Directorate of Economics and Statistics, Department of Agriculture and Cooperation.

ORIGIN

Lentils probably originated in the Near East and rapidly spread to Egypt, central and southern Europe, the Mediterranean basin, Ethiopia, Afghanistan, India and Pakistan, China and later to the New World including Latin America (Cubero, 1981; Duke, 1981; Ladizinsky, 1979). It is probably the oldest of grain legumes to be domesticated (Bahl *et al.,* 1993). It is now cultivated in most subtropical and also in the Northern hemisphere such as Canada and Pacific Northwest regions.

BOTANICAL DISCRIPTION

The botanical features of *Lens culinaris* (cultivated lentil) can be described as annual bushy herb, slender almost erect or suberect, much-branched, softly hairy; stems slender, angular, 15-75 cm height (Duke, 1981; Muehlbauer *et al.,* 1985). Ten to sixteen leaflets are subtended on the rachis (40-50 mm); upper leaves have simple tendrils while lower leaves are mucronate (Muehlbauer *et al.,* 1985). "The leaves are alternate, compound, pinnate, usually ending in a tendril or bristly; leaflets 4-7 pairs, alternate or opposite; oval, sessile, 1-2 cm long; stipules small, entire; stipules absent; pods oblong, flattened or compressed, smooth, to 1.3 cm long, 1-2-seeded; seed biconvex, rounded, small, 4-8 mm × 2.2-3 mm, lens-shaped, green, greenish-brown or light red speckled with black; the weight of 100 seeds range from 2 to 8 g; cotyledons red, orange, yellow, or green, bleaching to yellow, often showing through the testa, influencing its apparent color" (Kay, 1979; Duke, 1981; and Muehlbauer *et al.,* 1995). Flowers are small, pale blue, purple, white or pink, in axillary 1-4-flowered racemes; 1-4 flowers are borne on a single peduncle and a single plant can produce upto 10-150 peduncles each being 2.5-5 cm long (Muehlbauer *et al.,* 1985). Flowering proceeds acropetally. The size of seeds increase from the types grown in eastern regions to western types. Two types, namely; macrosperma, found mainly in the Mediterranean region and the New World (seed size ranging from 6 to 9 mm in diameter and yellow cotyledons with little or no pigmentation), and microsperma (2 to 6 mm with red orange or yellow cotyledons) found on the Indian subcontinent, Near East and East Africa, respectively, are known (Hawtin *et al.,*1980; Muehlbauer *et al.*, 1985). The first one includes the Chilean or yellow cotyledon types while the latter includes the small seeded Persian or red cotyledon lentils (Kay, 1979). Germination is hypogeal and this keeps the developing seedlings below ground level which reduces the effects of freezing and other desiccating environmental conditions (Muehlbauer *et al.,*1985).

CLIMATE

Lentil is adapted to cool growing conditions, and the young plants are tolerant of spring frosts. This allows for early spring planting dates. Lentils have been grown extensively in the semi-arid parts of the world, where they have slightly lower yields, but good seed quality. High humidity and excessive rainfall during the season encourages vegetative growth, which prevents good yield and can reduce seed quality. 10 to 12 inches of annual rainfall will produce high yields of good quality seed. Excessive drought and high temperatures during the flowering and pod-fill period also reduce yields.

SOIL

Lentil is adapted to soil types, from sand to clay loam, if there is good internal drainage. Lentil does not tolerate flooded or waterlogged soils, and does best on deep, sandy loam soils high in phosphorus and potassium. Good drainage is required, because even short periods of exposure to waterlogged or flooded field conditions kill plants. A soil pH near 7.0 is best for lentil production.

TYPES OF LENTIL

Lentil-(*Lens culinaris*)

Probably originating in Turkey or Syria, these pulses are smaller than most beans and disk shaped rather than bean shaped. Optical lenses take their name from this shape. Lentils were one of the very first cultivated crops, probably more than 9000 years ago, and are now grown worldwide with varieties in different sizes and colors. They are commonly sold whole, peeled and peeled and split. Cooking times are less than for beans, particularly in dal from so they are seldom soaked before cooking. In India small beans of genus Vigna are sometimes called "lentils".

Black Lentil-(*Beluga lentil*)

These tiny lentils are similar to Puy Lentils but are smaller and most are black rather than mottled, though a few mottled ones are likely to be in the batch. They hold their shape well and become shiny black when cooked, thus the name "beluga" after the black caviar. They are particularly used as an ingredient in salads and soups.

Brown Lentils-(*Green Lentil, Continental Lentil*)

This is your common grocery store in the USA, available in several sizes. It is most sold whole but also in the peeled and split from which is a medium yellow color and called "Yellow Lentils".

Egyptian Lentils

An inexact term but usually referring to either Masoor Dal or Red Lentil, but sometimes to others includes Brown Lentils.

Masoor

Similar to the Red Lentil but much smaller. It is sold whole, peeled and peeled and split. Masoor dal is often cooked mixed with rice because the cooking time is about the same. If a recipe calls for masoor to be soaked at all it probably means whole masoor, otherwise probably dal. Cooked masoor dal will turn a bright yellow color as will red lentils.

Pardina Lentils-(Spanish Brown)

While grown as a significant crop in the US and Canada the largest portion of production is exported to Spain where these lentils are popular.

Puy Lentils-(French green lentil)

These small greenish brown mottled lentils from Puy France are now grown in North America and Italy, but are still found mainly in gourmet outlets at high prices. They are often used in salads and soups because they stay firm and intact when cooked.

Red Lentils

These lentils are similar to Masoor but larger. The most popular cultivar in the US and Canada is Red Chief. They are almost always sold peeled and split to show off their salmon color. Cooked red lentils will be a bright yellow color as will masoor dal.

Tarahumara Pinks

A lentil from Mexico with mottled seeds, grown in semi arid regions.

White Lentils

White lentils are not lentils at all, but rather the split and peeled Urd Bean.

Yellow Lentils

Yellow lentils are the peeled and split form of the regular Brown Lentil.

GROWTH AND DEVELOPMENT STAGES OF THE LENTIL PLANT

The following is a uniform system for the description of the developmental stages of lentil (*Lens culinaris*) that is universally applicable to all growing environments and divergent cultivars. Vegetative growth stages are described by counting nodes on the main stem and continuing the count up the basal primary branch to include the highest fully developed leaf. Reproductive stages R1 and R2 are based on flowering, R3 to R6 on pod and seed development, and R7 and R8 on maturation.

VEGETATIVE GROWTH STAGES

Count the number of visible nodes on the main stem up to the node subtending the basal primary branch, and then continuing the node count up the basal primary branch to include the highest fully developed leaf. The basal primary branch usually develops between nodes 1 to 5.

VE – seedling emergence, cotyledonary node visible

V1 – the first simple leaf has unfolded at the first node

V2 – the second simple leaf has unfolded at the second node

V3 – the first bifoliate leaf has unfolded at the third node

V4 – the second bifoliate leaf has unfolded at the fourth node

V5 – the first multifoliate leaf has unfolded at the fifth node

Vn – the nth multifoliate leaf has unfolded at the nth node

REPRODUCTIVE GROWTH STAGES

Flowering in lentil is indeterminate, occurring from axillary buds on the main stem and branches. It proceeds acropetally from lower to higher nodes.

R1 – early bloom, one open flower at any node

R2 – full bloom, flower open or has opened on nodes 10-13 of the basal primary branch

R3 – early pod, pod on nodes 10-13 of the basal primary branch visible

R4 – flat pod, pod on nodes 10-13 has reached its full length and is largely flat

R5 – early seed, seed in any single pod on nodes 10-13 fill the pod cavity

R6 – full seed, seed on nodes 10-13 fill the pod cavities

PHYSIOLOGICAL MATURITY

R7 – the leaves start yellowing and 50% of the pods have turned yellow

R8 – 90% of pods on the plant are golden-brown

CULTURAL PRACTICES

Land Preparation

The soil should be made friable and weed free so that seeding could be done at a uniform depth. On heavy soils, one deep ploughing followed by two to three cross harrowing should be given. In the case of light soil less tillage is needed to prepare ideal seedbeds. After harrowing, the field should be levelled by giving a light slope to facilitate irrigation.

Varieties

Popular varieties of lentil are given in table 8.3.

Table 8.3: Popular Varieties of Lentil

S.No.	Varieties	Year of release	Sources	Duration	Special features	Average yield (q/ha)	Area of adoption
1	Pant L 406	1979	GBPUA&T, Pantnagar	140-145	Small seeds, resistant to rust, tolerant to wilt	15-18	NWPZ, NEPZ
2	Pant L 234	1980	GBPUA&T, Pantnagar	135-140	Medium large seeds, tolerant to rust and wilt	16-18	U.P.
3	Asha (B 77)	1980	Berhampore (WB)	120-125	Small seeds, white flowers	15-18	West Bengal
4	Pant L 639	1981	GBPUA&T, Pantnagar	130-135	Small seeds, resistant to rust, tolerant to wilt	16-20	NWPZ, NEPZ
5	VL Masoor 1	1982	VPKAS, Almora	165-170	Small & black seeds, torerant to rust & wilt	16-18	Uttarakhand
6	LL-56	1983	PAU, Ludhiana	150-155	Small seeds, resistant to rust	16-18	Punjab
7	Malika (K-75)	1986	CSAUA&T, Kanpur	130-135	Large seeds, tolerance to rust and wilt	18-22	NEPZ, CZ
8	LL 147	1987	PAU, Ludhiana	140-145	small seeds, tolerant to rust & wilt	15-20	Punjab
9	Sapna (LH 84-8)	1991	CCS HAU, Hisar	135-140	Large seeds, tolerance to rust and wilt	18-20	NWPZ
10	Jawahar lentil 1	1991	JNKVV, Jabalpur	120-125	Medium large seeds, early maturity	16-18	M.P.
11	Pant Lentil 4	1993	GBPUA&T, Pantnagar	130-135	Small seeds, resistant to rust & tolerant to wilt	18-22	NWPZ
12	Priya (DPL-15)	1995	IIPR, Kanpur	130-135	Large seeds, tolerance to rust and wilt	16-20	NWPZ
13	Pusa Vaibhav (L-4147)	1996	IARI, New Delhi	130-135	Small seeds, resistant to rust & tolerant to wilt	18-22	NWPZ
14	Narendra Masoor 1 (NDL 92-1)	1997	NDUA&T, Faizabad	120-130	Large seeds, resistant to rust, tolerant to wilt	18-20	U.P.
15	Sheri (DPL-62)	1997	IIPR, Kanpur	130-135	Extra large seeds, resistant to rust & tolerant to wilt	18-20	NWPZ
16	Pant L 5	1999	GBPUA&T, Pantnagar	130-135	Large seeds, resistant to rust, tolerant to wilt and ascochyt blight	18-22	U.P.

17	Jawahar lentil 3 (SLC-6)	1999	JNKVV, Jabalpur	115-120	Large seeds, wilt tolerant	18-20	CZ
18	Noori (IPL-81)	2000	IIPR, Kanpur	110-120	Large seeds, tolerance to rust and wilt	18-20	CZ
19	LL 699	2001	PAU, Ludhiana	140-145	Tolerant to rust & blight	12-15	Punjab
20	VL Masoor 125	2002	VPKAS, Almora	140-145	Small black seed, toerant to wilt and root rot	16-18	NHZ
21	KLS 218	2005	CSAUA&T, Kanpur	120-125	Small seeds	15-17	NEPZ
22	HUL-57	2005	BHU, Varanasi	120-130	Small seeds, resistant to rust	18-20	NEPZ & NHZ
23	VL Masoor-507	2006	VPKAS, Almora	160-170	Large seed, tolerant to wilt	15-17	NHZ
24	Angoori (IPL-406)	2007	IIPR, Kanpur	120-155	Extra large seeds, resistant to rust	16-18	NWPZ
25	Pant Lentil 6	2009	GBPUA&T, Pantnagar	125-145	Large seeds, resistant to rust, wilt, Ascochyta blight	16-18	Uttarakhand
26	Pant Lentil 7	2009	GBPUA&T, Pantnagar	125-145	Large seeds, light grey seed colour, resistant to rust, wilt, Ascochyta blight and pod borer	16-18	Uttarakhand
27	Shalimar Masoor-2	2013	SKUAST-K, Srinagar	200-205	Large seeds, Protein content of 23.03%, Mpderately resistant to wilt and rust resistant to white grub	12-13	Kashmir
28	RVL 31	2014	RAK, Sehore	110-115	Large seeds, resistant to wilt	18-19	M.P.
31	KLB 345 (Shekhar 4)	2014	CSAUA&T, Kanpur	11-115	Large seeds, resistant to wilt and rust	18-20	U.P.
29	KLB 2008-4 (Krati)	2015	CSAUA&T, Kanpur	115-120	Large seeds, resistant to wilt	18-20	U.P.
30	KLS 09-3 (Krish)	2015	CSAUA&T, Kanpur	105-110	Small seeds, resistant to wilt and rust	18-20	U.P.

NWPZ = North West Plain Zone, NEPZ – North East Plain Zone, CZ = Central Zone, NHZ = North Hill Zone

SOWING

The seed should be pure, free from inert matter, disease and insect. Free, true to the type and free from weed seeds. Very old seed should not be used as it has very low germinating capacity.

SEED TREATMENT

Dip the seeds in 5% salt solution after properly winnowing. The heavy seeds will remain at the bottom while light seeds, will float at the top. Then remove those seeds floating and carefully wash the heavy seeds with clean water for 3-4 times. Dry up these seeds in the sun before sowing. To avoid the attack of soil borne diseases, treat the seeds before sowing with fungicides such as Captan, Bavistin, Brassicol or Thiram @ 2.5 g per kg of seed. This treatment has proved very useful in bringing down the incidence of the soil as well as seed borne diseases in early stages of growth.

RHIZOBIUM INOCULATION

Rhizobium inoculation of lentil has been considered an important factor for increasing yield. Method of culture preparation and inoculation is described below:

1. Prepare a 10% sugar/gur solution and boil it for 15 minutes.
2. Cool the solution at room temperature.
3. Put the Rhizobium culture product of 250 gm with the solution and mix it thoroughly.
4. Mix the seeds with the solution properly, till all the seeds are covered with a thin layer of Rhizobium.
5. Spread the seed on gunny bags m the shade.
6. When the seeds dry, collect and keep it in bags for sowing.

It has been proved that the seeds treated with Rhizobium culture can yield 25-56% more yield than the untreated one.

SEED RATE

The normal seed rate is 30-40 kg/hectare. This is increased to 50-60 kg/ha in case of late sowing. But try to avoid the late sowing as it matures late and gives low yield.

SPACING

Lentil crop is preferred to be sown in lines than by broadcast method. The row to row spacing should be 20-30 cm and it is reduced to 20-25 cm in case of late sowing. Lentil seeds should be sown at a shallower depth of 3-4 centimeters.

TIME OF SOWING

The seed should be sown timely to get the optimum yield. Middle of October is the most suitable time for sowing lentil. Delay in sowing causes reduction in yield, but the magnitude of reduction is large after 15th November.

METHOD OF SOWING

Generally the seed is sown by broadcast method or by using a fertilizer cum seed drill. Utera cultivation is possible in the standing paddy crop, where moisture is sufficient for the germination of the seed. After harvest of the paddy the residual moisture in the soil can be made use for growing lentil. In moisture deficient soils, sowing may be done by pora method. The line sowing method should be given preference to get more yield and to perform inter cultural operation such as weeding, hoeing, irrigations, etc. easily and quickly.

CROP ROTATION

Lentil is generally grown after the harvest of kharif crops or as the whole crop of the year. The most common rotations are jowar-lentil, cotton-lentil, paddy-lentil, fallow-lentil, bajra-lentil, ground nut-lentil and maize-lentil.

INTERCROPPING

Lentil is grown with mustard, barley, toria, etc. Lentil and gram can be grown as mixed crop since both the crops have similar climatic requirements. But lentil being hardier than gram, is capable of withstanding drought, water logging and delayed sowing. So keeping in view the above benefits intercropping and mixed cropping system can be practiced widely to boost the production. Lentil is also grown as an intercrop in autumn sugarcane. Two lines of lentil may be sown 30 cm apart in the centre of two sugarcane rows. Thus, the distance between sugarcane and lentil rows will also be 30 cm.

MANURES AND FERTILIZERS

Generally lentil is grown without fertilizers and manures. Nodulation by adequate inoculation is essential for the growth of the crop. Get the soil tested, as it becomes important to assess fertility status of the soil. If the soil test is not possible add the following fertilizers as basal dose. Add 20-30 kg nitrogen, 50-60 kg phosphorus and 40-50 kg potash per hectare.

IRRIGATION

Lentil is mostly grown in unirrigated areas. It can tolerate drought conditions to some extent. It requires 5-6 irrigations depending upon the climate, rainfall, and availability of the irrigation facilities. First irrigation should be given 45 days after planting and second, if needed, at pod filling stage. Excess watering may affect the crop performance adversely.

WEED CONTROL

Weeds do much harm to the lentil crop. It is slow growing in early stages and, therefore, suffers adversely from competition with weeds. The first weeding is done 25-30 days after sowing and the second when the crop is 40-45 days old. The important weeds which infest lentil crop are bathua (*Chenopodium, alhum*), gajri (*Fumaria parviflora*), chatrimatri (*Lathyms spp*), ankari (*Vicia sativa*), kateli (*Cirsium arvense*), and senji (*Melilotus alba*). Weeds can be controlled by spraying, weedicides like Basalin 0.75 kg a. i. per hectare dissolved in 800-1000 litres of water as pre-planting spray or Pre emergence application of Pendimethalin @ 1.25 kg/ha. One manual hand weeding at 40-50 days after sowing can also effectively control the seasonal weeds.

DISEASE CONTROL

Lentil is attacked by a number of diseases at different stages of its growth. It has been observed that these diseases cause 30-50% loss in the yield. Therefore, these diseases must be kept under control. The important diseases of lentil are described here.

1. Powdery Mildew

The disease is caused by a fungus *Erysiphe polygoni*. On the lower surface of the leaves small whitish patches about three months after sowing the seed are seen. These patches spread as whitish powdery mass on pods, stems, leaves, etc. Under severe attack both the surface of these plant parts are affected. It is one of the serious diseases of the lentil-crop.

Control

1. Spraying of 3% wettable Sulfur 85% DP (500 l/ha) or benomyl 50% WP, tridemorph 80% EC (1 l/ha).
2. Remove or destroy the plant debris.
3. Use disease free seeds.
4. Follow long duration crop rotation.
5. Sow disease resistant varieties.

2. Rust

The disease is caused by fungus *Uromyces fabae*. Pink to brown pustules appear on sterns and leaves. Later, these pustules turn black. In severe cases the plants may dry (figure 8.2). All the green parts of the plant are affected. The disease appears the field from January onwards causing extensive damage to the crop.

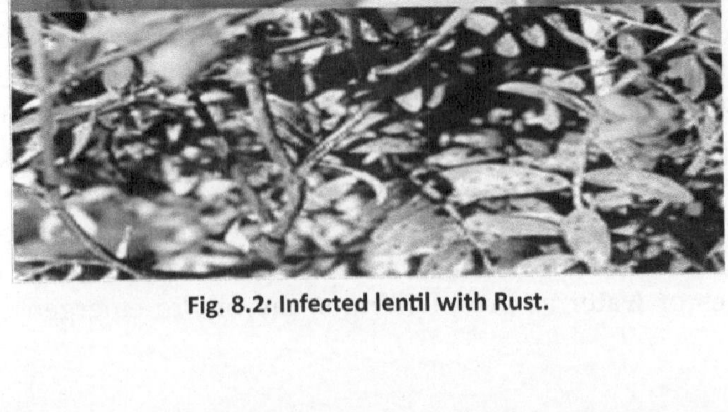

Fig. 8.2: Infected lentil with Rust.

Control

1. Spray Dithane M-45 (75%). Two sprays at an interval of 15 days are needed.
2. Grow resistant varieties like Pant-L-406, L-9-12, etc.
3. Remove the affected plants and burn them.

3. Seedling Mortality

The disease is caused by a fungus *Fusarium oxysporum.* The seedlings start drying up within a month after sowing. The seedlings may turn yellow and then dry up.

It is one of the most dangerous diseases of the lentil. It is found in almost all the lentil growing areas. If not controlled properly well in the, the crop loss may go up to 30-40 per cent.

Control

1. Grow only resistant varieties like Pant-L-406.
2. Treat the seeds with Benornyl, a systemic fungicide, @ 2 g/kg of seed.
3. Delay planting up to mid-November.
4. Remove the affected plants and burn them.
5. Adopt 4-5 years crop rotation.

4. Downy Mildew

It is caused by *Peronospora lentis*. Light greenish to yellow spots appear on the upper surface of the leaf, whereas brownish cottony growth of fungus appears on the lower side of the leaf opposite to the upper side spots. The plant growth is stunted and plant remains dwarf. The plant in the later stages of growth is af fected by this disease. It is a dangerous disease as it affects the whole part of the leaf. The leaflets of the lower branches are more severely affected by this disease.

Control

1. Treat the seeds with Agrosan G.N. (0.2 g/kg of seed.
2. Adopt 3-4 years crop rotation to reduce borne inoculum of the fungus.
3. Remove all the affected plants and bur.

5. Wilt

This disease is caused by a fungus *Fusarium oxysporum lentis*. The disease affects the plant in two stages viz seedling stage and adult stage. The disease appears after 20 days of planting. The roots of the plant remain undeveloped and become light brown in colour (figure 8.3). Leaves become yellow. Plants start drying and then die. It is a serious disease of lentil. The disease is more common in sandy loam soils. It causes 20-30% loss in crop yield.

Fig. 8.3: Showing Wilt in Lentil.

Control

1. Grow disease resistant varieties like Pant-L-406.
2. Follow a four-year crop rotation. This will help in reducing the disease incidence.
3. Use healthy seeds.
4. Remove the affected plants from the field and burn them.
5. Keep the field clean from weeds, etc.

PEST CONTROL

Lentils are attacked by insects wherever they are cultivated. Preharvest pests include soil insects that attack seeds soon after planting or that attack the stems and roots of seedlings. These include seedcorn maggots [*Delia platura* (Meigen)], wireworms (*Limonius* spp. and *Ctenicera* spp.), cutworms (*Agrotis* spp.), and larvae of weevils (Sitona spp.). Thrips (*Frankliniella* spp.), aphids [*Aphis craccivora* (Koch) and *Acyrthosiphon pisum* (Harris)], leaf weevils [*Sitona lineatus* (L.)], lepidopterous larvae (*Helicoverpa* and *Spodoptera* spp.), and grasshoppers feed on leaves, stems, and flowers. The important pests which attack the lentil crop are described below:

1. Pod Borer

Pod borer damages the crop at pod formation stage. The caterpillar defoliates the tender leaves, bores the green pods and feeds upon the ripening grains (figure 8.4).

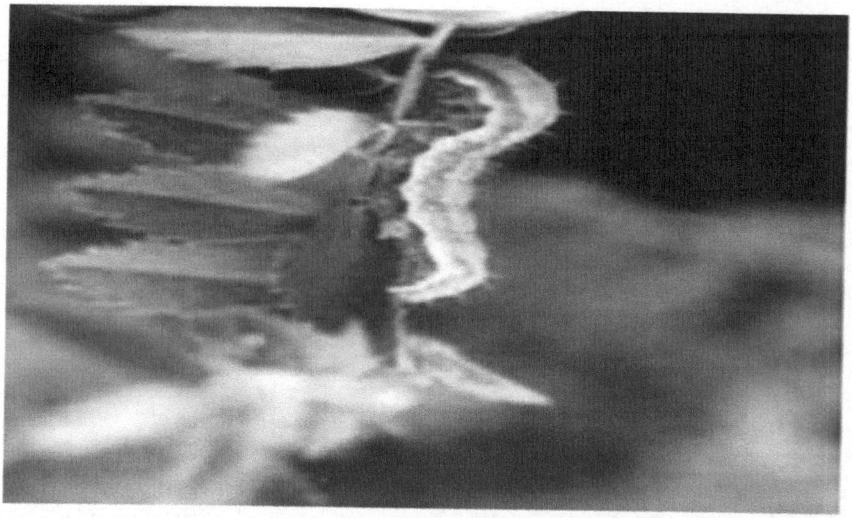

Fig. 8.4: Showing pod borer infestation in lentil.

Control

1. Spray with monocrotophos 36% SL, Chloropyriphos 20% EC, synthetic pyrethroid and Deltamethrin 11% EC and other at a time of flowering early pod setting.
2. Grow pest resistant varieties.

2. Cut Worm

The cut worm is a serious pest in low lying areas where fields are cloudy. The larvae of this insect remain hidden during the day time and cause damage during night hours. The caterpillars cut the plant at ground level. The pest is sporadic in nature. Cloudy fields are worst hit by this pest. The caterpillars are gray in colour.

Control

1. Deep plough the field between crops.
2. Cutworms are difficult to control especially in epidemic situation.
3. Flood the field during the morning or evening hours. The caterpillars will float on water. Thus can be separated mechanically.

3. Aphids

Aphid clusters are observed on the branches and leaves (figure 8.5). They slick the sap of plant resulting in suppressed growth.

Control

1. Spray with neem oil 3000 ppm @2 ml/l slse spray with systemic or contact insecticides to protect susceptible crops.

Fig. 8.5: Showing aphids infestation in lentil.

HARVESTING AND YIELD

The crop matures in 100-160 days depending upon the variety, climatic condition, soil fertilizers, etc. The leaves turn reddish-brown and the plant becomes dry. The pods also turn reddish brown. When pressed with thumb or finger, the pods open and seeds corne out. The plants and pods should not be allowed to become I too ripe, otherwise a large quantity of produce may be lost due to shattering.

The crop should be harvested in the morning hours when dew is there and the shattering of seeds may not take place. The plants are usually cut with a *gandasa* or sickle from 7-10 cm above the ground. The harvested plants should be left in the sun for drying before threshing. The remaining portion of the plant after harvest of the crop is cut and used as fuel. The leaves are fed to cattle or used as fuel. The leaves are also decomposed in compost pits and used as compost.

The harvested plants are dried in the sun on turpoline or cement floor. Threshing is done either by beating the plants, with sticks or by trampling under the feet of bullocks. In advanced countries, the farms are big enough and the production is also large, so the threshers are used for threshing the crop. The thresher mini mise the cost of threshing (figure 8.6).

After threshing the grains are cleaned by removing the pods, leaves, etc. The dead grains are also removed. Since they are lighter in weight, they can be removed by winnowing easily. The cleaned product is then dried in the sun. The average yield of grains obtained is about 20-25 quintals per hectare under proper management practices.

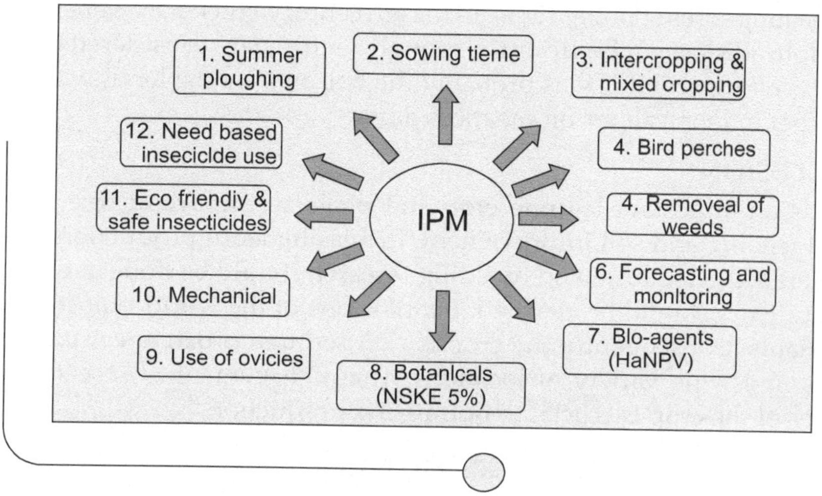

Fig. 8.6: Integrated Pest Management Strategies for lentil

STORAGE

Bring down the moisture of grains to 12% by drying in the sun. The grains are then packed in gunny bags. The bags are sealed. The store rooms should be properly cleaned and fumigated. Close all the holes of rats, keep the bags on the wooden racks in stalls. Keep some distance between the two stalls (6-8 bags in one stall).

USES

Because of its high average protein content and fast cooking characteristics lentil is the most desired legume in many regions (Raghuvanshi & Singh, 2009). Lentil seeds contain 1-2% fat, 24–32%. Some important uses are mentioned below:

1. Lentil is used as a dal. The grain is just converted into split pulse by the removal of skin and separation of the fleshy cotyledons. It is a rich source of calcium, iron, niacin, etc.
2. It is a good source of protein in the Indian diets as majority of population is vegetarian. It contains about 11% water, 25% protein and 60% carbohydrates.
3. It is grown as mixed crop and thus compensates the failure of the companion crop.
4. It is used as a cover crop to check the soil erosion in problem areas.
5. The dry leaves, stems, branches, empty pods, and broken bits are used as cattle feed.

MEDICINAL USES

Lentils are supposed to remedy constipation and other intestinal afflictions. "In India, lentils are poultice onto the ulcers that follow smallpox and other slow-healing sores" (Duke, 1981). In the 6th century, chickpeas were believed to be an aphrodisiac; while curiously enough, lentils were considered to have the opposite effect, and this was probably the reason why the lentil was included in the diet in monasteries on meatless days.

CONCLUSION

Lentil is an important legume crop and plays an important role in human, animal feeding and soil improvement. Increasing lentil production should be considered. Agricultural and breeding research should be done and its genetic characteristics should be clarified. Lentil is one of the world's most important food plants. Consequently the crop is exposed to a broad spectrum of insect species in a wide variety of locations. The management of insect pests and diseases of the crop is crucial to optimizing production.

REFERENCES

Adsule, R.N., S.S. Kadam, and H.K. Leung. 1989. Lentil. In: CRC Handbook of World Food Legumes (eds. D.K. Salunkehe and S.S. Kadam). Boca Raton, Florida, USA: CRC Press.

Bahl, P.N., S. Lal and B.M. Sharma. 1993. An Overview of the Production and Problems in Southeast Asia. p. 1-10. In: W. Erskine and M.C. Saxena (eds.), Lentil in South Asia. Proceedings of the Seminar on Lentils in South Asia. ICARDA, Aleppo, Syria.

Cubero, J.I. 1981. Origin, Taxonomy and Domestication. p. 15-38. In: C. Webb and G. Hawtin (eds.), Lentils. C.A.B., London, UK.

Cokkizgin A., Munqez J.Y. (2013) Lentil: Origin, Cultivation Techniques, Utilization and Advances in Transformation. Agricultural Science 1(1): 55-62.

FAOSTAT (2013) Agricultural Data on Primary Crops.

Duke, J.A. 1981. Handbook of Legumes of World Economic Importance. Plenum Press, New York. p. 52-57.

Food and Agriculture Organization of the United Nations. 1996. Production Yearbook. Rome, Italy.

Hawtin, G.C., K.B. Singh and M.C. Saxena. 1980. Some Recent Development in the Understanding and Improvement of Cicer and Lens. pp. 613-623.

In: R.J. Summerfield and A.H. Bunting (eds.), Advances in Legumes Science. Proceedings of the International Legume Conference, Kew, 31 July-4 August 1978, Royal Botanic Garden, Kew, the Missouri Botanical Garden, and the University of Reading, UK.

Huisman, J. and A.F.B. van der Poel. 1994. Aspects of the Nutritional Quality and Use of Cool Season Food Legumes in Anmal Feed. p. 53-76.

In: F.J. Muehlbauer and W.J. Kaiser (eds.), Expanding the Production and Use of Cool Season Food Legumes. Kluwer Academic Publishers. Dordrecht, The Netherlands.

Hulse, J.H. 1990. Nature, Composition and Utilization of Grain Legumes. p. 11-27.

In: ICRISAT. Uses of Tropical Grain Legumes: Proceedings of a Consultants' Meeting, 27-30 Mar, 1989. ICRISAT Center, India, Patancheru, A.P. 502 324. India: ICRISAT.

Jumbunathan R., H.L. Blain, K.S. Dhindsa, L.A. Hussein, K. Kogure, L. Li-Juan and M.M. Youseef. 1994. Diversifying Use of Cool Season Food Legumes Through Processing. pp. 98-112. In: F.J. Muehlbauer and W.J. Kaiser (eds.) Expanding the Production and Use of Cool Season Food Legumes. Kluwer Academic Publishers. Dordrecht, The Netherlands.

Kay, D. 1979. Food legumes. Tropical Development and Research Institute (TPI). TPI Crop and Product Digest No. 3. p. 48-71. UK.

Ladizinsky, G. 1979. The Origin of Lentil and Wild Gene Pool. Euphytica 28:179-187.

Muehlbauer, F.J., R.W. Short, R.J. Summerfield, K.J. Morrison and D.G. Swan. 1981. Description and Culture of Lentils. Cooperative Extension, College of Agriculture, Washington State University and USDA-ARS. EB 0957.

Muehlbauer, F.J., J.I. Cubero and R.J. Summerfield. 1985. Lentil (Lens culinaris Medic.). p. 266-311. In: R.J. Summerfield and E.H. Roberts (eds.), Grain Legume Crops. Collins, 8 Grafton Street, London, UK.

Muehlbauer, F.J., W.J. Kaiser, S.L. Clement, and R.J. Summerfield. 1995. Production and Breeding of Lentil. Advances in Agronomy 54:283-332.

Muehlbauer, F.J., 1996. Advances in the Production of Cool Season Legumes. American Journal of Alternative Agriculture 11:71-76.

Murray, G.A., D. Eser, L.V. Gusta and G. Eteve. 1994. Winter Hardiness in Pea, Lentil, Faba Bean and Chickpea. p. 831-843. In: R.J. Summerfield (ed.), World Crops: Cool Season Food Legumes. Kluwer Academic Publishers, Dordrecht the Netherlands.

Robertson, L.D., K.B. Singh, W. Erskine and Ali M. Abd El Moneim. 1996. Useful Genetic Diversity in Germplasm Collections of Food and Forage Legumes from West Asia and North Africa. Germplasm Resources and Crop Evolution 43:447-460. Kluwer Academic Publishers, Dordrecht, The Netherlands.

Simon C.J. and R.M. Hannan, 1995. Development and Use of Core Subsets of Cool Season Food Legume Germpasm Collection. Hort Science 30:907.

Van der Maesen, L.J.G. 1972. *Cicer* L., A Monograph of the Genus, with Special Reference to the Chickpea (*Cicer arietinum* L.), Its Ecology and Cultivation, Commun. Agric. University. Wageningen.

Van Emden, H.F., S.L. Ball and M.R. Rao. 1988. Pest Disease and Weed Problems in Pea Lentil and Faba Bean and Chickpea. p. 519-534. In: R.J. Summerfield (ed.), World Crops: Cool Season Food Legumes. ISBN 90-247-3641-2. Kluwer Academic Publishers, Dordrecht, The Netherlands.

Williams, P.C., R.S. Bhatty, S.S. Deshpande, L.A. Hussein and G.P. Savage. 1994. Improving Nutritional Quality of Cool Season Food Legumes. p. 113-129. In: F.J. Muehlbauer and W.J. Kaiser (eds.), Expanding the Production and Use of Cool Season Food Legumes. Kluwer Academic Publishers, Dordrecht, The Netherlands.

Williams, P.C. and U. Singh. 1988. Quality Screening and Evaluation in Pulse Breeding. p. 445-457. In: R.J. Summerfield (ed.), World Crops: Cool Season Food Legumes. Kluwer Academic Publishers, Dordrecht The Netherlands.

Zohary, D. 1973. The Wild Proginator and Place of Origin of the Cultivated Lentil: *Lens culinaris*. Economic Botany 26:326-332.

Medicinal and Nutritional Values of Plants
Edited by: Alka Chauhan and Pawan Kumar 'Bharti'
ISBN: 978-93-5056-883-5
Edition: 2017
Published by: Discovery Publishing House Pvt. Ltd., New Delhi (India)

9 Influence of Potassium Nutrition on Physiology, Yield and Nutritional Quality of Vegetables

[1]Priyanka Pal, [1]Narender Singh

ABSTRACT

Vegetables adorn a significant role in human nutrition and necessary for cognizant diet as they supply plenty of phytonutriceuticals. Every vegetable has its benefits in human diet since ensure an adequate intake of most vitamins and nutrients, dietary fiberwhich imports lots of desired nutrients accord to fix several problems regarding nutrition. Vegetables act as source of phytochemicals which help in get rid of many malignant human disease. Vegetables help to fight malnutrition and obesity especially in developing countries. Over increasing world population demand higher food which derives need to increase vegetable yield. Considering this demand, efforts are being contrived to use conventional methods of applying nutrient for increasing the yield per unit area.Foliar spray of nutrients is important in enhancing vegetable growth and development. Potassium is the most important inorganic osmotic active substance and 'quality element' for crop production with strongest influence on various biochemical and physiological parameters of vegetables. This article constructs a review and confers the use of methods which enhance growth and yield, nutritional quality and health prosperity of vegetables.

INTRODUCTION

Vegetables crops are important constituents of agriculture and nutritional security due to their short duration, nutritional richness, high yield, economic viability and ability to generate on-farm and off-farm employment. Vegetables are essential in the diet of humans in many parts of the world as they make available many vitamins (C, A, B1, B6, B9, E), plant fiber, mineral elements, carbohydrates, proteins and phytochemicals (Wargovich, 2000; Dias and Ryder, 2011). It hold a wide variety of minerals and biologically active compounds well known as phytochemicals like alkaloids, flavonoids, tannins and steroids imparting health benefits beyond basic nutrition. Some phytochemicals acting

[1] Plant Physiology Lab, Department of Botany, Kurukshetra University, Kurukshetra, Haryana, India

as strong antioxidants protects against free-radical damage by modification in metabolic activity and processes that alter the course of tumor cells, so help in reducing the risk of many deadly human diseases (Southon, 2000; Herrera *et al.*, 2011).

A world Health Report 2007showed that unbalanced diets with stumpy vegetable intake and little consumption of carbohydrates and dietary fiber are estimated to account 2.7 million deaths per year and contributes to the top 10 risk factors leads to mortality (Dias, 2011). Intake of vegetables in the daily diethold overall soundhealth, improvement in vision and cut down hazard for some forms of cancer, heart disease, diabetes, stroke, anaemia, gastric ulcer, rheumatoid arthritis and other cardiovascular diseases (Mullie and Clarys, 2011).

In 2014-15, 2019342 tons of the total vegetables produced while in 2013, 950 million tonsvegetables were produced in world. China produces half of worldwide vegetables, ranks first in vegetable production. Major vegetable producing countries of the world: China (51.6% world production), India (14% world production), USA (3.1% world production), Turkey (2.2% world production), and Egypt (2% world production) in 2013-2014. India with vegetable production of 146.55 million tons is the second largest producer of vegetables contributing 14% of world's vegetable production. During 2012-13, India produced 162.19 million metric tons of vegetables covering area under cultivation of 9.21 million hectares as per National Horticulture Database (National Horticulture Board, India, 2013). Major vegetable growing states in India are West Bengal, Bihar, Andhra Pradesh, Uttar Pradesh, Karnataka, Gujarat, and Tamil Nadu. Total vegetable exports from India was accounted for Rs. 4702.78 crores in 2014-15, sharing 2.25% of total agricultural exports and 0.23 % of total national exports during the period. Nonetheless India shares only 0.1% in the global market. With this projected population growth 1330 million in 2020, 1570 million in 2040 and 1650 million in 2050, provoke increase in production by 190, 225 and 240 million tons of vegetables by respective years. New practices needed to enhance the vegetable yields for production of more and better food in order to meet the demand of over increasing world population, especially in the developing countries.Production targets are likely to further increase by understanding physiological and biochemical regulation of growth and development.

Fertilization is a dynamic process for soil and crops. Foliar nutrient spray is an environmentally friendly fertilization method which provides rapid and effective response to plant requirement, regardless of soil conditions. Its application during the growth and development can improve nutrient balance of crops, which may in turn lead to an increase in yield and quality (Kolota *et al.*, 2001). Fertilizers are the most important factors that affect vegetable crop production. In vegetables, the foliar application of nutrients results in positive economic effect and increase yield (Jaskulski *et al.*, 2007). Application of nutrients as foliar spray is preferred for intensive and profitable cultivation of tomato crop (Oded and Uzi, 2003). Foliar application is also results in less ground water pollution.

Among all the nutrients, potassium(K) is the third macronutrient after nitrogen and phosphorus required for plant growth and sustainable crop production as it predominantly exists as a free or absorptive bound cation which can be displaced very easily on the cellular level as well as in the whole plant(Abbas *et al.*, 2011). It is the most important inorganic osmotic active substance and 'quality element' for crop production with strongest influence on various biochemical and physiological parameters of vegetables (Marschner, 1995; Cakmak, 2005). Potassium is not an incorporated component of plant molecules, in opposite to P and N which are constituents of nucleic acid, proteins, phospholipids, ATP, etc. It is also important for pH stabilization and neutralization of negative charge of organic acids and inorganic anions such as Cl^- and SO_4^{2-} (Bennett, 1993). Potassium improves nitrogen utilization by enhancing utilization of amino acids for protein synthesis (Xu *et al.*, 1992). K involves in regulation of vegetative growth,photosynthesis, respiration, protein synthesis, stomatal regulation as contributes in enhancing water and gaseous exchange (Eshghi *et al.*, 2012; Shafeek *et al.*, 2013). Potassium involve in activation of many enzymes needed for growth and metabolism, phloem transport, maintenance of the osmotic potential of the cells in addition to cell extension, wallthickness and stability, energy, plant stress responses and postharvest shelf life (Cherel, 2004; Marschner, 2012). Potassium is essential in meristematic growth through its involvement in maintenance of optimum osmotic potential and turgor pressure required for cell expansion. Potassium play also essential role in enhancing the effect of phytoharmones involved in growth of meristematic tissues (Mengel and Arneke, 1982). Adequate K nutrition improves tissue stability and crop resistance to lodging, pest and diseases through thickened leaf cuticle and epidermal cell wall, stimulation of lignification's and silicification by its influence on plant metabolism (Hardter, 2003; Pervez *et al.*, 2007).

Over increasing population growth demand higher food which derives need to increase vegetable yield. Considering this demand, efforts are being contrived to use conventional methods of applying nutrient for increasing the yield per unit area. Vegetables help to fight malnutrition, obesity and have many other medicinal properties as it contains plenty of vitamins and minerals. Some vegetables are eaten as raw so nutrients are not loss during cooking (Kimura and Itokawa, 1990). Adequate potassium intake helps in maintain blood pressure, bone mineral density (Zhu *et al.*, 2009). Consumers concern in total foods with adorn nutritional qualities is at an all-time high and too many consumers are choosing foods on the basis of their health benefits. This article makes a review and discusses the nutritional quality and health benefits of the major groups of vegetables and moreover enhancing their nutritional quality by applying potassium.

Nutrition Requirement

Potassium (K) is the seventh most lavish element in the earth's crust. Essentiality of potassium in plant growth was first time recognized by Liebig (1841). K is a non-constitutive element serve as buffers, necessary for the maintenance of conducting tissues which is not replaceable, so the plant needs to maintain the K concentration between 80-200 mm mol^{-1} for its cytoplasmic functions (Leigh and jones, 1984). Requirement of potassium in vegetable crops is high and its failure in meeting K demands may result in development of symptoms which lower their quality. K requirement of crops largely depend on plant species, yield, levels, varietal differences, plant associations competition. Total potassium requirement of a crop is a function of K content in various plant parts and the dry weight produced in a single growing period. Root and tuber crops are heavy feeders of potassium. Plant which show high K utilization result in large dry matter yield. Generally K needed by crops followed the order: fruit crops > vegetables > pulses and oil seeds > cereals. Uptake concentrations of K in some horticultural crops, expressed as mmol $l^{-1}$and in percent of the total sum of ions in mmol l^{-1}.

Table 9.1: Uptake Concentrations of K in Some Horticultural Crops, Expressed as mmol l^{-1} and in Percent of the Total Sum of Ions in mmol l^{-1}.

Crop	K	%
Cucumber	6.6	27
Lettuce	8.7	40
Radish (summer)	4.5	28
Radish (winter)	16.5	27
Sweet pepper	4.5	25
Tomato	6.5	31
Rose	1.9	21

Source: Soneeveld (1997), Voogt (1988,1993) and Soneeveld and Van den Bos (1999)

Growth and Development

K scarcity affect many metabolic processes, like the rate of photosynthesis, the rate of translocation and enzyme systems while the rate of dark respiration is increased at the same time, resulted in reduction of plant growth and quality.

Potassium vs. Growth of Crops

Potassium requirement of plants during growth period

(*a*) *Seedling stage:* Most crop seeds contain 0.4 to 1.00 percent potassium. For very early development, this quantity is sufficient for germination but will not sustain growth for long period. There is not much rapid uptake of K at this stage in most of the vegetables.

(b) *Vegetative growth stage:* In most annuals, the phase of rapid vegetative enlargement is characterized by progressive increase in the absolute amounts of inorganic elements such as potassium. In potato crop, 14 pounds of soil potassium was removed by the crop in the first 50 days after setting the seed on an acre basis. Twenty pounds was absorbed in the next 10 days and during the period between 60 to 80 days, an average of 4 pounds was absorbed per acre per day.

(c) *Flowering:* It is well established that during anthesis, little much acceleration particularly in vegetables mineral uptake and synthesis of organic compounds occur which results ingradual increase in K uptake.

(d) *Fruit or seed formation:* Many investigations have found that, during early stages of fruit or seed formation, there may be a marked increase in mineral absorption by roots as well as metabolism in younger tissues of the plant. Bidari *et al.,* (2004) noted a substantial gain in potassium in chilies during this period. The main physiological change at this stage involves the diversion of inorganic and organic reserves to reproductive organs. Adequate supply of potassium has been found vital to secure a high rate of fruit set and good quality.

Source: B. I. Bidari and N. S. Hebsur (2010).

The findings of the experiments indicated that the vegetative growth and yield of Vegetable crops was greatly improved by different concentrations of K. K. treated plants showed significantly higher value for plant height and leaf area, fresh and dry weight, Leaves per plant, fresh and dry weight of plants.

Table 9.2: Effects of Potassium on Growth Attribues of Vegetable Crops

Vegetable crop	Conc. of K	Plant	Leaf no.	Leaf	Fresh wt. of plant (g)	Dry wt. of plant (g)	No. of fruit/ plant	Average fruit wt.(g)	Total yield g/ Plant
Cucumber	0 (g/l)	117	140.0	34	466	67.0	20.80	115.0	2392.0
	2.5 (g/l)	250.5	165.0	48	584	107.0	31.6	142.7	5141.3
Cabbage	0 (mg/l)	36.4	20.2	—	46.4	—	—	—	1200
	120 (mg/l)	41.5	22.2	—	57.3	—	—	—	1740
Tomato	KNo_3 (119 mg/l)	223.71	—	—	—	69.01	40.9	120	4848
	KNo_3 (181 mg/l)	119.25	—	—	—	75.67	40.0	119	4760

Source: Priyanka Pal (2016), Mazumdar (2013), B.P. Chapagain, Z. Weisman/Scientia Horticulture (2004).

Water Relation and Gaseous Exchange

In the plants, small pores provide passage for the gaseous exchange called stomata found in epidermis of the leaves, which are open or close under the control of a pair of kidney-shaped guard cells. The CO_2 is taken and O_2 is evolved during photosynthesis and O_2 is taken and CO_2 is liberated in respiration through stomata. They also indirectly involve in passive absorption of water, ascent of sap and absorption of mineral salts by regulating the transpiration. (Pospíšilová, 2003; Taiz and Zeiger, 2006).

Potassium take part in guard cells found around the stomata, its uptake into guard cells increases turgorpressure therefore, control the opening and closing of stomata (Epstein and Bloom, 2005; Marschner, 2012). In plants leaf movements, cell extension are driven by K^+ generated turgor pressure and helps in osmoregulation of plant cell (Philippar *et al.*, 1999; Yang *et al.*, 2004). Brag (1972) observed that the plants grown with adequate K has shown low water loss. Potassium accumulates in cell vacuole where, with sugars, it contributes to osmotic pressure, water uptake and turgor potential (Mengel and Arneke, 1982). The source of K^+ ions is the neighbouring subsidiary and epidermal cells, in so doing increasing the concentration from 50 mM to 300 mM in guard cells. Levitt (1974) ascertained that uptake of proton (H^+) by guard cells lead to increase in pH value of guard cells. With rise in pH converts starch into organic acid like malic acid. Increased K^+ concentration and malate

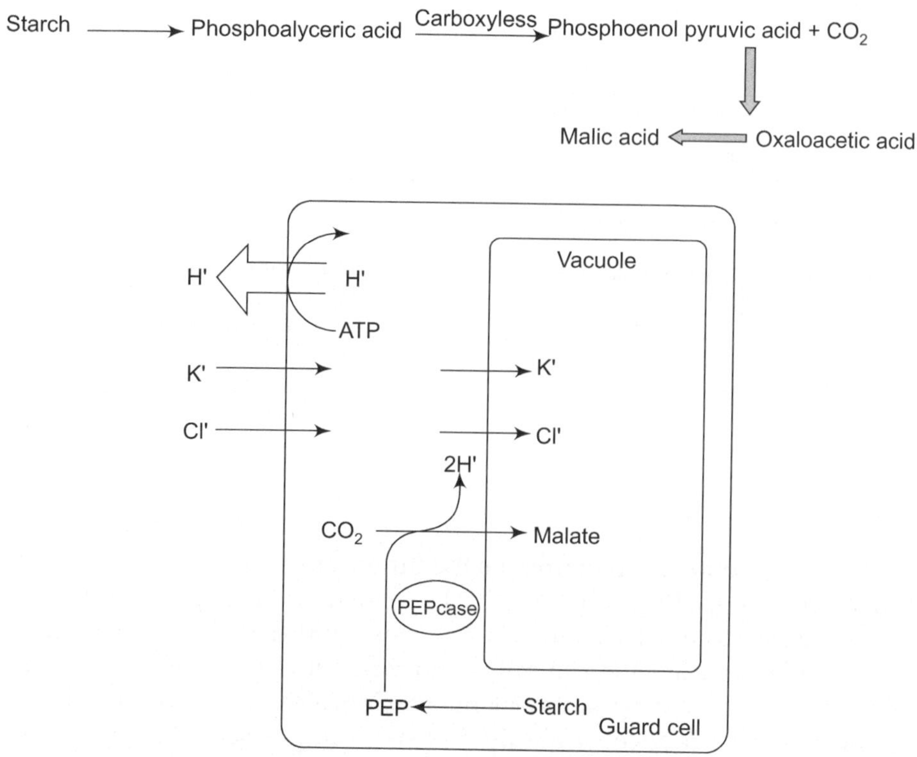

Fig. 9.1: Role of K^+ and malate ions (plus Cl^-) in waterrelation and gaseous exchange

ions (plus Cl^-) in the vacuole of guard cells causes sufficient increase in solute concentration and decrease in osmotic potential (e.g., 0.5 M K^+ concentration can cause a decrease in the osmotic potential by about 2.0 megapascals) that evoke reduction in water potential, results in entry of water from surrounding cells lead to opening of stomata. When decrease in turgor of guard cells results in closing of stomatal pore (Figure 9.1).

K^+ ion uptake is balanced by:

- Uptake of chloride (Cl^-) ions
- Movement of H^+ ions released from malic acid
- By negative charges of organic acids when they lose H^+ ion

The stomatal closure is considered to be brought about by a passive or highly catalyzed excretion of K^+ ions and Cl^- ions from the guard cells tothe epidermal tissue in general and the subsidiary cells in particularly when K moves into the guard cells around the stomata, the cells accumulate water and swell, causing the pores to open and allowing gases to move freely in and out. When water supply is short, K is pumped out of the guard cells (figure 9.1). The pores close tightly to prevent loss of water and minimize drought stress to the plant (Thomas and Thomas, 2009).

It has been proved that the accumulation of K^+ ions bring the opening of stomata and closing of stomata with loss of K^+ ions and ATP helps in entry of K^+ ions into the guard cells. **Source:** Fujino (1967).

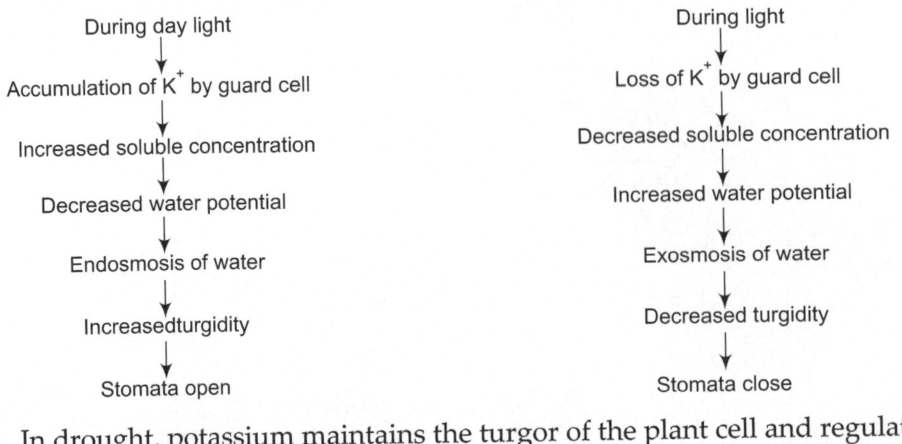

In drought, potassium maintains the turgor of the plant cell and regulates stomatal functions (Waraich *et al.*, 2011). Inadequate K supply, inhibit water stress induced stomatal closure via ethylene synthesis, the stomata Closure may take hours rather than minutes and when it is incomplete plant much more susceptible to water stress (Benlloch-Gonzalez, 2010). Accumulation of K in plant roots produces a gradient of osmotic pressure that draws water into the roots. Plants deficient in K are thus less able to absorb water and are more subject to stress when water is in short supply. The stomata were able to function properly during airborne pathogen infections in presence of sufficient K (Hardter, 2003; Pervez *et al.*, 2007).

PHOTOSYNTHESIS

The role of K in photosynthesis is very complex. The activation of enzymes by K and its involvement in adenosine triphosphate (ATP) production is probably more important in regulating the rate of photosynthesis than its role of K in stomatal activity. When the energy come from sun is used to combine water and CO_2 to form sugars, the initial high-energy ATP product. The electrical charge balance at the site of ATP production is maintained with K ions. When plants are K deficient, the rate of photosynthesis decreases which also contributes to slower growth and development. An increased K concentration in root can increase leaf photosynthetic efficiency possibly by increasing the number of chloroplast per cell, number of cells per leaf and consequently leaf area (Possingham, 1980). Lopez and satti, (1996) examined a huge decrement in photosynthetic activity with decreasing supply of K to the roots. In some plants, leaf blades re-orient toward light sources to increase light interception or away to avoid damage by excess light, as they assist to regulate the rate of photosynthesis. K application in plants increasing leaf chlorophyll concentration (Taiz and Zeiger, 2002) and also involve in formation of chlorophyll precursor (Fageria, 2009). Shafeek *et al.*, (2013) demonstrated greater concentration of leaf pigments in plants with foliar application of K as compared to those in the plants without foliar fertilization. El-Tohamy *et al.*, (2006) reported that foliar K fertilization reduced electrolyte leakage, thus increased total chlorophyll content as compared to that of the plants without foliar fertilization and also found that spray of pepper with potassium chloride or calcium chloride maintained higher total chlorophyll content in leaves. Potassium is involved efficiently in capturing sunlight to produce sugars (Milford and Johnston, 2007). Higher rates of photosynthesis have also been associated with stomatal regulation by K^+ (Marschner, 2012) as stomatal closure under K deficiency inhibit photosynthetic rates in several crop plants (Tomemori *et al.*, 2002; Jin *et al.*, 2011).

Table 9.3: Relationship between Potassium Content in Leaves, CO_2 Exchange and RuBP Carboxylase Activity in Alfalfa (Marschner, 1995)

Leaf Potassium	Stomatal Resistance	Photo-synthesis	RuBP carboxylase activity	Photo respiration	Dark respiration
mg/g dry wt	s/cm	mg CO_2/ dm^2/h	µmol CO_2/mg protein/h	dpm/dm^2	mg CO_2/ dm^2/h
12.8	9.3	11.9	2.8	4.0	7.6
19.8	6.8	21.7	4.5	5.9	5.3
38.4	5.9	34.0	6.1	9.0	3.1

Enzyme

Potassium is involved in the activation of more than 60 enzymes, including synthetases, oxidoreductases, dehydrogenases, transferases and kinases (Marschner, 2012; Bushkh *et al.*, 2011). These enzymes are necessary for essential plant process such as energy utilization, starch synthesis, N metabolism, respiration and regulate the metabolite pattern of higher plants ultimately changing metabolite concentrations (Mengel, 2001; Marschner, 2012). The enzyme starch synthase which is responsible of the synthesis of starch that catalyzes the incorporation of glucose into long chain starch molecules. Potassium is the most efficient cation stimulating of this enzyme. Optimum K nutrition results in higher concentration of starch in the plant and therefore on quality of crops grown for this material. Vegetables that storage starch can have a total carbohydrate content of more than 30% (Mengel, 2001). The high energy status provided by starch accumulation is also important for water stress and winter hardiness. Potassium deficiency also changes carbohydrate metabolism, with negative consequences such as accumulation of soluble carbohydrates and also decrease in starch content (Mengel and Kirk, 1987). Accumulation of reducing sugars and decrease of starch in potato tubers are the cause of undesired dark-coloured potato chips which occur under low K nutrition levels (Martin-Prevel, 1989). The amount of K present in the cell determines how many of the enzymes can be activated and the rates at which chemical reactions can proceed. Thus, the rate of a given reaction is controlled by the rate at which K immigrate in the cell (Van Brunt and Sultenfuss, 1998). Potassium activates starch synthesis (starch synthetase) consequently it plays critical role in water and nutrient transport (Pettigrew, 2008). K^+ ion needed for stimulating the plasma lemma ATPase which produces the necessary conditions for the metabolites, such as amino acids and sucrose (Barker and Pilbeam, 2007). Potassium involved in the synthesis of vital enzymes, boosts the oxidizing dynamism of root, plays a crucial role in sustaining plant cell physiological function and coordinated intracellular osmotic pressure and has an intimate connection with plant growth (Eun *et al.*, 2000; Giertha and Maser, 2007).

Energy

Willingford (1980) reported that plants need K for the production of high energy molecules (ATP) which are release both in photosynthesis and transpiration processes.Potassium nurtures the balance of electric charges in chloroplasts, which is prerequisite for ATP formation. Consequently, transfer of radiation energy into primary chemical energy in the form of ATP (photophosphorylation) and NADPH ($Fe^{\hat{o}*}$cyanide reduction in chloroplast improved by K (figure 9.2). A requisite K surplus assures high level of energy in the form of ATP and NADPH and energy transfer is an integral process in the plant

(Pfluger and Mengel, 1972). Entire synthetic process in plant metabolism, resulted in carbohydrates, lipids andproteins generation which explicit the quality of the crops. Mengel (1997) observed that K application results in high energy status in crops stimulate the synthesis of secondary metabolites, like vitamin c). Potassium has a crucial role in the energy status of the plants (Imas and Bansal, 1999).

Translocation

Potassium play an important role in the transport of assimilates and nutrients. Photosynthates must be transported from the leaves (sources) to the site of their use or storage. Herlihy (1989) observed that K promotes phloem transport of photosynthates mainly sucrose and show positive role in phloem loading with sucrose, in enhancing the transport rate of phloem sap solutes and in

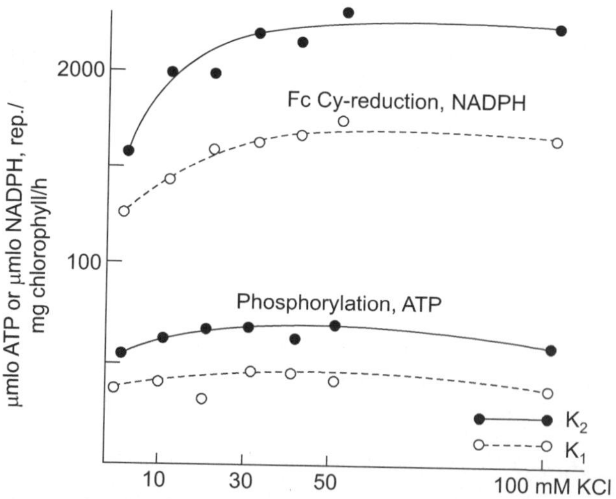

Fig. 9.2: Photoreduction (reduction of Fe^{III} cynide) and photophosphorylation in chloroplast as a function of K concentration (K_1 suboptimum K supply, K_2 optimumK supply) (Pflugera and Mengel, 1972).

phloem unloading. This role of K is related to its contribution to the osmotic potential in the sieve tubes and its function in ATP synthesis which provides the energy for the loading of photosynthesis. In well K supplied plants, the amount of potassium, the osmotic potential of the phloem sap and the volume flow rate are all higher than in plants supplied with a lower potassium level. As a result, increment in sucrose concentration in the phloem sap (Marschner, 1995). Potassium not only promotes the translocation of newly synthesized photosynthates but also has a beneficial effect on the mobilization of stored material (Mengel and Kirky, 1987). Potassium also acts as counter ion for nitrate transport in the xylem. After nitrate reduction in shoot charge balance has to be maintained by corresponding net increase in organic acid anions. Part of these organic anions (mainly malate) can be retranslocated with K as the accompanying cation through the phloem to the roots (Marschner, 2012). A requisite supply of K helps to keep all of these processes and transportation systems functioning normally (Van Brunt and Sultenfuss, 1998). Potassium is involved in metabolic and transport processes, charge balances, and generation of turgor pressure in the cells (Dorais *et al.*, 2001). Potassium is important in carbohydrates formation and translocation of sugars (Acquaah, 2005).

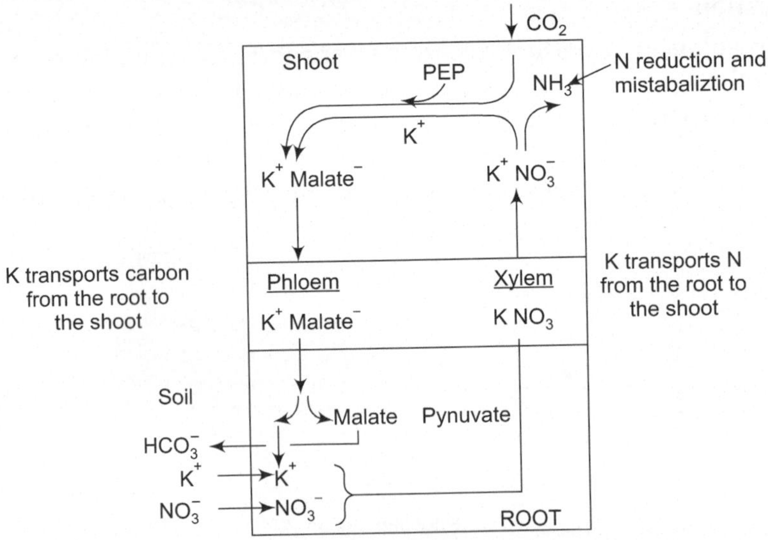

Fig. 9.3: A simplified schematic for circulation of potassium between root and shoot in relation to nitrate and malate transport (PEP, phosphoenolpyurvate).

Source: Kirky and Knight, 1977).

Yield and its attributes

Golcz *et al.,* (2012) have reported that the total yield, marketable yield, commercial fruit yield and total average yield per plant were increased by increasing application rates of potassium (K) fertilizers. Picha and Hall (1982) found that increased application of K resulted in enhanced yield of tomato (*Lycopersicon esculentum Mill.* Fruits, flower production but through larger proportion of flower forming fruits. The tomatoes are one of the crops that require high level of K nutrition to achieve quality in addition to higher yields (Kazemi, 2014). A very similar response was also obtained when grown on peat bags; a potassium level of 50 mg/l in liquid feed by fertigation produces a mean yield of 9.98 kg/plant of cucumbers. Yield was increased by 91% to 19.1 kg/plant when the potassium level was raised from 50 to 250mg/l (Adams *et al.*, 1992). In a field experiment carried out by Prince *et al.* (1988), capsicum yields were highest with N:K ratio of 1:1.2. Several studies have been done on the effect of K fertilization on yield of potatoes (Chapman *et al.*, 1992). Chapman *et al.* (1992) reported significant increases in size and yield of potatoes (*Solanum tuberosum*) with increasing rate of K fertilization in soils where the initial soil K status were low. Evers (1989) reported a positive effect of fertilization yield, dry matter, and dietary fiber content of carrots (Daucus carota L.). Haripraksha Rao (1994) observed increase in the yield of tomato fruits with increased levels of potassium. The highest yield (35.4 t ha^{-1}) was obtained at 150 kg K_2O ha^{-1} which signifies non-significant differences between the sources of potassium (KCl and K_2SO_4) with respect to yield. IPI-PRII-CPRI project (1997) on effect of K on number and size of potato tubers reported that K application in potatocrop increases the yield of large and medium-sized tubers and decreases weight loss from the tubers after harvest. Nanadal *et al.* (1998)conducted a field experiment on sandy loam soil at Gurgaon(Haryana) to know the effect of phosphorus and potassium on growth, yield and quality of tomato (cv. Arun) and reported that, application of 120 kg K_2O per ha has registered highest plant height (77.8 cm)which was significantly superior over control (58.0 cm)t. Gunes *et al.* (1998) who investigated critical nutrient elements in young tomatoes found that K concentration in the plant increases with increasing K in nutrient solution. Singh *et al.*, (1998) reported that, plant height of okra *(Abelmoschus esculantus)* was significantly increased with increasing levels of potassium upto 75 kg K_2O ha^{-1}. Highest plant height (104.1 cm) was recorded at 100 kg K_2O ha^{-1} which was on par with 75 kg K_2O ha^{-1} (103.0 cm), but it was significantly superior over 25 kg K_2O ha^{-1} (99.9 cm). Imas (1999) noticed that high potassium concentrations increased fruit total soluble solids of tomato fruit. Singh (1999) found that potassium give positive effect on photosynthesis, phloem loading and translocation as well as synthesis of large bulking of the potato tubers. Majumdar *et al.*, (2000) reported that, increased levels of K had significant influence on the fruit yield of tomato with highest yield (525.33q ha^{-1}) under 90kg K_2O ha^{-1}. Vitamin C is perhaps the most popular vitamin. Soil and foliar treatmentof K has been shown to enhance the level of vitamin C in many crops, like cucurbits, cauliflower, onion, banana, guava and papaya. Wu-Zhong, 2001 reported that, applying K increased the vitamin C content of sweet pepper. Thakre *et al.*, (2005) conducted a field experiment to know the effect of levels of potassium on yield and quality of brinjal *(Solanum melongeana)* at Nagpur. The results revealed that, application of 25 kg K_2O per ha has resulted in highest fresh fruit yield (144.52 q ha^{-1}) which was on par with 50 kg K_2O per ha (140.60 q ha^{-1}).The results showed that adequate amounts of K decrease the incidence of fungal diseases by 70%, of bacterial diseases by 69%, of insect and mite damage by 63%, and of viruses by 41%. Kazemi (2014) examined that potassium application increase plant height, number of leaves, fruits and fruit yield. The positive effect of potassium also shows increment in total,economic yield in cabbage (Majumdar, 2013).

Striking differences in total K uptake were found between crops, compared on basis of a year round growing cycle. Total yield, total dry matter production and K uptake of crops based on a year round growing period (tomato, cucumber, sweet pepper), or year round cropping cycle (radish). K, as important nutritional elements, plays its part in regulation of many physiological criteria in plant which in turn affect the resulted total yield. The trends of obtained results are in good accordance with that of the investigators such as Kaya *et al.*, (2002) and Al-Hamzawi (2010), Shafeek *et al.*, (2013) on cucumber plants.

Table 9.4 Total Yield, Total Dry Matter Production and K Uptake of Crops Based on A Year Round Growing Period (Tomato, Cucumber, Sweet Pepper), or Year Round Cropping Cycle (Radish, Lettuce, Chrysanthemum).

Crop	Total yieldkg m^{-2} yr^{-1}	Total dry matterkg m^{-2} yr^{-1}	Total Kkg m^{-2} yr^{-1}
Tomato	50	3.8	1750
Cucumber	65	3.0	1500
Sweet pepper	25	2.5	1500
Radish	25	1.2	900
Lettuce	23	1.2	1200
Chrysanthemum	16	2.1	1100

Source : Sonneveld (1997), Voogt (1993)

Quality

'Quality' refers to several aspects that affect the marketability of the product, including: uniform and large size, good shape and attractive color, freedom from blemishes, markings, mechanical injuries and signs of disease, enhanced flavor and aroma, higher content of proteins and vitamin C, Longer shelf life, Adequate processing quality for industry.

Quality improvement of vegetables has been observed as one of the beneficial effect of K fertilization. Hassan (2002) and Khayyat *et al.*, (2007) stated that potassium improves fruit chemical composition via increasing protein and starch content, total soluble solids, ascorbic acid content and extends fruit shelf life. Lucas (1968) observed that increase in K application up to 166kg/ha enhanced carrot yield on Houghton muck soil. Trudel and Ozbun (1971) studied the influence of potassium levels on carotenoid content of tomato fruits. Results of this experiment revealed that, most of the carotenoids especially lycopene increased with increment in K supply. Application of K nutrient solution resulted increase in lycopene content of fruit, whereas without K fruit show very less ltcopene. Likewise, Widders and Lorenz (1982) found higher rate of K intensification to accord with maximum uptake of K by tomato fruits. Habben (1972) noted that increasing K fertilization increased both glucose and fructose contents in carrot and also seen positive improvement in sucrose content with increasing K fertilization. Potassium is related to improved fruit shape, the reduction of ripening disorders and an increase in fruit concentration, which improves taste (Adams *et al.*,1978). With improve K nutrition, fruit is generally higher in total soluble solids, acids, sugars, lycopene and carotenes has a better keeping quality (Munson,1985). Application of high rates of K economized severity of bruising in potatoes (Chapman *et al.*, 1992). Potassium enhances storage quality of potato and also extends their shelf life (Perrenoud, 1993). Imas and Bansal (2002) have reported that rapid bulking potato varieties producing large size tubers retort more to K than the varieties with small size tubers as application of K is known to increase the tuber size. Bagal *et al.* (1989) reported improved lycopene content in tomato fruits with elevated potassium utilization. Evers (1989) noted a significant increase in root K content with fertilization as compared to unfertilized treatments in carrots. The effect of potassium on shelf life was dominantly favorable both through slowing of senescence and through decrease of numerous physiological diseases (Martin-Prevel, 1989). Mitra *et al.*, (1990) found increase in reducing sugars, dry weight and pH of fruits with increased application of K up to 744 kg/ha. Subbiah and Raniperumal (1994) studied the effect of five levels of nitrogen and three levels of potassium on tomato. The results indicated that, individual as well as combined application of nitrogen and potassium significantly increased the nitrogen concentration of tomato fruits. Ibrahim (1996) also reported that sugar and vitamin c content increased with K application. Nanadal *et al.*, (1998) tried four levels of potassium viz., 0, 40, 80 and 120 kg per ha on tomato and found highest lycopene content (214.7 μg g-1) obtained with 120 kg K_2O ha-1. Thakre *et al.*, (2005) governa field experiment at Nagpur to know the effect of different levels of potassium on quality of brinjal. They concluded that, highest ascorbic acid content (17.96 mg/100 g) was resulted with 50 kg K_2O per ha which was significantly superior over 25 kg K_2O per ha (17.16 mg 100 g-1). In tomato it was found that fruit dipped in 2% potassium nitrate perpetuate good quality (Bombelli and Wright, 2006). The foliar K application improved fruit marketable quality by increasing firmness, sugar content and fruit human health quality by increasing ascorbic acid, beta-carotene, and K levels in a soil (Lester *et al.*, 2007). Foliar spray of potassium show positive effects on fruit size, yield and nutritional quality by enhance total soluble solid, percent dry matter and phenolic activity (Pal *et al.*, 2016).

Effect of K on number and size of cucumber. C.E.V, Indo-Isreal project. Karnal, Haryana, India. **Source:** (Pal *et al.*, 2016)

PLANT STRESS RESPONSES

An adequate K nutrition may facilitate osmotic adjustment, which maintains higher turgor pressure, lower osmotic potential and relative water content, thus improving the ability of plants to tolerate drought stress (Egilla, 2005; Marschner, 2012). Potassium is essential in maintain water uptake and had a positive impact on stomatal closure which increases tolerance to water stress and enhances water use efficiency (Nguyen *et al.*, 2002). The K application under drought moderates the adverse effects of water shortage on plant growth (Sangakkara *et al.*, 2001; Singh and Kumar, 2009). Photosynthetic rate was decreased under drought stress in K-deficient plants (Egilla, 2005; Tsonev *et al.*, 2011). Tissue with higher K concentrations reduced chilling damage and increased cold resistance, ultimately increasing yield production (Mengel, 2001; Kant 2002). The exogenous application of K in soil and as foliar spray alleviated the adverse effects of waterlogging (Ashraf *et al.*, 2011).

SUPPRESSION OF DISEASE AND INSECT

K is a highly mobile element in the plant and is translocated from the older to younger tissue. Consequently, K deficiency symptoms usually occur first on the lower leaves of the plant and then progress toward the top as the severity of the deficiency increases (Hoffer, 1938). Most common signs of K deficiency are the yellow scorching or chlorosis along the leaf margin. K deficiency occurs frequently on soils which are light and sandy, acid and common in heavy soils with calcareous and heavily cropped soils (Anderson, 1973). K deficiency results in poor quality of leaf vegetables due to extensive marginal chlorosis with interveinal brown necrotic spots and rolling, cupping, curling and distortion of the midrib of younger leaves and reduction in the length and diameter of stem internodes and root development (Singh and Sharma, 1988). K deficiency is indicated by development of an acute rosette in beets, celery and parsnips (Hewitt, 1963) and by chlorosis, browning of leaves, spindly roots and short growth in carrots (Ulrich and Ohki, 1966). K insufficiency also downturn the rate of photosynthesis and the rate of respiration thereby causing a decline in sugar concentration and accumulation of nonstructural carbohydrates due to reduced protein synthesis (Oparka and Wright, 1988). Plants with squat levels of K are susceptible to pathogen attack due to nitrogen accumulation which favors growth of microorganisms which may reduce the storability of vegetables (Locascio, 1993). K deficiency reduces vegetative growth, yield and often in severe situations can result in loss of older leaves and lead to crop death (Clarkson and Hanson, 1980). Hobson *et al.*, (1977) examined that the K status is inversely related to incidence of blotchy ripening in tomatoes. K also provides resistance against pest, diseases, drought and frost stresses.Insufficiency of K in the fruit leads to poor fruit quality and yield loss (Bar Tal and Pressman, 1996). It has been recognized for decades that K enhancesplant's ability to resist pest and diseases which is not isolated to a few crop species, but includes a wide range of both plants and pathogens. The role of K in crop resistance to diseases was extensively examined in an IPI review of 2,450 literature references. Adequate K fertilization produces a strong, vigorously growing plant, which can tolerate disease and insects much more effectively than those suffering stress. By its favorable action in regulating plant metabolism and counteracting the harmful effects of excessive

N, K normalizes plant development and ensures proportionate growth. This guarantees the health and hardiness of the plant tissues, providing resistance to damage by pests and diseases. In general, an inverse relationship is found between available soil K and the severity of disease. It is a common practice to add K fertilizers to diminish certain diseases. Leaf spot in cotton is mainly related to low soil K, low plant tissue K and low petiole K. K deficiency in late-season soybeans can lead to reduced yields and poor seed quality caused by pod and stem blight and purple seed stain. In potatoes, K fertilization has been found to diminish the incidence of certain diseases, likewise late blight, dry rot, powdery scab and early blight. The foliar sprays of Multi-K results incontrolling powdery mildew in cucumbers by produce systemically induced disease resistance (Reuveni *et al.*, 1996). The airborne pathogen invasion is also prevented (especially from bacteria and viruses) in plant by rapid stomatal closing under sufficient K (Hardter, 2003; Pervez *et al.*, 2007).Different K fertilizers, applied as foliar sprays which are highly effective as inducers of systemic protection against powdery mildew in cucumbers.

Effect of K application on the incidence of late blight disease (Phytophthorainfestans) in potato. IPI-PRII-CPRI project. Jalandhar, Punjab, India. 1998. **Source:** IPI Coordination India.

CONCLUSION

Daily intake of vegetable rich diet is vital for health as supplied many phytoneutricals much needed by human to get rid of death dealing human diseases. Nutrient such as potassium helps in regulating blood pressure, deal with malnutrition and obesity. Foliar fertilization is very important method to provide direct absorption of nutrients through leaves. Foliar application show better results regarding productivity of vegetable crops in comparison to soil fertilization. Potassium functions as the key nutrient elements for enhancing productivity of vegetable crops. A sound K fertilization management balances both P & N nutrient uptake for high yield and quality. K contributesin enhancing carotenoids syntheses in chilies, tomato and other vegetables. In many crops, tomato and sweet pepper, the K application seems to be walking a tightrope, with possibilities of enhancing storage quality. Adequate supply of K mainly at the time of fruit development and maturation is required by plants and positive relationship with quality attributes. It not only performs the important physiological functions as discussed in the review, but shows positive effects on nitrogen use efficiency. As we know, nitrogen is directly related to yield. Now, these days Consumers are much aware of nutritional quality. Vegetable is main part of our regular diet. There is low production of vegetables due to less knowledge of fertilizers used by farmers and plant diseases. Due to which prices of vegetables increases and not in keep of poor people pocket. With much more production the availability of vegetables to people at a moderate price reduce malnutrition, many deadly disease and help in other health benefits and also thereby making a necessary marketing incentive to plant breeding.

REFERENCES

Abbas, G., Aslam, M., Malik, A.U., Abbas, Z., Ali, M. and Hussain F. (2011): Potassium Sulphate Effects on Growth and Yield of Mungbean (*Vigna radiata* L.) under Arid Climate. International Journal of Agriculture and Applied Science, 3:72-75.

Acquaah, G. (2005): Principles of Crop Production: Theory, Techniques and Technology. 2nd Ed. Pearson Prentice Hall, New Jersey.

Adams, P., Davies, J.N. and Winsor, G.W. (1978): Effects of Nitrogen, Potassium and Magnesiumon the Quality and Chemical Composition of Tomatoes Grown in Peat. Journal of Horticulture Sciences, 53:115-122.

Al- Hamzawi and Abbas, M.K. (2010): Effect of Calcium Nitrate, Potassium Nitrate and Anfaton on Growth and Storability of Plastic House Cucumber. American Journal of Plant Physiology, 5(5): 278-290.

Anderson, G.D. (1973): Potassium Response of Various Crops in Eat Africa. IN: Potassium in Tropical Crops and Soils. Proc. 10th Colloq., International Potash Institute, Bern, Switzerland. pp. 287-309.

Ashraf, M., Karim, F. and Rasul, E. (2002): Interactive Effects of Gibberellicacid (GA3) and Salt Stress on Growth, Ion Accumulation and Photosynthetic Capacity of Two Spring Wheat (*Triticum aestivum* L.) Cultivars Differing in Salt Tolerance. Plant Growth Regulation, 36:49–59.

Bagal, S.D., Shaikh, G.A. and Adsule, R.N. (1989): Influence of Different Levels of N, P and K Fertilizers on the Protein, Ascorbic Acid, Sugars and Mineral Contents of Tomato. Maharashtra Agriculture University, 14:153-155.

Barker, A.V. and Pilbeam, D.I. (2007): Handbook of Plant Nutrition by Taylor & Francis Group, LLC CRC Pressis an Imprint of Taylor & Francis Group, an Informa Business, pp. 244.

Bar-Tal, A. and Pressman, E. (1996): Root Restriction and Potassium and Calcium Solutions Concentrations Affect Dry-matter Production, Cation Uptake and Blossom-end Rot in Greenhouse Tomato. Journal of the American Society for Horticulture Science, 121: 649-655.

Benlloch-Gonzalez, M., Romera, J., Cristescu, S., Harren, F. and Fournier, J.M. (2010): K^+ Starvation Inhibits Water-stress-induced Stomatal Closure via Ethylene Synthesis in Sunflower Plants. Journal of Experimental Botany, 61:1139–1145.

Bennett, W.F. (1993): Nutrient Deficiencies and Toxicities in Crop Plants, APS Press, St. Pau.

Bidari, B. I. and Hebsur, N. S. (2004): Potassium in Relation to Yield and Quality of Selected Vegetable Crops. Journal of Agriculture Science, 24:55-59.

Bombelli, E.C. and Wright, E.R. (2006): Tomato Fruit Quality Conservation During Postharvest by Application of Potassium Bicarbonate and Its Effect on Botrytis Cinera. Cienciae Investigacion Agraria, 33:167-172.

Brag, H. (1972): The Influence of Potassium on the Transpiration Rate and Stomatal Opening in Triticum Aestivum and Pisum Sativum. Physiological Plantarum, 26:250-257.

Bushkh, M. A. A. H. A., Ahmad, R., Malik, A. U., Hussain S. and Ishaque M. (2011): Profitability of Three Maize Hybrids as Influenced by Varying Plant Density and Potassium Application. Journal of Animal and Plant Sciencea, 21(1): 42-47.

Cakmak, I. (2005): The Role of Potassium in Alleviating Detrimental Effects of Abiotic Stresses in Plants, Journal of Plant Nutrition and Soil Science, 168: 521-530.

Chapagain Bishnu P. and Wiesman Zeev. (2004): Effect of Potassium Magnesium Chloride in the Fertigation Solution as Partial Source of Potassium on Growth, Yield and Quality of Greenhouse Tomato. Scientia Horticulturae, 99: 279–288.

Chapman, K.S.R., Sparrow, L.A., Hardman, P.R., Weight, D.N. and Thorp, J.R.A. (1992): Potassium Nutrition of Kennebec and Russet Burbank Potatoes in Tasmania: Effect of Soil and Fertiliser Potassium on Yield, Petiole and Tuber Potassium Concentrations and Tuber Quality. Australian Journal of Experimental Agriculture, 32:521-527.

Cherel, I. (2004): Regulation of K^+ Channel Activities in Plants: Physiological to Molecular Aspects. Journal of Experimental Botany, 55:337-351.

Clarkson, D.T., and Hanson, J.B. (1980): The Mineral Nutrition of Higher Plants. Annual Review of Plant Physiology, 31:239-298.

Epstein, E., Bloom, A. J. (2005): Mineral Nutrition of Plants: Principles and Perspectives, 2nd ed. Sunderland: Sinauer Associates Inc.

Dias, J. S. (2011): World Importance, Marketing and Trading of Vegetables. Acta Horticulturae, 921:153-169.

Dias, J. S. and Ryder, E. (2011): World Vegetable Industry: Production, Breeding, Trends. Horticultural Reviews, 38: 299-356.

Dorais, M., Papadopoulos, A. and Gosselin, A. (2001): Greenhouse Tomato Fruit Quality. Horticultural Review, 26: 239-319.

Egilla, J.N., Davies, F.T. and Boutton, T.W. (2005): Drought Stress Influences Leaf Water Content, Photosynthesis, and Water-use Efficiency of Hibiscus Rosa-sinensis at Three Potassium Concentrations. Photosynthetica, 43:135–140.

El-Tohami, W.A., Ghoname, A.A. and Abou - Hussein, S.d. (2006): Improvement of Pepper Growth and Productivity in Sandy Soil by Different Fertilization Treatments under Protected Cultivars. Journal of Applied Sciences and Research, 2:8-12.

Eshghi, S., Safizadeh, M.R., Jamali, B. and Sarseifi, M. (2012): Influence of Foliar Application of Volk Oil, Dormex, Gibberellic Acid and Potassium Nitrate on Vegetative Growth and Reproductive Characteristics of Strawberry cv. 'Merak'. Jornal of Biological and Environmental Sciences, 6: 35-38.

Eun, S., Youn, H.S., and Lee, Y. (2000): Cadmium Disturbs Microtubule Organization in the Root Meristem of Zea Mays. Physiological Plantarum, 110: 357-365.

Evers, A.M. (1989). Effect of Different Fertilization Practices in the Yield and Quality of Carrot. Journal of Agriculture Science, 61:329-360.

Fageria, N.K. (2009): The Use of Nutrients in Crop Plants. CRC Press Taylor NW, pp: 430.

Fujino, M. (1967): Role of Adenosinetriphosphate and Adenosinetriphosphate in Stomatal Movement. Sci. B. Fac. Nagasaki University, 18:1-47.

Giertha, M. and Mäser, P. (2007): Potassium Transporters in Plants-Involvement in K^+ Acquisition, Redistribution and Homeostasis, FEBS Letters, 581: 2348-2356.

Golcz, A., Kujawski, P. and Markiewicz, B. (2012). Yielding of Red Pepper (Capsicum annuum L.) Under the Influence of Varied Potassium Fertilization. [Article]. Acta Scientiarum Polonorum-Hortorum Cultus., 11(4):3-15.

Gunes, A., Alpaslan, M. and Inal, A. (1998): Critical Nutrient Concentrations and Antagonistic and Synergistic Relationship among the Nutrients of NFT Grown Young Tomato Plants. Journal of Plant Nutrition, 21: 2035-2047.

Habben, J. (1972): Quality Constituents of Carrots as Influenced by Nitrogen and Potassium Fertilization. Acta Horticulturae, 29:295-305.

Hassan, Z.F. (2002): Effect of Some Sources of Organic Manure and Level of Potassium on Growth, Yield, Quality and Chemical Composition of Pepper (Capsicum annum L.) Ph.D. Thesis, Cario University, Cario, Egypt.

Hardter, R. (2003): Potassium and Biotic Stress of Plants. In Feed the Soil to Feed the People: The Role of Potash in Sustainable Agriculture; Johnston, A.E., Ed.; International Potash Institute: Basel, Switzerland, pp. 345–362.

Hariprakasha Rao, M. and Subramanian, T.R. (1991): Effect of Potassium Application on the Yield and Content of K, Ca and Mg in Cabbage, Okra, Tomato and Beetroot. Journal of Potash Research, 7 (3): 190-197.

Herrera, E., Jimenez, R., Aruoma, O. I., Hercberg, S., Sanchez-Garcia I. and Fraga, C. (2009): Aspects of Antioxidant Foods and Supplements in Health and Disease, Nutrition Reviews, 67(1):S140-S144. doi:10.1111/j.1753-4887.2009.00177.

Herlihy, M. (1989): Effect of Potassium on Sugar Accumulation in Storage Tissue. In: Proceedings of the IPI 21 st Colloquium on: Methods of K Research in Plants, held at Louvain-la-Neuve, Belgium, 19-21 June 1989. International Potash Institute, Bern, Switzerland, pp. 259-270.

Hewitt, E.J. (1966): Sand and Water Culture Methods Used in the Study of Plant Nutrition. 2nd ed. Commonw, Agr. Bur. England.

Hobson, G.E., Davies, J.N. and Winsor, G.W. (1977): Ripening Disorders of Tomato Fruit. Growers' Bulletin No 4. Glasshouse Crops Research Institute. Littlehampton, England.

Hoffer, G.N. (1938): Potash in Plant Metabolism Deficiency Symptoms as Indicators of the Role of Potassium, Industrial and Engineering Chemistry Research, 30(8): 885–889.

Ibrahim, M. (1996): Research and Development Project on the Use of Muriate of Potash, (MOP) in Pakistan, Technical Progress Report of Rabi 1995-96, PARC, Islamabad, Pakistan.

Imas, Patricia. (1999): Quality Aspects of Potassium in Horticulture Crops, International Potash Institute, Isreal.

Imas, Patricia and Bansal, S.K. (2002): Potassium and Integrated Nutrient Management in Potato. In, Potato Global Research and Development (Proceedings of the Global Conference on Potato, New Delhi, India 06-11, December 1999) Khurana SMP, Shekhawat GS, Singh BP and Pandey, SK (eds), 2: 744-5.

Jaskulski, D. (2007): Comparison of the Effect of Foliar Fertilization on Economic and Production Effect of Growing Some Field Crops. Fragmenta Agronomica (Poland), 24(93):106-112.

Jin, S.H., Huang, J.Q., Li, X.Q., Zheng, B.S., Wu, J.S., Wang, Z.J., Liu, G.H. and Chen, M. (2011): Effects of Potassium Supply on Limitations of Photosynthesis by Mesophyll Diffusion Conductance in *Carya cathayensis,* Tree Physiology, 31:1142–1151.

Kaya C., B. Ak, B.E, Higgs, D. and Murilli Amador (2002): Influence of Foliar Applied Calcium on Cucumber and Melon Plant Drip Irrigated with Saline Water, Journal of Plant Nutrition, 26:1665-1681.

Khayyat, M., Vazifeshenas, M.R., Rajee S. and Jamalian S. (2007): Potassium Effect on Ion Leakage, Water Usage, Fruit Yield and Biomass Production by Strawberry Plants Grown Under NaCl Stress Journal of Fruit and Ornamental Plant Research, 17:79-88.

Kimura, M. and Itokawa, Y. (1990): Cooking Losses of Minerals in Foods and Its Nutritional Significance, Journal of Nutritional Science and Vitaminology, 36: 25-32.

Kolota E. and Osinska M. (2001): Efficiency of Foliar Nutrition of Field Vegetables Grown at Different Nitrogen Rates. Acta Horticulturae (ISHS), 563:87-91.

Liebig, J. (1841): The Organic Chemistry and Its Application on Agriculture and Physiology, Verlag, Viehweg, Braunschweig.

Leigh, R.A. and Wyn Jones R.G. (1984): A Hypothesis Relating Critical Potassium Concentration for Growth to the Distribution and Functions of this Ion in the Plant Cells. New Phytologist, 97:1-13.

Lester, G.E., Jifon, J.L. and Stewart, W.M. (2007): Better Crops. 91: (1)24-25.

Kant, S. and Kafkafi, U. (2002): Potassium and Abiotic Stresses in Plants. In *Potassium for Sustainable Crop Production;* Pasricha, N.S., Bansal, S.K., Eds.; Potash Institute of India: Gurgaon, India, pp. 233–251.

Levitt, D.G. (1974): A New Theory of Transport for Cell Membrane Pores. General Theory and Application to Red Cell, Biochimica Et Biophysica Acta, 373: 115–131.

Locascio, S. (1993): Cucurbits: Cucumber, Muskmelon and Watermelon. *In*: Nutrient Deficiencies and Toxicities in Crops Plants. W. Bennett. APS. Press, Minnesota, pp. 123-130.

Lucas, R.E. (1968): Potassium Nutrition of Vegetable Crops. IN:N.J. Kilmer, S.E. Younts, and N.C. Brady (eds.), The Role of Potassium in Agriculture, ASA, CSSA SSSA. Madison, W.I., pp. 489-498.

LOPEZ, M.V. and SATTI, S.M.E. (1996): Calcium and Potassium-enhanced Growth and Yield of Tomato under Stress. Plant Sciences, 114: 19-27.

Marschner, H. (1995): Mineral Nutrition of Higher Plants. 2nd Ed. Academic Press, London and Newyork, pp. 200-255.

Marschner, P., (2012): Marschner's Mineral Nutrition of Higher Plants, 3rd ed., Academic Press, London, UK.

Martin–Prevel P.J. (1989): Physilogical Process Related to Handling and Storage Quality of Crops. *In* Proceedings of the 21st IPI Colloqulum on "Methods of K Research in Plants" held at Louvin-La-Neuve, Belgium 19-21 June, 1989. International Potash Institute, Bern, Switzerland: 219-48.

Majumdar, S.P., Meena, R.L. and Baghel, G.D.S. (2000): Effect of Levels of Compaction and Potassium on Yield and Quality of Tomato and Chilli Crops Grown on Highly Permeable Soils. Journal of the Indian Society of Soil Science, 48 (2):215-220.

Mazumdar, F. (2013): Response of Gibberellic Acid and Potash Nutrient on Growth and Yield of Late Planting Cabbage, MS Thesis, Department of Horticulture, Sher-e-bangla Agricultural University, Dhaka, Bangladesh, pp. 62-86.

Mengel, K. and Kirk, E.A. (1987): Principles of Plant Nutrition. 4th ed. Intern, Potash Inst., Berne, Switzerland.

Mengel, K. and Kirkby, E. (2001): Principals of Plant Nutrition, 5th Ed.: International Potash Institute, Bern, Switzerland.

Mengel, K. and Arneke, W.W. (1982): Effect of Potassium on the Water Potential the Osmotic Potential and Cell Elongation in Leaves of Phaseolus Vulgaris. Physiological Plantarum, 54:402-408.

Mitra, S.K., Sadhu, M.K., and Bose, T.K. (1990): Nutrition of Vegetable Crops, Naya Prokash, pp. 18-19.

Milford, G.F.J. and Johnston, A.E. (2007). Potassium and Nitrogen Interactions in Crop Production. Proceedings International Fertiliser Society, 615: 63.

Mullie P. and Clarys, P. (2011): Association between Cardio-vascular Disease Risk Factor Knowledge and Lifestyle. Food and Nutrition Science, 2(10):1048-1053.

Nanadal, J.K., Ramesh, V. and Pandey, U.P. (1998): Effect of Phosphorus and Potassium on Growth, Yield and Quality of Tomato. Journal of Potash Research, 15 (1-4): 44-49.

Nguyen, H.T., Nguyen, A.T., Lee, B.W. and Schoenau, J. (2002): Effects of Long-term Fertilization for Cassava Production on Soil Nutrient Availability as Measured by Ion Exchange Membrane Probe and by Corn and Canola Nutrient Uptake. Korean Journal of Crop Science, 47: 108-115.

Oded, A and Uzi, K. (2003): Enhanced Performance of Processing Tomatoes by Potassium Nitrate Based Nutrition, Acta Horticulturae, 613:81–87.

Opkara K.J. and Wright K.M. (1988): Osmotic Regulation of Starch Synthesis in Potato Tubers? Planta. 174, 123-129.

Pal P., Yadav K., Kumar K. and Singh N. (2016): Effect of Potassium and Gibberellic Acid Combination on Growth and Development of Cucumis sativus L. cv. Sevenstar. Fascicula Biologiae (accepted).

Pfluger, R. and Mengel, K. (1972): The Photochemical Activity of Chloroplasts from Various Plants with Different Potassium Nutrition. Plant and soil, 36: 417-425.

Perrenoud, S. (1993): Fertilizing for High Yield of Potato. IPI Bulletin 8. Second edition, International Potash Institute, Basel, Switzerland, pp. 138-86.

Pervez, H., Ashraf, M., Makhdum, M.I. and Mahmood, T. (2007): Potassium Nutrition of Cotton (Gossypium hirsutum L.) in Relation to Cotton Leaf Curl Virus Disease in Aridisols. Pakistan Journal of Botany, 39: 529–539.

Pettigrew, W.T. (2008): Potassium Influences on Yield and Quality Production for Maize, Wheat, Soybean and Cotton. Physiological Plantarum, 133: 670-681.

Philippar, K., Fuchs, I., Luthen, H., Hoth, S., Bauer, C.S. and Haga, K. (1999) Auxin Induced K^+ Channel Expression Represents an Essential Step in Coleoptile Growth and Gravitropism. Proceedings of National Academy of Sciences of the USA, 96: 12186–91.

Picha, D.H. and Hall, C.B. (1981): Influences of Potassium, Cultivar and Season on Tomato Graywall and Blotchy Ripening. Journal of the American Society for Horticultural Science, 106:704-708.

Prince, C.A., Sanders, D.C. and Campbell, C.R.(1988): Response of Pepper to N Fertilizer and N/K Ratios. Proc. 4th Int. Micro. Irrig. Cong. Inst., Australia, 2: 478-480.

Pospíšilová, J. (2003): Participation of Phytohormones in the Stomatal Regulation of Gas Exchange during Water Stress. Biologia Plantarum, 46 (4): 491-506.

Possingham, J.V. (1980): Plastid Replication and Development in the Life Cycle of Higher Plants. Annual Review of Plant Physiology, 31: 113-129.

Reuveni, M., Agaropov, V., and Reuveni, R. (1996): Controlling Powdery Mildew Caused by Sphaerotheca Fuliginea in Cucumber by Foliar Sprays of Phosphate and Potassium Salts. Crop Protection, 15:49-53.

Sangakkara, U.R., Frehner, M. and Nosberger, J. (2000): Effect of Soil Moisture and Potassium Fertilizer on Shoot Water Potential, Photosynthesis and Partitioning of Carbon in Mungbean and Cowpea. Crop Science, 185:201-20.

Shafeek, M.R., Helmy, Y.I., El-Tohamy, W.A. and El-Abagy, H.M. (2013): Changes in Growth, Yield and Fruit Quality of Cucumber (Cucumis sativus L.) in Response to Foliar Application of Calcium and Potassium Nitrate under Plastic House Conditions. Research Jornal of Agriculture and Biological Sciences. 9: 114-118.

Singh, R.P., Rajput, C.B.S. and Chaurasia, S.N.S. (1998): Effect of Different Levels and Methods of Potassium Application on Growth and Green Pod Yield of Okra (Abelmoschus Esculentus L. Moench) cv. Parbhani Kranti. Haryana Journal of Horticulture Sciences, 27 (4) : 288-292.

Singh, J.P. (1999): Potassium Fertilization of Potatoes in North India. In Proceeding of IPI Workshop on "Essential Role of Potassium in Diverse Cropping System", held at the 16th World Congress of Soil Sciences, Monnte Pellier, France 20-26 August,1998. International Potash, Institute, Basel, Switzerland, pp. 123-27.

Singh, A.K. and Kumar, P. (2009): Nutrient Management in Rainfed Dryland Agro Ecosystem in the Impending Climate Change Scenario. Agri. Situ. India, 66(5):265-270.

Singh, S. and Sharma, C.P. (1988): Effect of Potassium on Leaf Diffusive Resistance and Transpiration. Current Science, 57:393-394.

Southon, S. (2000): Increased Fruit and Vegetable Consumption within the EU: Potential Health Benefits. Food Research International, 33: 211-217. doi:10.1016/S0963-9969(00)00036-3.

Sonneveld, C. (1997): Mineral Absorption of Greenhouse Crops. pp 35, Internal Report, Glasshouse Crops Res. Station, Naaldwijk, The Netherlands.

Sonneveld, C. and van den Bos, A.L. (1999): Effects of Nutrient Levels on Growth and Quality of Radish (Rapahanus sativus L.) Grown on Different Substrates. Journal of Plant Nutrition, 18: 501-513.

Subbiah, K. and Raniperumal (1994): Change in N, P, K, Ca and Mg Contents in Tomatoes as Influenced by Different Nutrient Regimes. Madras Agricultural Journal, 81(6):299-302.

Taiz, L. and Zeiger, E. (2002): Plant Physiology. 3 rd Ed., Sinauer Association, Inc, Publishers Sunderland, Massachusetts, USA. pp: 286: 673.

Taiz, L. and Zeiger, E. (2006): Plant Physiology, Forth Edition. Sinaur Associates, Inc. Sunderland, MA.

Thakre, C.M., Badole, W.P., Tiwari, T.K. and Sarode, P.B. (2005): Effect of Different Levels of Sulphur, Phosphorus and Potassium on Yield and Quality of Brinjal. J. Maharashtra Agricultural University, 30 (3): 352-353.

Thomas, T.C. and Thomas, A.C. (2009): Vital Role of Potassium in the Osmotic Mechanism of Stomata Aperture Modulation and Its Link with Potassium Deficiency. Plant Signal Behaviour, 4(3): 240–243.

Tomemori, H., Hamamura, K. and Tanabe, K. (2002): Interactive Effects of Sodium and Potassium on the Growth and Photosynthesis of Spinach and Komatsuna. Plant Production Science,5: 281–285.

Tsonev, T., Velikova, V., Yildiz-Aktas, L., Gurel, A. and Edreva, A. (2011): Effect of Water Deficit and Potassium Fertilization on Photosynthetic Activity in Cotton Plants. Plant Biosystems, 145:841–847.

Trudel, M.J. and Ozbun, J.L. (1971): Influence of Potassium on Carotenoid Content of Tomato Fruits. Journal of the American Society for Horticultural Science. 96 (6) : 763-765.

Ulrich, A. and Ohki, K. (1966): Potassium. In H.D. Chapman (ed.) Diagnostic Criteria for Plants and Soils. University of California, Division of Agriculture Science, Davis, CA. pp. 362-393.

Van Brunt, J.M., and Sultenfuss, J.H. (1998): Better Crops with Plant Food. In Potassium: Functions of Potassium, 82(3): 4-5.

Voogt W. (1988): K/Ca Ratios with Butterhead Lettuce Grown in Recirculating Water. Proceedings of 7th International Cong. Soilless Culture, pp. 469-482.

Voogt, W. (1993): Nutrient Uptake of Year Round Tomato Crops. Acta Horticulture, 339: 99-112.

Waraich, E. A., Ahmad, R., Saifullah., Ashraf, M. Y. and Ehsanullah. (2011). Role of Mineral Nutrition in Alleviation of Drought Stress in Plants. Australian Journal of Crop Science, 5(6): 764-778.

Wargovich, M. J. (2000): Anticancer Properties of Fruits and Vegetables, Hort Science, 35: 573-575.

Widders, I.E. and Lorenz, O.H. (1982): Effect of Graded Levels of K Fertilization on Uptake and Composition of Tomato Fruits. Journal of the American Society for Horticultural Science, 107: 960-964.

Willingford, W. (1980): Function of Potassium in Plants. In: Potassium for Agriculture. Potash and Phosphate Institute, Atlanta, GA, pp. 10-27.

Wu-Zhong (2001): Effect of K Application on Yield and Vitamin C Content of Sweet Pepper, Zhejiang Agricultural University, China.

Xu, Y.W., Zou, Y.T., Amjad, M.H., Zeng, J.W., Guan, L.L., Liu, Q. and Wu, W. (2011): Optimization of Potassium for Proper Growth and Physiological Response of Houttuynia Coradata Thunb. Environment and Experimental Botany, 71: 292-297.

Yang, X.E., Liu, J.X., Wang, W.M., Ye, Z.Q. and Luo, A.C. (2004): Potassium Internal Use Efficiency Relative to Growth Vigor, Potassium Distribution, and Carbohydrate Allocation in Rice Genotypes. Journal of Plant Nutrition, 27:837–52.

Zhu, K., Devine, A. and Prince R.L. (2009): The Effects of High Potassium Consumption on Bone Mineral Density in a Prospective Cohort Study of Elderly Postmenopausal Women. Osteoporosis International, 20:335-40.

Index